Ideas in seventee

To the memory
of
William Sykes Booth

IDEAS IN SEVENTEENTH-CENTURY FRANCE

*The most important thinkers
and the climate of ideas
in which they worked*

EDWARD JOHN KEARNS

MANCHESTER
UNIVERSITY PRESS

© EDWARD JOHN KEARNS 1979

All rights reserved

Published 1979 by
Manchester University Press
Oxford Road
Manchester M13 9PL

First paperback edition 1982

British Library Cataloguing in Publication Data
Kearns, Edward John
  Ideas in seventeenth-century France.
  1. France — Intellectual life
  I. Title
  194   DC33.4
  ISBN 0-7190-0907-3

Printed in Great Britain by Whitstable Litho Ltd.,
Whitstable, Kent

CONTENTS

Foreword   vii

1 *The intellectual situation in seventeenth-century France*

(i) Absolutism   1
(ii) Counter-Reformation and neo-scholasticism   6
(iii) The 'New Philosophy': scientific revolution and early enlightenment   11
(iv) The changing world-picture   18

2 *Descartes*

(i) The formation of Descartes' thought   32
(ii) The *Discours de la méthode*   42
(iii) Descartes as scientist   63
(iv) The controversy Gassendi–Descartes   68
(v) Malebranche: a modified Cartesianism   73
(vi) Attitudes to Descartes   75

3 *Pascal*

(i) Biographical background and Pascal as scientist   82
(ii) Pascal and Jansenism: the *Lettres provinciales*   94
(iii) The *Pensées*: Pascal on reason, man and God   98

4 *Bossuet*

(i) The classical Catholic   117
(ii) The political theorist   123
(iii) The historian   126

5 Fénelon
(i)	The priest	132
(ii)	The educationalist	137
(iii)	The political and economic theorist	140

6 Pierre Bayle — 147

7 Fontenelle — 161

Notes — 177

Bibliography — 200

Index — 215

FOREWORD

In this book I have attempted, on a scale designed not to intimidate the student reader, a synthesis of the state and development of ideas in French culture during the reigns of Louis XIII and Louis XIV (1610–1715). It is intended primarily for students of French civilisation, and French quotations are given in the original; but I hope that the book may also be of good use to students of the history of ideas, of philosophy and of science and, to some degree, to students of the philosophy of science.

Obviously, the study of an era of thought, and especially one as critical for modern civilisation as the era of the 'New Philosophy', offers ramifications which could justify, and have justified, numerous monographs on a monumental scale. I have attempted to follow important developments in such a way as to help the student towards a balanced but not simplistic understanding of the era's thought without smothering him under a welter of detail, fascinating as that detail is. I hope that most historians of ideas will agree with the proportions of the studies I have given to a number of individual thinkers, and with the depth of enquiry into certain aspects of thought which has required other aspects to be indicated with greater brevity. I trust also that the very sophisticated reader will not find the fields of enquiry suggested by the notes unworthy of his attention.

Where quotations given are from books listed in the Bibliography, I have given in the notes only the author, title and page reference, and occasionally, where particularly illuminating, the date of the edition.

In quotations from seventeenth-century French sources I have modernised the spelling but retained the original punctuation even where at variance with modern usage. Occasionally, a twentieth-century critical edition used will already have modernised both spelling and punctuation.

I wish to express my gratitude to the following: Dr and Mrs P. J. Whyte and Dr J. Ann Moss for their painstaking reading and criticisms of large parts of the text; Professor John Lough for the kind patience with which he allowed me to draw on his vast knowledge of the period; Professor George Saunders of Bath University for clarifying for me the mathematical principles involved in certain discussions; Dr Robin Howells of Birkbeck College, London, for helpful bibliographical indications on Bossuet, and for several useful comments; Dr Richard Maber for helping me through the complexities of Pascal editions; Drs David and Ann Loades for their enlightenment on some historical problems; Mrs Elizabeth Clifford and Miss Carol L. Kirkley for their careful preparation of the type-script from a sometimes mangled manuscript; the Library Staff of Durham University for their patient help with many problems and especially the tracing of texts through Inter-library loan; the Research Fund Committee of Durham University for the grant which financed my final bibliographical check at the British Museum.

CHAPTER ONE
THE INTELLECTUAL SITUATION IN SEVENTEENTH-CENTURY FRANCE

(i) Absolutism

Central to any discussion of ideas in seventeenth-century France must be the question of authority, and it is largely aspects of this question that we shall examine in this introductory chapter. It will become apparent that questions relating to intellectual authority cannot be discussed independently of those relating to moral authority and political authority. This is why we begin with an enquiry into the nature of authority in the political structure during the reigns of Louis XIII and Louis XIV, since it is the profound changes in the mental climate of France during these reigns that we wish to study.

From a mediaeval situation in which the kings of France in their 'royal domain' were scarcely more powerful than many of the dukes of France in their duchies and were often indeed less wealthy than individual nobles, the power and wealth of the monarchy had slowly increased until, by the mid sixteenth century, at which time the geographical unification of the country was almost complete, a king such as Henri II can properly be said to have reigned (1547–59) as an absolute monarch. From that time on, the monarchy increased in power, wealth, organisation, prestige and authority until absolutism reached its peak in the twenty-five years that followed 1661, the date when Louis XIV's personal reign began. Yet this peak was not attained without the nation's going through periods of great internal stress and danger, and these periods left their mark on the French mentality—of whatever class, religious persuasion or intellectual category—and undoubtedly on the minds of the Bourbon monarchs.

The greatest period of threat to the nation was that of the Wars of Religion between Catholics and Huguenots, from

1563 to 1593. During the reigns of Charles IX (1560–74) and Henri III (1574–89), the last of the Valois, royal authority over a disintegrating nation at times almost ceased to exist. Ronsard (1524–85), France's most illustrious poet of the time, lamented this state of quasi-anarchy in the *Discours des misères de ce temps* and its *Continuation*:

> O toi historien, qui d'encre non menteuse
> Ecris de notre temps l'histoire monstrueuse,
> Raconte à nos enfants tout ce malheur fatal,
> Afin qu'en te lisant ils pleurent notre mal,
> Et qu'ils prennent exemple aux péchés de leurs pères,
> De peur de ne tomber en pareilles misères . . .

Ronsard, strongly imbued with a sense of hierarchical authority inherited from the Middle Ages, sees theological dispute as the direct cause of national disorder:

> Et tout à abandon va sans ordre et sans loi.
> Les enfants sans raison desputent de la foi . . .

Yet it is interesting to note that he blames not Calvinism as such, but the psychological phenomenon which he sees underlying Calvinism—namely, the spirit of individual enquiry. This he expresses by the word 'opinion', and he allegorises it as 'l'Opinion, peste du genre humain', a monster sired by Jupiter in his anger against human curiosity upon 'Dame Présomption'.

Three observations may be made briefly at this point. One is that numerous historians of ideas have seen an affinity in outlook between the Calvinists and the protagonists of the 'New Philosophy' (which we shall go on to outline in this chapter), precisely in a commonly asserted right of the new generation seen as individuals to engage in intellectual enquiry without regard to traditionally authoritative values and views. The second observation is that as late as the 1680s Bossuet is still pointing the finger at the same enemy—the enquiring disposition—in his sustained battle to persuade the Huguenots to return to the Catholic fold: he consistently upholds the antiquity and universality of the Catholic Church against 'ceux qui ont une opinion particulière'. The third observation is that the French monarchy was based not on a constitution but on a complex network of rights and privileges authorised by tradition.

Henri IV, the first of the Bourbon kings of France, managed to restore order and to begin rebuilding the economy in his reign from 1589 to 1610. It was only when he abjured Calvinism in 1593 that he truly gained control of the State. His attitude towards the Huguenots remained liberal. The economic reconstruction was carried out by his two ministers, the duc de Sully and Barthélemy de Laffemas, both Protestants. In 1598, Henri issued the Edict of Nantes, which not only promised the Protestants freedom of worship but gave them privileges, not the least of which was the right to certain fortified towns. Henri became a popular king, and one may say that with him the cult of royal personalities began. It was indeed strength of personality rather than good organisation on his part that put the monarchy in a position to become all-powerful.

During the minority of Louis XIII and the Regency of Marie de Médicis (1610–24) it became quite clear that no alternatives to monolithic absolutism were viable. The regional *parlements*, of which there were twelve, had very little to do with our conception of parliamentary rule. They were essentially judiciary bodies, and applied laws made by the monarchy, though with royal assent they could make their own *arrêts*, such as prohibitions against the publishing of new ideas—even in the classroom—and so they did, more than once. One of their main tasks was to register royal edicts, and they had the right of remonstrance before doing so. How real this right was depended on the relative strengths of *parlements* and monarchy, and faced with the intransigence of Marie de Médicis in 1615 the *Parlement de Paris* proved very weak.

The Estates General (*Etats généraux*), the only body offering anything resembling national representation (though the Third Estate was in no sense representative of the proletariat but only of the upper middle class) convened in 1614–15 and proved to be entirely without a common purpose. After this fiasco, they did not meet again until 1789, even though about the beginning of the eighteenth century Fénelon and others had hopes of seeing them become, under a revised charter, a real political force. It thus became apparent under the Regency that there was simply no alternative to absolute rule by the monarch, with the only kind of working representation to him being by his own selected body, the *Conseil du roi*.

Then, during the reign of Louis XIII, the minority of Louis XIV (1643–51) when Anne of Austria was regent, and for ten more years to the death of Mazarin, came the great ministerial periods of Richelieu (1624–42) and Mazarin (1642–61). These two men were during their ministerial periods the real masters of France, but they worked to build up the authority of the monarchy. In particular, Richelieu put an end to the sectarian militancy of the Protestants, whom he tended to regard as a 'State within the State'. During the regency of Marie de Médicis the Protestants had been alarmed by the growth of ultra-Catholicism and had taken up arms, only to be forced to submit at the siege of La Rochelle in 1625. Then the *Grâce d'Alais* gave them freedom of conscience and a restricted freedom of worship, but removed the privileges granted by the Edict of Nantes.

With regard to the cult of absolutist monarchy, Corneille gives a clear indication of loyalist feeling under the not especially charismatic Louis XIII, in *Le Cid* (1636). In the quarrel between the antipathetic Count, father of Chimène, and the venerable Don Diègue, father of Rodrigue, the Count asserts that:

> Pour grands que soient les rois, ils sont ce que nous sommes:
> Ils peuvent se tromper comme les autres hommes . . .

to which Don Diègue, the voice of patriotism, replies:

> Mais on doit ce respect au pouvoir absolu,
> De n'examiner rien quand un roi l'a voulu.

During the Thirty Years' War, which ended only in 1648, such views as this last were no doubt at a premium.

None the less, in 1648, while Louis XIV was still a minor, he learned what revolt meant in the shape of the Frondes, and in the following year experienced the humiliation of having to flee with his court to Saint-Germain; he was not able to return to Paris till the end of the sequence of revolts in 1652, a year after his legal majority. Certainly he never forgot this, and when he decided to rule for himself in 1661 without filling the ministerial gap left by Mazarin's death, he was very clear in his mind about what he understood by absolute authority, and was to express himself frequently on the subject:

... La tranquillité des sujets ne se trouve qu'en l'obéissance, ... il y a toujours moins de mal pour le public à supporter qu'à contrôler même le mauvais gouvernement des rois dont Dieu seul est le juge ...

Rien n'est si dangereux que la faiblesse, de quelque nature qu'elle soit. Pour commander aux autres, il faut s'élever au-dessus d'eux ...

... Les rois sont *seigneurs absolus* et ont naturellement la disposition de *tous les biens*, tant des séculiers que des ecclésiastiques ... [1]

It is also interesting to note how often in his writings Louis XIV takes it as understood that absolutism is the natural order and is grounded in good sense. When one is familiar with Descartes' concept of good sense, it does not seem too extravagant to suggest that Louis XIV was in one way something of a Cartesian. He writes: ' ... La fonction des rois consiste à laisser agir le *bon sens* qui agit toujours *naturellement et sans peine* ... '[2] Bearing in mind that most historians agree that it is difficult to know what religious motives led the king to the disastrous and inhuman Revocation of the Edict of Nantes in 1685, and even more difficult to know what real political or religious reasons he could have had for throwing his weight against Jansenism, one is tempted to suggest that he was motivated by a kind of Cartesian passion for simplification and 'clarity' in his nation's structure and that Protestantism and Jansenism were impediments to the kind of politico-religious monolithic rule he desired simply because they introduced into it complications which offended him in a purely psychological way.

In another sense, of course, Louis XIV's views were the reverse of Cartesian. Louis held that he himself was authority and that authority must be obeyed *indiscriminately* ('sans discernement').[3] Descartes, on the other hand, held that all individuals have *bon sens* and that every man is therefore entitled to discriminate as to what constitutes authority and what does not. We shall see that Descartes never seriously thought of applying this principle in the realm of politics or of religion, but we shall also see that he left the way open for others to do so.

(ii) Counter-Reformation and neo-scholasticism

During the seventeenth century, the Catholic Church in France tried hard to acquire power with the growth of monarchic absolutism. It is clear that the Church party, the so-called 'parti des dévots', had a considerable part in persuading Louis XIV to revoke the Edict of Nantes. It is clear too that the Catholic Church, and especially the Jesuits, exerted influence on the *parlements* and the universities. However, it was never the policy of either Richelieu or Mazarin, both cardinals, to allow their Church to acquire too much political power, and Louis XIV was careful to follow these earlier ministerial examples, at least until a late stage in his reign.

The Catholic Church had its own intestine conflicts: between Jesuits and Jansenists (as we shall see in discussing Pascal), between Gallicans and Ultramontanes (as we shall see in our chapter on Bossuet), between Quietism and Catholic orthodoxy (as we shall see in discussing Fénelon) and between the clerical and the monastic orders. The greatest challenge to the Catholic Church came, however, from outside: from Protestantism.

The first major phase of the Protestant Reformation of the Church is of course associated with Germany and Luther (1483–1546). French Protestantism however derives from a French source, the great follower of Luther, Calvin (1509–64), a theologian as noted for his mastery of the French language as Bossuet was later to be. In 1541 Calvin settled in Geneva, and had much to do with the founding of its university in 1559; and it is mainly to Geneva that the intellectual sources of the civil wars in France and the revolt of the Netherlands can be traced. In the seventeenth century and particularly about the time of the Revocation of the Edict of Nantes in 1685 one finds French Protestant intellectuals, as well as simple refugees, taking flight to Geneva or to the so-called 'Refuge' of Rotterdam. Bayle, for example, born a Protestant, converted to Catholicism and then 'lapsing', as the term was, obtained his Calvinist intellectual formation first from his father, then in Geneva, and finally did most of his publishing from Holland.

The Catholic Counter-Reformation in France is then essentially a combat with Calvinism (though in the first half of the sixteenth century there had been a Zwinglian element in France to take account of also) and it is to French Calvinists that reference was commonly made as 'huguenots' or 'réformés' or, more usually and more ironically, 'les prétendus réformés'. The intellectual and theological position of the Counter-Reformation was largely worked out by the Council of Trent (1545–63), the ecumenical council which had been conceived with a view to finding out first how Catholic elements stood in relation theologically to each other so that they could the better redefine doctrine and restore the Catholic Church's discipline and moral, with the aim of stemming the tide of the Reformation in Europe.

In France the long-term results of the conclusions reached at Trent were complex. Up to 1660 there was indeed a considerable revival of Catholic fervour: new church buildings, new convents; new seminaries and a much-improved education for the priesthood, especially in its lower echelons in which priests had been appallingly lacking in knowledge both theological and secular; a proliferation of twenty-seven new French saints, from Saint François de Sales (1567–1622), whose gentle teaching of joyful meditation, the *Introduction à la vie dévote* (1608), was a publisher's dream, to the great activist of Catholic missions and charities, Saint Vincent de Paul (1581–1660).[4] One may say that, in respect of the laity and a number of mystically disposed clerics, this part of the Counter-Reformation was largely fideistic in tone, that is, grounded in faith in the dogmas of the Church and in 'the word of God', especially through the New Testament, without intellectual criticism.

In contrast with this fideism, however, there was an intellectual current, flowing from a long tradition of 'rational theology' and strongly championed by many clerics, theologians and teachers of philosophy. To understand this current and to see why it may be called neo-scholasticism, we must briefly take stock of its origins.[5]

These origins go back to the time when, with the enormous

hierarchical growth of Christendom, the tradition of the 'Fathers of the Church' gave way to a breed of thinkers who became the 'Doctors of the Church', whose ambition was the rational justification of the dogmas of the Church in intellectual terms that would convince even those who were not fideistically inclined and which were teachable. Scholastic philosophy thus has as its axiomatic truths the dogmas laid down by the Church, as its methodology rational logic derived from the Greeks—particularly the Aristotelian syllogistic method—and as its objective the 'rational justification of faith', *ratio fidei*.

Thus, the man who is regarded as the founder of mediaeval scholasticism, Saint Anselm of Aosta (1033–1109), who was to end his career as Archbishop of Canterbury, takes the mystery of the Incarnation as an established truth on the authority of scripture and the Church and then explains with a terrifyingly rigorous logic why it was necessary for God to become man and in precisely the way he did: this is Anselm's *Cur Deus homo*. He was also the author of the proof from pure logic of God's existence, the so-called 'ontological' proof, later used by Aquinas and then by Descartes, with little modification.[6]

However, scholasticism was concerned not only with rationalising the dogmas of Christian theology, but aimed at a total rational description of the universe, which includes of course the need for a physics in addition to a metaphysics. Seeking a physics at first in Plato, the schoolmen, in course of time, believed that they had found what they were seeking in Aristotle, though they knew him at first only through the Arabic commentators, Avicenna (Ibn Sīna, eleventh century) and Averroes (Ibn Rushd, twelfth century). In course of time, the element of pantheism in Averroes was to make him *persona non grata* with Catholic officialdom, but in the heyday of scholasticism there came, through study of the Arabs, a fusion of Christian theology with Aristotelianism which remains one of the strangest amalgams known to the history of ideas.

Aristotle's physics constructed a universe not unlike the Ptolemaic. With Earth at the centre it consisted of a series of concentric spheres carrying Moon, Sun, planets and, beyond, the sphere of the fixed stars. It was divided into two regions, the sublunary and the celestial (or supralunary). The sublunary region was made up of four elements—earth, air, fire, water—having the four qualities, hot–cold, moist–dry, in various proportions, and was the region of change and corruption. The celestial region was composed of a unique element, the aither, and was changeless and incorruptible. The whole was dominated by God as Unmoved Prime Mover, and it was this concept which made it possible to envisage Aristotle's theory as being simultaneously theological and physical.[7]

The great synthesis of Aristotelianism with Christian theology was achieved by Saint Thomas Aquinas (1225–74) in his *Summa theologica*, and for the seventeenth century this was the high point of scholastic philosophy. Yet about the time Aquinas died was born John Duns Scotus (c. 1265–1308) whose questioning of Thomism was to lead in the fourteenth century to a growing division between theology and philosophy, particularly through William of Ockham (1270–1347) whose work implied that belief in God is a matter of fideism and that 'rational theology' is impossible, and attacked certain fundamental aspects of Aristotelian physics, particularly in respect of motion. Ockham was extremely influential, and since to challenge 'rational theology' is to challenge scholasticism itself, it is fair to say that from the fourteenth century onwards, scholastic philosophy was atrophying, particularly in its failure to provide any major new departures. This is not to say that it was authoritatively recognised as atrophying. Nor is it to say that Thomism was ever entirely eclipsed.

In fact, during the Counter-Reformation the reverse was true. From even before the Council of Trent, Thomas Aquinas was elevated to a position of prestige that he had never held in the heyday of scholasticism and it is this new ascendancy of Thomism that can reasonably be called 'neo-scholasticism'. It is true that some of the great intellects of the Counter-Reformation—such as the Spaniard Suárez (1548–1617) and the Italian Saint Robert Bellarmine (1542–1621)—though sometimes called neo-scholastics, were men who recognised many of the decadent aspects of scholasticism and rejected slavish devotion to Aristotle and Aquinas. Yet though both Suárez and Bellarmine were Jesuits, it was above all the Jesuits who worked to re-impose the authority of Thomism in France in every matter except that of divine grace.

The Jesuits had been expelled from France after an assassination attempt on the life of Henri IV in 1594—a plot which may or may not have been rightly attributed to them—but, as a show of magnanimity, the king allowed them back in 1603. From that moment on, the Jesuits sought to foster Aristotelian Thomism in France. They taught it in their own famous colleges, they infiltrated the University of Paris, they tried to gain influence over the one independent college of Paris, the new Collège Royal (today Collège de France), they influenced the *parlements* to harass teachers of new thought.

The new ascendancy of Thomism came only just before the dawn of the New Philosophy, and so, for men like Galileo, Descartes and, for somewhat different reasons, Gassendi, Aristotelianism was the great enemy. In fact the Aristotelian schoolmen had no one among their number who could rival intellectually the three men we have just named, yet for Descartes the 'schools' as he calls them were a constant source of irritation and scholasticism was 'ante omnia exterminanda'—the thing to be destroyed above all else. In the *Discours de la méthode* he names Aristotle only once, to express admiration for him as a natural scientist in his own day, and to rail against the parasitic 'ivy' of the neo-scholastics, which can rise no higher than, nor even as high as the philosophic tree it feeds off. The Aristotelian syllogism he rejects as being capable of teaching what we already know but not capable of leading to new understanding.[8]

Yet, although all historians recognise that by 1650 or at the latest 1670 it was clear in France that scholasticism was intellectually dead, Descartes never, before his death in 1650, nor for long afterwards, won what he longed for so much, the approval of the University of Paris. If the Cardinal de Bérulle had as early as 1628 realised that scholasticism was decayed and that Descartes was the main hope for a new Catholic rationalism to replace it, there was still much authority behind Aristotelian Thomism, and as late as 1671 the Faculty of Theology in Paris, the Sorbonne, sought to persuade the *Parlement de Paris* to forbid the teaching of any philosophy but

Aristotelianism. We shall have more to say on this in our discussion of 'attitudes to Descartes'. For the moment it will suffice to observe that, through the Jesuits, the Catholic Church in France lent its authoritative support to the Aristotelian philosophy (which included physics and the deductive method through syllogism) long after the heliocentric system had been accepted by all the leading intellectuals and Descartes' mechanistic cosmology was already coming under critical scrutiny from the Newtonians in England.

(iii) The 'New Philosophy': scientific revolution and early enlightenment

Let us look first at the terminology set out in the title of this section. It must be appreciated that for the French of the seventeenth century the term 'philosophie' had wider applications than it does for us: it subsumed not only the categories of enquiry which we now accept as philosophic, such as metaphysics, epistemology, logic, ethics, but also others which we would now distinguish as 'scientific', such as cosmology, physics and even the 'natural' sciences such as botany or palaeontology in so far as they existed at that time.

Thus, when near the end of the century Fontenelle constantly sings the praises of the 'New Philosophy' or the 'True Philosophy' he is referring, among other things, as much to Descartes' physics as to his metaphysics. He saw the totality of Cartesianism as the triumph of the authority of 'reason' over every other kind of authority, and in particular over the authority of antiquity, whether Judaeo-Christian or Hellenistic, whatever religious or secular powers might lend it their weight: 'La Philosophie a entièrement secoué le joug de l'autorité, et les plus grands Philosophes ne persuadent plus que par leurs raisons . . .', he wrote in 1699.[9]

Today, we quite clearly see the attack on a static Aristotelianism by the physics of Galileo and Kepler, the empiricism of Francis Bacon and the mechanistic cosmology of Descartes, all in the first half of the seventeenth century, as the initiation of our own scientifically orientated society and the inauguration of a massive cultural transformation.[10] This transformation we envisage as happening in all essentials between Galileo and Newton and we call it the 'Scientific Revolution'. Though they did not use this expression, there were a number of thinkers before 1740 who were fully aware of what an enormous scientific breakthrough had taken place. Fontenelle was well aware of it before 1700, even though he could not accept Newton as its necessary outcome. In the 1720s, Montesquieu, who was a keen naturalist, felt—astonishing as it may seem to us—that the great scientists of the seventeenth century had left his own generation little or nothing to discover in the way of fundamental scientific truths. Voltaire, in his *Lettres philosophiques* (1734) affirms that: 'Un nouvel univers a été découvert par les philosophes du dernier siècle, et ce monde nouveau était d'autant plus difficile à connaître qu'on ne se doutait pas même qu'il existât . . .' and goes on to sing the praises of Galileo, Kepler, Descartes ('brilliant even in error'), Harvey and, above all, Newton.

The term 'Scientific Revolution' is therefore clear and reasonable in its present-day application. The term 'early enlightenment' is more complex. Generations of scholars in the earlier part of our century saw Bayle and Fontenelle essentially as precursors of the *philosophes* of the eighteenth century, the so-called 'Enlightenment', and so they called the period from the appearance of these two until the death of Louis XIV (*c.* 1680–1715) the 'Pre-Enlightenment'. This term has not entirely dropped out of use, though recent scholarship tends to call this period from 1680 to 1715 the 'crise de la conscience européenne', the name given to it by Paul Hazard in the title of his authoritative study published in 1935.[11] Today scholars tend, while not failing to see the sense in which Bayle and Fontenelle can be regarded as precursors of the *philosophes*, to consider it important to understand them as part of the century in which nearly all their important work was done—the seventeenth. It is recognised that their aspirations towards religious and civil tolerance through the spread of sweet reason, while giving them a clear affinity with the *philosophes*, can only be understood in relation to the fight for intellectual freedom in the sciences, which began as early as Galileo, and the tradition clearly established in France by 1650. It is true that one could trace a shift in the use of the terms 'bon sens', 'droite raison', 'lumière naturelle' from Descartes' use of these terms to mean 'that faculty which tells me that the part may not be greater than the whole' to Bayle's use of them to mean, for example, 'that faculty which tells me that Jesus did not intend his parable of the guests forced to come to the wedding-feast as a justification for religious conversion by force'. Yet this second sense, directed towards a more civilised *ethos* for mankind, cannot be separated from the first sense, directed towards the understanding of physical reality. The two kinds of preoccupation are part of the quest for man's right to be free of established authority and to create a new, 'modern' world-picture, or even, if appropriate, to accept old authority in a free and rational act of modification.

Thus, though it is true that as far as France is concerned the fundamental scientific breakthroughs came before the death of Pascal in 1662 and that the preoccupations of thinkers after this date were more orientated towards criticism—historical, biblical, theological, political—and towards the *popularisation* of the new science, it is to some extent a falsification to speak of the years 1680 onwards as the 'Pre-Enlightenment' without understanding that this term must be subsumed under the more recent term 'Early Enlightenment' whose beginnings cannot be dated any later than Descartes' *Discours de la méthode* (1637), and are, in a general way, appreciable earlier than that. The *'esprits forts'*, the followers of the New Philosophy, whom La Bruyère attacks in his *Caractères* (1688), were, under a different appellation, the same sort of men as the *'libertins'* or 'free-thinkers' of the first half of the century, and indeed the term *'libertin'* was still frequently used in the 1680s of Bayle for example.

For these free-thinkers, whom we shall go on to consider now, the attempt to understand the physical world in terms of modern reason was closely interwoven with the attempt to understand man's position *vis-à-vis* nature and society in similar terms. We shall not examine these 'libertins' or free-thinkers of the first half of the seventeenth century at great length, since various good studies of the movement are readily available.[12] It is important to consider them, however, in order to understand that Descartes' idea of making a clean sweep, his *tabula rasa*, so as to produce a brand new philosophy, was not a totally unpredictable undertaking. His principle of 'systematic doubt' was born in a climate of enquiry, examination and scepticism regarding traditional intellectual authority.

In France, such a climate had been fostered before the end of the sixteenth century not only in the theological context of Calvinism but also by Montaigne (1533–92) whose moral scepticism was to be much studied by Descartes[13] and was methodically expounded by Charron (1541–1603) in his *Traité de la sagesse* (1603). It is sometimes suggested that Montaigne's scepticism was so complete that it was actually discouraging for anyone who wanted to build a new system, but this is to suggest an outright Pyrrhonism which is true of his influence in only one important case, that of La Mothe le Vayer. At the same time Montaigne was neither philosopher nor scientist: he believed that there was no certain knowledge in his own day, but his scepticism was more likely to clear the ground for new lines of enquiry than to discourage faith in 'modernism': one can imagine Descartes nodding approval of lines like these: 'Le Dieu de la science scolastique, c'est Aristote; c'est religion de débattre de ses ordonnances . . . Sa doctrine nous sert de loi magistrale, qui est à l'aventure tout aussi fausse qu'une autre . . .'[14] while choosing, since he lived in less troubled times, to ignore Montaigne's fears of innovation and anarchy, expressed in *De la présomption* and *De la vanité*. It is true that Montaigne had attacked all claim to certainty on the part of the Italian thinkers, but Montaigne died in 1592, whereas Italian ideas continued to flow north in the seventeenth century, through Aix-en-Provence and the activities there of an intellectual well-known through Gassendi in Paris, Nicolas Peiresc (1580–1637).[15]

Atheistic free-thought came largely from the university of Padua and the 'Averroist' teaching of Pomponazzi, which included the denial of miracle, of the immortality of the soul, and of the concept of a universe created in time and destined to end in time. A different element was the concept of an intelligence infused in nature, a doctrine called 'naturalism' and lying somewhere between hylopathism—the belief that matter has feeling—and hylotheism—the belief that God and matter are identical.[16] This came from the Italians Cardano (1501–76) and Giordano Bruno, who had taught in Paris and was burned for heresy in Rome in 1600, and was brought into France by two Italian travellers: Campanella (1568–1639), who also fought against scholasticism and favoured the experimental method in science—he spent twenty-seven years in prison; and Vanini (1585–1619), whose 'naturalism' was labelled 'atheism' and took him to the stake in Toulouse.

It must be understood that the French free-thinkers were a small erudite band, and the number who left a public record of their views was small indeed. Yet influence in the first half of the seventeenth century was largely through personal contacts and private correspondence, and the significance of the attitudes propagated by this minority should not be underestimated, nor should we fail to note how important they, belonging to the generation of Descartes, seemed as a 'tradition' to men like Bayle and Fontenelle who were of a decidedly later generation.[17] They were essentially of two kinds: some who, like La Mothe le Vayer (1588–1672), Gabriel Naudé (1600–53) and Pierre Gassendi (1592–1655), who were all friends, all believed in caution, had a certain social status, were patronised by men of power, and on the whole showed no desire to overthrow the establishment, but only to be free in their private intellectual doubts; and others who, like the unfortunate foreigner, Vanini, had little money, status or hope of relying on powerful protection. It was, ironically, this second category that tended to be more extravagant in risking official displeasure. The first category is represented by Gassendi in our Chapter 2.

We shall look closely here only at the most famous of the second category, Cyrano de Bergerac, in order to see the extreme form that free-thinking could take.

Cyrano (1619–55) cannot be regarded as a philosopher, since although he is quite erudite, he throws off ideas piecemeal and does not systematise.[18] His most important work was in fact presented in story form and there are numerous interlocutors who offer different views of which none are given explicit preference. There are two stories: *Les états et empires de la lune* (1657) and *Les états et empires du soleil* (1662), now given the joint title *L'autre monde*. There are two points to be made about these works which reduce the image of Cyrano as an incredibly outspoken polemicist: one is that he was already dead before the publication of his science-fiction journey to the moon, the other is that the 1657 editor expurgated the most pointed details on a massive scale.

L'autre monde remains however an astonishing work for its time, a work that attacks Aristotelianism, Ptolemy, Cartesianism, Revelation, Christianity and scripture, the clergy, the dignity of man in the universe, the authoritarian principle, the closed mind, and much else, in a fictional form that is polemical like the *contes* of the eighteenth-century *philosophes* and ranges from the comical to the burlesque. One has only to flick through the pages of *L'autre monde* to capture the tone of almost indiscriminate mockery, and there is hardly a paragraph without something calculated to outrage the 'gens bien pensants' of the era: mockery of 'God's inspiration' which has led the author to enlighten mankind on the inhabitants of the moon,[19] mockery of the 'science' of Saint Augustine,[20] mockery of Genesis—landing on the moon Cyrano finds himself in the Earthly Paradise and is saved from the effects of his crash by diving head first into the Tree of Life and having an apple forced down his throat—with a sexual burlesque on the serpent and the words of God, closely followed by a sequence of music-hall repartee between Cyrano and Elijah.[21]

Yet apart from the joy in causing outrage, Cyrano is prepared to propound thoughts which require serious consideration, and there are the rudiments of a system which it took courage to put forward. For example, whereas in the 1620s (as Baillet, Descartes' biographer, reported) the Church agreed that the heliocentric system of Copernicus could be propounded as a working hypothesis but not a theory, and whereas Gassendi discussed it as a hypothesis and Descartes withheld from publication his *Le monde* in which he had propounded it as a theory, Cyrano publicly maintains it as a theory (even though his reasoning on the subject is wrong). He even maintains that 'bon sens' shows that it can be true, since it can be demonstrated that our sense impressions, which might appear to contradict it, when reasoned about do not do so.

However, his heliocentric system is infinite in time and space. It consists of material, atoms, which have existed for all time whether in chaos or organisation. There was no creation, nor is there any finalism (any divine intention). Worlds form

The intellectual situation in seventeenth-century France 17

and unform themselves, but matter remains. Beyond matter there is no spirit, from which it follows that all metaphysics must disappear. The universe is an accident and there is no special destiny for man. The nearest thing to divine providence is instinct, which is benign in that it fosters self-preservation. Cyrano in his stories does put weak arguments for God into his own mouth as participant in the narrative, but they are clearly not intended in earnest.

What we have then, when we can separate it out from the welter of conflicting detail, is an atheistic materialism, which for Cyrano in no way implies cosmic loneliness as Pascal thought it must do. On the contrary, it becomes clear that this world-view is intended to free man from metaphysical terror and to encourage him to work out his own future. Indeed, that was also the intention of Epicurus in his modifications of the atomism of Democritus, and it was almost certainly from Epicurus—discovered through Gassendi or pupils of Gassendi—that Cyrano developed his view.[22] But whereas Gassendi modified his own Epicureanism in favour of the view that only trust in a benevolent deity could set man free from cosmic terror, Cyrano seems bent on propagating the reverse view.

Such then was the extreme of *libertinage* in a generation slightly younger than Descartes'. Cyrano was no Cartesian in physics or metaphysics, but most of his mocking humour stems from a contrast between the view he is attacking and simple 'bon sens'—a kind of *reductio ad absurdum*—and like Descartes he maintains the right of the individual to follow his own reason:

Je ne défère à l'autorité de personne, si elle n'est accompagnée de raison, où si elle ne vient de Dieu . . . Ni le nom d'Aristote plus savant que moi, ni celui de Platon, ni celui de Socrate ne me persuadent point, si mon jugement n'est convaincu par raison de ce qu'ils disent.
   La raison seule est ma reine . . . (*Lettre contre les sorciers*[23])

Cyrano, as we see, was fundamentally perfectly serious. But his generally mocking and burlesque manner of writing puts him somewhere between *libertinage érudit* and another form of polemical writing which usually expresses itself in verse. It was commonly maintained that a man could not be a free-thinker without being generally licentious. Théophile de Viau (1590–1626), a poet of real merit, was called a *libertin* and was denounced for immoral verse. He spent two years on trial, and though he was eventually released the experience in prison during these two years virtually killed him. After him there was a flow of verse which is patently irreligious, mostly anonymous, and which clearly shows that impatience with the principle of obedience to the Church's authority was not uncommon:

> [Qu'] on parle de Dieu le Père,
> De toute la Trinité
> Qu'une Vierge soit la mère
> D'un Sauveur ressuscité
> Et que l'esprit en colombe
> Descende comme une bombe,
> Je me fous de leurs destins
> Pourvu que j'aie du vin.[24]

Though this brief survey of free-thinking in Descartes' generation shows that the movement was not on a vast scale in respect of the numbers involved, we have yet to add to it its other dimension, that of the effect that scientific discovery was having on the 'world-picture'. Once we have added this dimension, we may hope that the *rationale* of the term 'Early Enlightenment' will have become quite clear.

(iv) The changing world-picture

Despite increasing urbanisation, seventeenth-century France was still largely a nation of peasants. The proportion of illiteracy, though it cannot be accurately assessed, is commonly estimated at about seventy per cent of the total population. There was a considerable cultural gulf between the bulk of the population and the educated upper middle class together with the aristocracy, and, if anything, with the coming of the Scientific Revolution, this gulf widened.[25] Whereas, about 1500, we can assume that there was not a great difference between the world-pictures held by illiterates and the educated, during the seventeenth century the world-picture of the cultured minority changed rapidly, and we can have only a very general idea of what the world-picture of the rest of the populace was.

Before attempting to reconstruct in outline the world-picture of the educated in the Early Enlightenment, we shall do well to survey briefly the social structure from the point of view of the dissemination of ideas among them. Education was the privilege of a moneyed minority, and Descartes and Pascal are good examples of men of the 'classes aisées' who could enjoy a good education and develop it further. The Jesuits were known as offering the best humanistic and up-to-date education, but when we say 'up-to-date' we must remember that in philosophy they still taught Aristotelian Thomism, even though they were quick to acquaint their pupils with such discoveries as that of the moons of Jupiter by Galileo. Descartes was educated at their college of La Flèche, which he describes as 'l'une des plus célèbres écoles de l'Europe'.[26] As the century advanced the *petites écoles* of the Jansenists came to rival Jesuit education, and their most famous pupil was Racine. Pascal was privately educated, largely by his father, and towards the close of the century Fénelon's educational theory clearly holds that private tutorship is the norm for a gentleman.

The French universities, and especially the University of Paris, were extremely conservative, indeed static throughout the whole of the century.[27] Descartes spent two years at the University of Poitiers and graduated in law. Pascal did not go to university at all. Self-education through reading was of course possible for those with money, though it was a decidedly minority activity even among the wealthy. There was strict control over 'privileges' granted for the publication of books in France—through the Crown, the *parlements*, the Church and the Congregation of the Index and, after 1667, by the lieutenant of police. Yet there was a flourishing trade in books so banned, published in Holland, Germany or Geneva and brought illegally into France. The truly erudite had one great advantage in international scholarship, which was having Latin as a *lingua franca* (though reading Latin was not an occupation favoured by the 'mondains'); at the same time one is impressed by the speed with which texts in English, German, Italian appeared in French versions, and *vice versa*.

By far the greatest advantage for the would-be scholar was having the right social contacts, and particularly belonging to a scholarly group. Such a group was that held together by Marin Mersenne (1588–1648), the Minorite Friar who acted as liaison officer in Paris for several of the most advanced thinkers of the day, in spite of his caution regarding *libertinage*.[28] Slightly later there was the group formed in Paris by a *gentilhomme*, Habert de Montmort.[29] We have already mentioned Peiresc in Aix-en-Provence, friend of Galileo and Gassendi.

Eventually the value of such groups was recognised by Colbert, and the Académie Royale des sciences was founded in 1666 (very close in time to the founding of the Royal Society in London—1660—and there were friendly exchanges between the two). In the 1670s and 1680s Louis XIV took a close interest in the Académie, an interest which caused its members some discontent since they found themselves forced into the rôle of glorified public servants. After the reorganisation of 1699 the Académie was given greater freedom of action, while the king guaranteed continued financial help with research and experimental projects. How extensive the financial help for non-utilitarian projects actually was, history does not know.[30] As part of the same trend, the first French scholarly journal, the *Journal des savants*, came into being in 1665, while in 1667 the Paris Observatory was founded, with laboratories for research in physics, chemistry and anatomy as well as astronomical facilities.

Another social aspect of the dissemination of ideas is the rôle of the *salons*. All students are familiar with this phenomenon—the rôle of entertaining at home by great ladies—in respect of its influence on literature and social refinement, but the *salons* also played a 'philosophical' rôle of considerable importance at the peak of classicism (*c.* 1660–85). A significant number of great ladies were happy to call themselves 'cartésiennes', and it must be appreciated that Molière in *Les femmes savantes* (1672) was not mocking this interest in the New Philosophy (he himself indeed was suspected of being a free-thinker and was called 'fit for the stake' by some in spite of the hellfire to which he sends the atheistic anti-hero of *Dom Juan*); he was satirising the pretentious aping of it by ladies of lesser standing who tried unsuccessfully to emulate the conversation of the great *salons*.

The intellectual situation in seventeenth-century France

Letter-writing was of extreme importance in the propagating of ideas. Nearly all the major *savants*, as well as the more important clerics, left a large body of correspondence, and one finds in Descartes, for instance, that many scientific problems are dealt with in his letters and nowhere else. The classic case of the letter-writer as philosophical and scientific newsagency is that of Mersenne, whose vocation was in fact letter-writing (he was *Epistolier des frères minimes*) and who not only kept his friend Descartes in touch with new developments while the latter was in Holland, but had correspondents all over Europe. Here again, the use of Latin overcame language-barriers. Sometimes a complex network of letter-writing would give publicity to such events as Pascal's contest for the best solution to the problems of the cycloid.

Having given this outline of the modes of spreading of ideas, we can reiterate our opening remarks, namely that the gulf between the learned minority and the proletariat could only, given these conditions, grow wider. It is worth noting that the *savants* had no desire for this to be the case. Francis Bacon, early in the century, had fostered hope for the generalisation of new knowledge, and it is interesting to see that in 1675 Leibniz, whose thought was largely fashioned during his years in France, had the idea of a vast exhibition, which he clearly intended at least to win over the imagination if not entirely the comprehension of the common people. Such an exhibition on the scale Leibniz envisaged did not take place until the various world fairs of the nineteenth century.[31]

One thing that many educated people had in common with the uneducated was a taste for prodigies, 'le merveilleux', anything that savoured of miracle, magic, the unfamiliar, the sensational. To some extent the educated could satisfy this taste—this craving even—in their entertainments. The *machine* which would produce astonishing effects was the essence of the baroque entertainments favoured alongside the classical drama. But one is given pause for thought when Racine in *Phèdre*, his finest tragedy, as late as 1677, retains the legendary death of Hippolytus, killed in his runaway chariot when Neptune sends a monster from the sea to terrify his horses. Of course we do not see the monster—in a baroque entertainment such a *machine* would have been the high-point of the evening—but it is described in lengthy and lurid detail. How exactly did this square in the mind of the *élite* public with the classical demand for verisimilitude? Was their reaction a willing suspension of disbelief? Or did they regard such monsters as quite possible, just as many intellectuals gave credence to strange tales of grotesque creatures, rains of blood and other chilling phenomena manifesting themselves—even if usually in outlandish places?[32] The Calvinists mocked the Catholic penchant for relics, holy medals (which they called 'talismans') and seeing divine apparitions. The Catholics in their turn could mock the 'petits prophètes' among the Huguenots after 1685 who claimed to read signs from heaven. But from the widespread panic caused by comets in the first half of the century (and there were several) as being signs of 'God's animadversion' to the mass hysteria in a Paris cemetery where a miracle was held to have occurred in the early eighteenth century (the *affaire des convulsionnaires*), the free-thinkers and followers of the New Philosophy never had occasion to cease attacking a national habit of 'superstition', to use their own word.

This 'superstition' had a very dark side: the extremely widespread belief in witchcraft and the occult. Michelet, the nineteenth-century historian, gave an account of it in *La sorcière* which, though he was commonly regarded as overimaginative, modern scholarship maintains as essentially accurate. Busson describes the study of seventeenth-century documents in this field as a 'stupefying and humiliating' experience.[33] Huxley maintains that in such areas as the Jura, Lorraine and the Basque country it is possible that the majority of the population worshipped the Christian God by day and the 'Old Religion' (or Dianic cult) by night.[34] A recent specialist in seventeenth-century French history goes so far as to speak of a 'contre-société', in all milieux, of those who believed in witchcraft and even to discuss 'diabolocentrisme', especially in rural areas.[35]

The most notorious example of the official attitude to witchcraft was the case of the priest Urbain Grandier who became the unfortunate object of the sexual hysteria of the whole convent of Loudun, and was tortured and burned in 1634 for 'possessing' the nuns. Louis XIII believed in witchcraft. Richelieu was prepared to do so on this occasion, as

The intellectual situation in seventeenth-century France

Grandier was something of a thorn in his side for political reasons. Many people of prestige who came from far and wide to the trial believed the whole thing to be a travesty of justice and totally unedifying on the part of the Catholic Church.[36] After 1640 the Paris *parlement* would no longer bring accusations of witchcraft, but others—those of Aix, Grenoble, Rouen—continued to do so.

In 1680 there broke on the capital the most sensational mystery of the century. The prosecution of a woman named La Voisin as a poisoner revealed a whole murderous and satanic network, largely among the aristocracy. La Voisin was burned in Paris and as a result of the efforts of the specially convened *Chambre ardente* 367 persons were arrested, 218 convicted and thirty-six put to death after torture 'ordinary and extraordinary'. Eventually, in 1683, Louis XIV had the proceedings stopped, because things got too close to home when the mistress who bore him seven children, Madame de Montespan, was implicated. An edict of this time speaks only of 'prétendue sorcellerie', which could mean that even those who admitted charges of witchcraft could be self-deluded or hiding crimes of a secular order. The public on the other hand was convinced that La Voisin was a witch, that Madame de Montespan had instigated several Black Masses and participated in at least one, and that other great ladies such as the Comtesse de Soissons (who was discreetly allowed to flee to Flanders) had the devil in them.[37] After that time, trials for witchcraft in France generally ceased, but where witchcraft was suspected it was usually possible to convict the accused on some other charge, or to treat him as criminally insane.

Other less morbid forms of occultism—astrology and alchemy—were rife in the first half of the seventeenth century. Even so superb a mathematical astronomer as Kepler (1571–1630) had to demean himself by drawing up horoscopes for great personages—or did he have a lingering belief in astrology, since in his earlier years he had cast his own horoscope?[38] In fact, astrology and alchemy can be held to be not disfavoured either by accepted Aristotelianism or by Italian 'pantheistic animism' ('Averroist Aristotelianism'). Both were grounded in the view that there are *sympathies* between all parts of the universe—in the case of astrology between the planets as macrocosm and the individual person as microcosm, in the case of alchemy between the chemical processes of the *opus magnum* and the processes within the soul of the operator. One can see that this theory of sympathies or *correspondences* does not conflict violently with the Aristotelian sublunary physics, which is qualitative. Thus, bodies in which the predominant elemental qualities are 'earthy' will seek the earth with which they have affinity—that is, they will fall. Similarly, with the 'pantheistic animism' of Giordano Bruno brought into France by Vanini and Campanella: if all parts of the universe are invested with mind or with God there must be a world-mind or world-soul which causes affinities or sympathies between various parts of the whole. Obviously, alchemists and astrologers were not illiterate men since they had to be able to make calculations or read the *grimoires* in which their lore was set out, and they were taken seriously by a large part of the literate population as well as by the uneducated.

The attitude of that minority from whom the Scientific Revolution and Early Enlightenment developed was constantly one of opposition to belief in magic or witchcraft, astrology and alchemy. We have mentioned already the attacks on belief in witchcraft by *libertins* like Naudé and Cyrano. For the rest we need at this point only refer to Descartes who in his very first major publication, the *Discours de la méthode*, mentions specifically the triple issue of magic, astrology and alchemy simply to dismiss these activities out of hand as 'les mauvaises doctrines'.[39] This stance left the intellectual *élite* free to develop its world-picture without reference to any kind of occultism. Every phenomenon would be explicable, comprehensible and eventually measurable. Even Cyrano, with his animistic view of the world-substance, held magic to be merely physics of which the causes were unknown but rational.[40]

In attempting to reconstruct a world-picture and the way it may have developed during a given period, one is usually well advised to look at the way the era envisaged cosmology, and this is certainly the central issue with regard to the New Philosophy. There are three aspects to its cosmology which we shall consider in turn—firstly, concepts concerning the structure of the universe, secondly, concepts concerning the dimensions and age of the universe and, thirdly, concepts concerning its essential nature.

Regarding the structure of the cosmos, the most important question was concerned with whether it is geocentric, as maintained in the Aristotelian and Ptolemaic systems, or heliocentric, as maintained by Copernicus. The sun-centred system of Copernicus did not become well known with any great speed.[41] It was set out in his *De revolutionibus orbium coelestium* in 1543, but as late as 1600 it was unknown generally, and of those who knew it many rejected it on religious grounds (in a curious way the geocentric view was held to be quite compatible with the story of the Creation in Genesis as well as being in line with authoritative scholastic teaching) or on grounds of 'common sense'. A greater willingness to give the newer system at least some consideration became obviously necessary when Galileo greatly improved on the early Dutch telescopes in 1610 and discovered the moons of Jupiter, the waxing and waning of Venus, and the fact that the Milky Way is not just a blurred light but is composed of a myriad of stars never previously seen by man.

A crisis came in 1633 when news spread through Europe that Galileo had been forced by the Inquisition in Italy to recant in respect of his support for Copernicus expressed in his *Dialogue concerning the two great World-Systems, Ptolemaic and Copernican*. In fact, the coercion against Galileo was not motivated exclusively by this problem but also by 'particular reasons' relating to the person of Galileo and too complex to deal with here.[42]

It was at this date that the scientific initiative moved from Italy to France, and the French *savants* had to assess their position: Gassendi thought the Catholic Church mistaken in the posture it had adopted, but, even though there was no Inquisition in France, he was cautious in saying so. Descartes was on the point of publishing his *Le monde*, which was in part based on the Copernican system, and he withdrew it, apparently in all honesty applying one of the principles he was four years later to publish as his 'provisional morality' in the *Discours de la méthode*, part 3—that of obedience to the Church. Descartes has sometimes been considered cowardly for this, but it is fairly certain that both he and Gassendi (who was, of course, a priest) could read the signs of the times and knew that the Church would inevitably give way on the Copernican issue before long.

In fact, in the 1640s, the spread of the Copernican view had found its way even into poetry.[43] By 1650 all the leading intellectuals considered the geocentric system as the most decayed part of an out-dated scholasticism. By 1686, Fontenelle was able to take for granted and give a popularising exposition of the heleocentric system in his *Entretiens sur la pluralité des mondes*. With the displacing of earth from the centre of the universe, there necessarily came a reconsideration of Aristotle's division of physics into two—sublunary and celestial. Copernicus himself had made statements in Latin on this subject which were not easy to interpret and still cause some controversy.[44] Johannes Kepler probably believed that there existed a single universal set of physical laws, and Descartes certainly did.[45]

We shall see that the move towards the heliocentric system and a universal physics had important psychological effects. Another scientific discovery was also to do so, and this was Kepler's work on planetary motion. Kepler, an Austrian, took over as Imperial Mathematician to Rudolf II in Prague on the death of Tycho Brahe, a Dane. Brahe had been an extraordinarily good observer rather than a theorist, and Kepler studied his records of planetary positions with a regard for fine detail rare until then and characteristic of the new rigorous application of the experimental method. In fact, the Ptolemaic system of epicycles executed by the planets around their own basically circular orbits had accounted for apparent aberrations in planetary motion (such as retrogression) with a degree of predictability previously considered quite acceptable, certainly by astrologers. Kepler however found in Brahe's records of Mars a small aberration which Ptolemy could not account for, and by 1605 he had shown that it could only be explained by postulating that planetary orbits are elliptical and not circular. This of course challenged the Aristotelian physics of the celestial region according to which the 'perfection' of the heavens included natural movement in circles (whereas the corruption of the sublunary region entailed natural movement in straight lines). Kepler went on, almost without realising it, to set out the three laws of planetary motion that hold today.

Now let us consider the questions of the dimensions and age of the cosmos. In general what we see is a change from a universe comfortably within the grasp of human imagination (what Koestler calls the 'walled-in' universe) towards a cosmos of almost unimaginable vastness or, according to some, infinite.[46]

The dimensions of earth had been known since Eratosthenes, in the second century B.C. The dimensions of the heavens were a different matter. A common scientific estimate of the distance from the earth to the sun in the early seventeenth century was six and a half million kilometres instead of the actual mean of nearly one hundred and fifty million kilometres. The fixed stars 'on the outermost sphere' were held to be at a distance from earth of seventy-nine million kilometres, about half the actual distance of the sun. To put it differently, the fixed stars were at a distance of five light-minutes, whereas the sun is actually at eight light-minutes and the nearest star after the sun, Alpha Centauri, is at four light-years.[47] The followers of Copernicus already suspected this estimate to be grossly in error, but could not prove it, since they tried to take a parallax from the surface of earth, a useless endeavour in view of the vast distances really involved. The idea of taking a parallax from opposite sides of earth's orbit was not regularly put into practice until the nineteenth century.[48] Yet in 1672, Picard gave a fair estimate of the real mean earth–sun distance, and in 1675 the Dane Olaf Roemer calculated the speed of light with only a modest error caused by underestimating the distance by about seventeen million kilometres. Perhaps nothing shows better the progress made by the New Astronomy than Roemer's work. Early in the century, most people maintained that the transmission of light was instantaneous. Galileo believed that it had a finite speed, but the crude experiments by which he is reputed to have tried to measure it show that he had no idea of the tremendous speed involved. Yet half a century later Roemer was able to conceive the sophisticated reasoning involved based on estimates and observations of remarkable accuracy.

As regards the age of the cosmos, the creation was commonly held to have taken place about three thousand years ago. In 1625 Mersenne affirmed that at least seven thousand years was nearer the mark. The discovery of sunspots by Galileo and Fabricius suggested to some cosmologists that the sun was cooling and that perhaps earth was a star that had cooled and taken a long time in the process.[49]

Descartes' thinly veiled theory that the universe had *evolved* from chaos in accordance with God-given laws could have suggested a very long period, but he does not seem to have pursued this thought.[50] In 1650 the Irish Archbishop James Usher calculated from the Bible that earth was created at 9 a.m. on 26 October of the year 4004 B.C. Bossuet, in his *Discours sur l'histoire universelle* (1681), though he was by no means unacquainted with Descartes' work, adopts the date 4004 B.C. and gives all his dates in two forms, one B.C. to A.D., the other *ab origine*. Bossuet was a very authoritative leader of thought in the Catholic world and it is easy to believe that the large majority of the reading public took his dates quite seriously. La Bruyère refers to the age of the cosmos as six thousand years in his *Caractères* ('Des esprits forts').

The third aspect of cosmology to be discussed is the views that were held on the essential nature of the universe, and these were probably the most important psychologically.

Firstly, the informed public was faced with the fact that they had not known the heavens. The telescope defined the Milky Way as a multitude of stars never previously seen and Galileo's 'starry messenger' (*Siderius nuntius*) announced among other things that Jupiter had four satellites revolving round it. The discovery was hailed at La Flèche at an open day when Descartes was a fifteen-year-old pupil there.

Secondly, there was a more disturbing realisation: the heavens were not perfect. The planets did not move in the divine perfection of the circle. The sun, common symbol for divine light, had spots which marred its appearance, and proved, against Aristotle, that the heavens were not unchanging. The moon was seen to have a rough surface like earth. What then of Aristotle's 'celestial region' as a fitting home for the deity and his angels?

Next, the universe could no longer be held unquestioningly

The intellectual situation in seventeenth-century France 29

to be geocentric. If earth was not at the centre of the universe, perhaps man was not at the centre of God's preoccupations. Cyrano argued that it is sheer accident that the sun warms the earth—it does not do so for man's benefit. Descartes in the 1640s warned against imagining that everything is disposed primarily for the good of man. The much discussed question of whether other planets are inhabited made men ask: Did Christ have to visit them all to atone for Original Sin? Only a very joyous faith could prevail against such doubts, and Fénelon, though he borrowed massively from Descartes, happily maintained in the 1680s that the universe is providentially disposed for man's physical and moral welfare. But Fénelon's kind of faith was ultimately the cause of the disgrace of his late years.

Next, there was controversy between the various forms of animistic theory of the universe and the mechanistic and 'lifeless' physics which appeared to triumph with Descartes. Matter had no soul, animals had no soul (though this was fiercely disputed), man's body was separate from his soul. Man's mind and God were entirely distinct from the rest of the mindless universe. The universe was becoming a bigger and lonelier place. Galileo's telescope had opened up the boundlessly vast. The microscope had opened up for Van Leeuwenhoek, Malpighi and Swammerdam the incredibly tiny and teeming life of a drop of pond-water.[51] For the faithful, such things were, if a little disturbing, marvels from God. For the doubtful, the swarming life seen under the microscope, and denied mind or soul, must have raised the question: Are we perhaps no more than that in the scale of things? Pascal argues the desperate need of faith as he portrays man lost between the infinitely great and the infinitely small in his *Pensées* (published 1670). Though he has sometimes been accused of 'intellectual shock tactics' on behalf of the faith, it is hard to doubt that many were beginning to share the cosmic loneliness of his cry: 'Le silence éternel de ces espaces infinis m'effraie' or the grief in his summing up of man as 'un milieu entre tout et rien', caught up in 'le néant'—not a physical nothingness, but a physical meaninglessness. Though Pascal's claim that Descartes only needed God to give the first flick of the finger ('la chiquenaude de Dieu') and that, beyond this, he had no use for God was, as we shall see, not quite fair, it is true that the mechanistic universe, at least as propounded by Descartes, is not Christocentric (though Malebranche sought to christianise it), nor is it anthropocentric except in so far as man, as the only rational being having a physical identity, is invited to make himself 'master and possessor of nature'. It is true, too, that before the end of the century, many people felt cosmic unease if not cosmic despair.[52]

A brief word on other sciences besides cosmology.[53] Undoubtedly, no other sciences showed so much development as physics, astronomy and mathematics. There were, however, great breakthroughs in physiology and anatomy through, for example, Harvey's discovery of the true function of the heart, crowned by Malpighi's discovery with the microscope of the capillaries of the lungs and the finding by Leeuwenhoek and Swammerdam—also with the microscope—of the corpuscles of the blood. Yet medicine was slow-moving in France, and was still largely based on the authority of the ancients (Hippocrates, Galen). Guy Patin, the most famous French doctor of the era, though often classed as a free-thinker, was not forward-looking and used bleeding as his all-purpose treatment; and in general curative medicine was, as one historian of ideas has put it 'replete with revolting absurdity'.[54] The common people tended to trust prayer, pilgrimage and folk-remedies or even spells sooner than doctors.

Considerable progress was made in botany, zoology and chemistry, but it is interesting to see that geology and palaeontology remained profoundly affected by the taste for the 'merveilleux' which we discussed earlier. A brochure by one Jacques Gaffarel, dated 1654, promises the potholer that he may stumble on 'grottoes of the nymphs, werewolves or imps'. More seriously, the priest Athanasius Kircher (*Mundus subterraneus*, 1678), a genuine *savant*, speaks of 'the remote and *sacred* places of Nature lying hidden'; and he also believed that the fossils he found in his caves were bones of giants and that Polyphemus had been thirty feet tall, even though Galileo had affirmed that bones gigantic in length would have to be of disproportionate thickness. The most fascinating example of this desire for marvels, or in this particular case to prove the scientific accuracy of the book of Genesis, comes as late as 1715, when Scheuchzer discovered the petrified remains of a Tertiary giant salamander which he believed till his death was the skeleton of a man drowned in the Flood and announced as *homo Diluvii testis*.[55] The news, though doubted before long by some, was a sensation throughout Europe.

Let us end this survey by asking: How much did the leading thinkers *expect* the world-picture to change? Did they have a concept of scientific progress? The tone was set early in the century by Francis Bacon (1561–1626): 'It is idle to expect any great *advancement* in science from the superinducting of new things upon old. We must begin *anew from the very foundations*, unless we would revolve for ever in a circle with mean and contemptible *progress*.'[56] The rejection of old authority is clear. The concept of progress is clear. The path is laid for Descartes to arrive at his *tabula rasa*. Bacon is thinking of a method based on induction, the arrival at general laws derived from observation of particular cases, in other words the empirical method, of the sensational possibilities of which Galileo was the living proof. Descartes, we shall see, did not consider Galileo to be giving enough thought to 'solid foundations'—he himself would supply them. He recognised the vast potential of the empirical method and encouraged it in others, but he himself, recognising that the experimental method requires one to do all the experiments necessary to rule out alternative theories in favour of a single explanation, felt this to be too time-consuming for himself and preferred the deductive method; this could have made his world-system as static and stultifying as Aristotle's, had it not been for the coming of Newton. What Bacon had that Descartes lacked—a real commitment to finding the potential of the experimental method—was supplied in France by Pascal, who set out clearly the nature of 'experimental proof' in dealing with the vacuum. What Descartes had that Bacon lacked was a true understanding of what could be done through the mathematisation of physics; this was understood by Pascal, Leibniz and Newton and was probably even more fundamental to the Scientific Revolution and change in the world-picture than was the replacement of authority by empiricism.

CHAPTER TWO

DESCARTES

(i) The formation of Descartes' thought

Of the great triumvirate of thinkers in the first half of the seventeenth century—Descartes, Galileo and Francis Bacon—it is Descartes (1596–1650) who is commonly accorded the title of 'Father of modern philosophy'. The main lines of his thought can be summarised in five points, as follows:

(a) *The 'tabula rasa'—the intention of making a complete break with scholastic philosophy and the Aristotelian cosmology and physics that were an integral part of its world-picture.* This break entailed the separation between the 'New Philosophy' and 'rational theology' for which Galileo had already asked, and which Descartes, though discreet on the subject, clearly sustains. The fact that Descartes required rational proof of God's existence for his ontology and for the guaranteeing of 'clear and distant ideas' should not blind us to the fact that he constantly evades being drawn on *any other* issue fundamental to 'rational theology', and that he might even be considered as a precursor of Bayle in the belief that 'rational theology' is valueless.

(b) *The mathematisation of physics*, which is at the very root of our scientific era. The doctrine of 'qualities' fundamental to Aristotelian physics is replaced in the new 'mechanistic' physics by a novel doctrine of 'quantification'. The laws of physics and indeed of reason will be seen henceforth to be of the same essence as the laws of mathematics and all phenomena will be measurable. In the building up of this new scientific system, improvements in mathematics itself, and in particular the fusing together of its different branches previously regarded as separate, were essential; and Descartes, together with his great contemporary, the French mathematician Fermat, brought about major developments (analytical and projective geometry) which were to lead through Pascal to Leibniz and Newton and the essential mathematical tool of modern science, the calculus.

(c) *'Cartesian dualism'*, the separating of reality into two elements, one existing 'not in extension' and comprised of God and the human mind (or 'soul'), the other existing 'in extension' (in three dimensions) and comprised of the human body and the whole of the existing universe, both animal and physical. From the very outset, in Descartes' lifetime, this 'dualism' was seen as a very mixed blessing if not an actual stumbling-block for philosophy, and was much more acceptable to physicists and natural scientists, so that the sciences eventually ceased to be considered as part of 'philosophy' in the wide sense in which Descartes himself understood the word. In our own day there is a marked movement on the fringes of the sciences towards what may, I believe, be called 'neo-animism', a quest based on the hope that it may be proved, *by the scientific method itself*, that mind and matter interpenetrate and that the universe may be shown to be monistic, not dualistic, almost as the sixteenth-century animists believed, yet as it were in compatibility with Cartesian methods of proof.

(d) Perhaps most fundamental of all, *the belief that man is destined to be master of himself and of the material universe*, and that for these two masteries he needs neither grace nor providence but only God's gift to all men, *assured* them from their birth, the capability of having 'clear and distinct ideas', which require nothing of men than that they should use them in accordance with Descartes' gift to mankind, *right method*. This belief, quite alien to the view of man's 'fallen state', which had a powerful hold on the mind of many in Catholic and Protestant Europe (and especially among the Jansenists), is at the root of the anti-clerical Enlightenment's myths of 'happiness on earth' and 'man by nature good'. In our time, it is regretted by many (such as Maritain, Gilson, Jaspers) as the disastrous triumph of an unbending and dogmatic *hubris*.

(e) Finally, Descartes' thought is characterised by a dislike of the 'specialist's' monopoly of philosophy and the desire to make his work accessible to all who are prepared to use simply 'bon sens'. The *Discours de la méthode*, written in French and avowedly intended for reading by women as well as men, clearly marks this intention (though Descartes was not unaffected by the disapproval of the University of Paris). In the 1680s, Fontenelle was to push the popularisation of Cartesianism a good deal further than Descartes himself did.

Let us now list the works of Descartes with which we need to concern ourselves.

The *Regulae ad directionem ingenii* (*c*. 1628) ('Rules for the directing of the mind') were incomplete, somewhat haphazard, and were not published in full until 1701 (*Opera posthuma*); this work is today held to be in a sense the 'method' before the Method.

Le monde, consisting essentially of scientific exposition, was withdrawn from publication in 1633 as a result of Galileo's recantation, and what survived of it was published posthumously, in 1664, as was *L'homme* which, according to Alquié, belongs with it.

The *Discours de la méthode pour bien conduire sa raison et chercher la vérité dans les sciences* was published in 1637, the year after Corneille's *Le Cid*, and remains the most easily accessible part of Descartes' work, though it should be read together with the *Méditations*. It was written as a preface to three technical works: *La dioptrique*, *Les météores* (on meteorology) and *La géométrie*, which rescued some of the material from *Le monde*.

The *Meditationes* were published in Latin in 1641, translated into French by the Duc de Luynes in 1644 and published in 1647. The full French title was *Méditations sur la philosophie première, dans laquelle l'existence de Dieu et l'immortalité de l'âme sont démontrées*. Shortly afterwards, Descartes replaced 'l'immortalité de l'âme' by 'distinction de l'âme et du corps', on the grounds that though his philosophy could vouch for the separateness of soul and body it could not vouch for the immortality of the soul. Though there is much that is unsatisfactory in this work, so that it received a fairly cool reception, there is also much that goes to elucidate the less clear parts of the *Discours de la méthode* and it is central in Descartes' thought. The series of *Objections*, together with Descartes' replies published along with the *Méditations*, are also of great interest, especially those of Hobbes and Gassendi.

The *Principia philosophiae* were published in 1644 and translated into French by the Abbé Picot in 1647. They contain much of Descartes' cosmology, and further develop *Le monde*.

Les passions de l'âme (1650) is largely concerned with physiology and psychology as well as ethics, and greatly expands what was written on these subjects in the *Discours* and in the letter to Elizabeth of Palatine.

We should also mention *La recherche de la vérité par la lumière naturelle*, an interesting though incomplete and brief fragment in dialogue form, which again helps to understand some of the most important reasonings in the *Discours*, and which was first published in the *Opuscula posthuma* of 1701 and is of uncertain original date.[1]

One must finally take into account the considerable volume of correspondence in which Descartes engaged with Mersenne, Princess Elizabeth of Palatine, and others, highly important for the numerous philosophical problems discussed and the many scientific problems solved therein and nowhere else.[2]

So much for the titles which will come under discussion. Now we may proceed to give a brief account of the development of Descartes' thought.[3]

René Descartes' father bought his way into the *parlement* of Rennes, so that the son, though not the eldest, is classed by Alquié as having been a *gentilhomme* and, being financially secure, René (who originally wrote his name Des Cartes—hence 'Cartesius' in Latin) was able to live as such throughout his life, and, even during his twenty years in Holland, with many changes of residence, was able to entertain liberally. He never married, but had one child, Francine, whom, though himself a practising Catholic, he had baptised in the Protestant faith, but who died at the age of five. There are six key points in Descartes' intellectual biography that we shall consider: the completion of his studies at La Flèche in 1614, his meeting with Beeckman in 1618, his experience at Neuburg in 1619 (the 'Dream of Descartes'), his contact with Bérulle in 1627, the recantation of Galileo in 1633, and the publication of the *Discours* in 1637. At that point we may consider that his thought was fully evolved, though of course its exposition kept him busy right up to his death in 1650, at the court of Queen Christina of Sweden.

At La Flèche he was taught the typical Jesuit curriculum in the humanities (including poetry, which he enjoyed) and in philosophy, which meant mostly some grounding in Aristotle and Aquinas, and in studying which Descartes showed a gift for the scholastic type of debate known as 'disputation'. Part 1 of the *Discours* is largely his autobiographical account of this education, and we must bear in mind that it is retrospective, for it is very doubtful that Descartes at La Flèche felt as much dissatisfaction as he later claimed. Be that as it may, his judgements on the Jesuit education—the best schooling to be had in Europe, as he says—are of great significance.

Having been given to believe that he would learn at La Flèche all that a man could usefully need to know, he was, he says, horrified to find himself entangled in doubt and faced with a growing awareness of his own (and by implication, all mankind's) ignorance (p. 6).[4] Languages, fables, history, poetry, mathematics, moral treatises, theology, philosophy, jurisprudence, medicine and the other sciences—he avows the merits of them all, and then leaves them with the stinging remark: ' . . . et enfin . . . il est bon de les avoir toutes examinées, même les plus superstitieuses et les plus fausses, afin de connaître leur juste valeur et se garder d'en être trompé' (p. 7).

What he derived from his studies was thus largely an attitude of scepticism. At all times, Descartes maintained that too much studying of books merely makes one a historian of thought and not a thinker. He then recapitulates in greater detail, saying what he admired in each subject, but not failing to add his criticisms: 'J'estimais fort l'éloquence, et j'étais amoureux de la poésie; mais je pensais que l'une et l'autre étaient des dons de l'esprit plutôt que des fruits de l'étude' (p. 8). Next we have a hint of what was to become Descartes' key idea, that of extending mathematical reasoning to all branches of science: 'Je me plaisais surtout aux mathématiques, à cause de la certitude et de l'évidence de leurs raisons;' (one notices the thirst of the young Descartes for certainty, for clarity) 'mais je ne remarquais point encore leur vrai usage' (he is commenting on the fact that mathematics have not been applied in physics and the description of the universe) 'et, pensant qu'elles ne servaient qu'aux arts mécaniques, je m'étonnais de ce que, leurs fondements étant si fermes et si solides, on n'avait rien bâti dessus de plus relevé' (pp. 8–9).

Then Descartes comes to the thorny subject of rational Christianity:'Je révérais notre théologie, et prétendais autant qu'aucun autre à gagner le ciel . . . ' (p. 9). Here it would seem that he could have written more truthfully : 'Je révérais notre religion . . . ', because theology he explodes in its entirety by the simple observation that he was taught in the first instance that the road to heaven 'n'en est pas moins ouvert aux plus ignorants qu'aux plus doctes', so that implicitly he raises fideism above rational Christianity. His scorn for 'rational theology' he ironically dissembles under the remark that the heights to which it aspires seem to him to require more than human faculties. In a letter to Burman he similarly remarked that simple folk—'idiotas ac rusticos'—are as well able to get to heaven as all the disputing monks; and it is in fact by their disputes on points of theology that the learned monks have given rise to all the sects and heresies; useless and dangerous disputation is indeed, he says, the very nature of that scholastic philosophy which is 'above all to be exterminated'. Even in the *Discours,* for all his dissembling, his scorn for scholasticism eventually shows through: 'Et je n'ai jamais remarqué non plus que par le moyen des disputes qui se pratiquent dans les écoles, on ait jamais découvert aucune vérité qu'on ignorât auparavant . . . ' (p. 65). As a gloss on this last quotation, we may observe that the key tool in scholastic disputation was the Aristotelian syllogism, and we noted in Chapter 1 that Descartes believed the syllogistic method could never discover new truths (p. 18).

Philosophy is disposed of with even less caution (p. 9). After so many centuries it is still a welter of doubt and confusion; seeing that it is possible for philosophers to hold so many conflicting opinions, it is better to be sceptical of them all: ' . . . je réputais presque pour faux tout ce qui n'était que vraisemblable' (p. 10). The other sciences, being built upon philosophy, (and this was of course as true of physics and medicine as it was of, say, jurisprudence), cannot be regarded as any more reliable than their foundation (p. 10). Finally, as for alchemy, astrology and magic, we have seen that Descartes shows his modernism by dismissing them out of hand (p. 10).

Truth, then, is not to be found in any book,[5] except, perhaps, for the fideist, in the Bible—provided that he takes it only as a source of spiritual and not scientific truth. Nor is truth the prerogative of any one civilisation (pp. 16–17), nor of any one tradition ('exemple' and 'coutume') (p. 11), or of any majority group ('pluralité des voix') (p. 17).

Descartes would have us then believe that he left La Flèche perhaps a fideist in Christianity but certainly a sceptic in everything else, and resolved to abandon books in favour of 'le grand livre du monde', which he would study by travelling, meeting people of all kinds, and observing courts and armies, but always guided by the desire to distinguish truth from falsehood (pp. 10–11). In fact, he went on to further teachers at the university of Poitiers, where he took a degree in law in 1616, and may have studied some medicine. Yet there seems to have been no clear direction in his studies, though he did seek the acquaintance of Mydorge, one of the outstanding mathematicians of the day, and met again his school friend, Mersenne, whose eventual rôle in the intellectual life of France we have already touched on and who was to be his regular correspondent. Yet it was not until 1618, when he enlisted in the army of Maurice of Nassau, Prince of Orange and director of the Ecole de Guerre internationale, that Descartes seems to have begun to take his intellectual vocation seriously. This happened in Holland and largely resulted from his meeting Isaac Beeckman, a Dutch *savant* and doctor of medicine, with whom he developed a friendship centring on discussions of mathematics, physics and logic. Though Descartes later resented the slightly patronising attitude of Beeckman, his senior by eight years, he acknowledged his debt to him in a letter: 'Je m'endormais, et vous seul m'avez éveillé'.

In the next year, 1619, Descartes moved from Holland to Denmark and then to Germany, where he joined the army of the Catholic Duke Maximilian of Bavaria to march against the Elector Palatine, Frederick, son-in-law of James I. Throughout the inactive winter of 1619 Descartes found himself in a small town, Neuburg near Ulm, spending his days shut up in a small room with a large stove: 'Je demeurais tout le jour enfermé dans un poêle' (p. 12). Here he meditated; and it was here that took place the most important single event—a purely intellectual event—in the history of the Scientific Revolution: the famous night of Descartes' intellectual crisis, denoted by the word 'enthousiasme', the night of 10 November 1619.

It is curious to notice how the 'irrational' or the 'subconscious' affected the 'Age of Reason'; the two men who tore the conscience of their age apart—Descartes and Pascal—are both remembered by the feverish November nights in which each had a vision that gave him a new vocation, though the vision of Pascal, the 'Illumination' of 1654, was, as we shall see, very different from that of Descartes.

It would be difficult to overestimate the importance of this night for Descartes. Baillet's account of it is detailed but dry, Descartes' own retrospective accounts are sober.[6] But a little imagination can help us to visualise an intense manic crisis emerging out of exhaustion caused by a longish period of intellectual excess. This phase had been set in motion by the twenty months Descartes had spent under Beeckman's influence. It was also possibly intensified by exchanges with the Rosicrucians, with their exalted and mystic views.[7]

We cannot here give a full account of the 'dream' (*songe*) or rather the three dreams, which can be found related elsewhere.[8] The dreams were strange and intense—Descartes regarded them as 'supernatural'—and all that we can understand from them for certain is that they answered for Descartes the question: 'Quod vitae sectabor iter?' ('What road in life shall I follow?') and that the answer was intimately related to a great discovery, one which implied spiritual danger but had to be followed through, the discovery of 'les fondements d'une science admirable' ('mirabilis Scientiae fundamenta').[9]

What this beginning of a wondrous knowledge was is nowhere stated explicitly, but all the later evidence is that it was the idea (germinating perhaps as far back as La Flèche) of extending mathematical method to all branches of enquiry, in the labours not of a multitude of *savants* but of one individual mind—Descartes'; in a few words, the ambition of inaugurating *and* bringing to fruition, single-handed, the era of modern rationalism. His letter to Mersenne of 13 November 1629 makes this clear. By the date of the *Discours*, Descartes had become aware that the harvest was too rich to be reaped in one lifetime, but he remained fired with the desire to create as much of a total system as time would allow.

This new science did not publicly show its proofs for eight years more, but though we know little of Descartes' life during those eight years we can be sure that his idea did not lie fallow, because of the speed with which he was able to respond to the next crucial event in his intellectual life, the meeting with Bérulle in 1627. The Cardinal de Bérulle (1575–1629) was an important figure in the Catholic revival in France. He brought the Congregation of the Oratory into France, aided the establishment of the Carmelites, and was a minister of Louis XIII, regarded with distrust by Richelieu as one of the leaders in the quest for political power by the Catholic church. He met Descartes on the occasion in 1627 which made the philosopher famous in Paris, when, in the house of the Papal Nuncio, he disputed the philosophical system set forth as an improvement on scholasticism by one Chandoux. Bérulle was well aware that scholasticism was not well armed to withstand the attacks of the new *libertins* inasmuch as authority alone could not satisfactorily counter their thinking. Recognising the brilliance of Descartes, he seems to have envisaged him as the potential champion of a new Catholic philosophy capable of convincing those who demanded reason and not authority; and for all the difficulties that were to be created for Catholicism by the Cartesian system, it is not unreasonable to believe that he persuaded Descartes to see himself in that rôle. There is little doubt that after his 'dream' Descartes cherished the secret ambition of ousting Aristotle as 'le Philosophe'; and he not only never willingly entered into confrontation with the Church, he did his best to win the Church's approval. As late as the 1680s, Bossuet approved of Descartes himself while fearing what the Cartesians were making of his system.

It seems to have been as a direct result of Bérulle's encouragement that Descartes, who frequently said that he hated the 'job' of writing books,[10] put pen to paper and had written the *Regulae* probably by 1628 (but not published then) and *Le monde* certainly by 1633. He also, in autumn 1628 or spring 1629, took the significant step of moving to Holland, where the remaining twenty-one years of his life were almost entirely spent. From Voltaire onwards it was customary to interpret this move as a flight from potential persecution from the Catholic Church, but modern scholarship mostly considers that Descartes risked nothing worse from the Church than adverse criticism and that indeed, as we have said, far from being ready to antagonise the Church, Descartes ardently sought its favourable opinion of him. In fact, some Protestant pastors and university men in Holland gave him sufficient trouble, accusing him indiscriminately of atheism *and* papism.[11] We may then accept for the most part Descartes' own explanation that he wished to escape the social commitments of France, though he was no recluse in Holland. But we can scarcely avoid thinking that he was also attracted by Holland's reputation as a seedbed of progressive intellectual activity and that he found the France of his day a tiresome place for an individualist like himself, where he would have been endlessly bothered with stupid questions. Descartes was arrogant and had little patience with questioners, reasonable or not, unless they played the rôle of humble disciple, like Elizabeth of Palatine.

So we come to 1633, when Galileo had to recant before the Inquisition (which, of course, had no jurisdiction in France) ostensibly for publishing his Copernicanism regarding the solar system. Descartes says in the *Discours* (p. 57) that, finding nothing in Galileo prejudicial either to state or religion he was totally bewildered by this event, and his private correspondence bears out the honesty of this statement. But, both publicly (in the *Discours*) and privately, he affirmed that he would not go against the decision of the Church ('les personnes à qui je défère') whose authority over his actions, like that of reason over his thoughts, he regarded as complete. Having made some study of Galileo, with whose work he was not very familiar in 1633, he found that this decision meant withholding his own *Le monde* from publication because its physics depended largely on acceptance of the heliocentric system; and so accordingly he did. This act has variously been described as 'biding his time', which in part it probably was (as we have discussed in Chapter 1), and as 'cowardice'. 'Astuteness' would certainly be a more accurate word than 'cowardice', but, in using any of these explanations, we must take note that Descartes' action was perfectly in accordance with the first of the four maxims set out as his 'provisional morality' in the *Discours* (p. 23).

When Descartes knew Galileo's work better, by 1638, he expressed admiration for the Italian's physics as being rid to a high degree of scholastic errors and as making excellent use of mathematics, but he found him unmethodical, and inadequate in that he did not seek 'les premières causes de la nature' and so had built 'sans fondement'.[12] Thus, at no time was Descartes morally obliged to support Galileo, even though he secretly shared Galileo's resentment of interference by the Church in matters concerning physics.[13] Furthermore, Descartes could not in 1633 have been satisfied that his own cosmology was fully worked out. It was not until 1644 in the *Principia*, part 3, that he expounded fully his own theory of vortices ('tourbillons'), according to which each planet was fixed in a vortex of 'fluid' ('matière subtile'); then, he could argue that, though earth's vortex moves round the sun, earth *does not move* in relation to its own vortex. This argument, Descartes admitted, could be erroneous, but he genuinely thought that he had found a better theory than Copernicus. Our view has to be that his own explanation has much in common with that of Copernicus. 'The views which he expressed in *Le monde* have been modified, not abandoned'.[14]

So we come to 1637, when Descartes' thought became known to a much wider public through the *Discours,* which though by no means a complete exposition of his system, gives clear indications of just why Descartes was to be the most important innovator in the New Philosophy and the Scientific Revolution.

(ii) The Discours de la méthode

The degree of optimistic enthusiasm that Descartes brought to the *Discours*, the vast ambitions that are barely concealed by its modesty and the frequent cautionary remarks it contains, are indicated clearly in the astonishing title he originally intended for it: 'Le projet d'une Science universelle qui puisse élever notre nature à son plus haut degré de perfection'. The title he ultimately chose is more cautious, but it is still of note that he is proposing what he considers to be *the* method and not just *a* method for reaching truth in the sciences (and American translators are therefore right in calling it *Discourse on the Method*), and it is still apparent in the text that nothing less than the perfecting of the human situation is his ambition. The *Discours* was intended by Descartes mainly as an introduction to the practical demonstrations of the method to be witnessed in *La dioptrique*, *Les météores* (meaning meteorological phenomena in general—effects of weather) and *La géométrie*, which themselves in part recreate the material of the withheld *Le monde*.[15] It could not have been predicted that the success of this modest introduction should be so enormous. In appearance, at least, it does little more than show autobiographically how the author arrived at certain of his concepts and then gives these concepts in a succinct form which is much elaborated on in the later works.

The use of French for a 'philosophical' work was unprecedented, and Descartes specifically intended by using it to appeal to those who use 'leur raison naturelle toute pure' as against those who believe only in 'the ancient books'. Descartes can be called a good but not a great stylist in French. His training in Latin makes him sometimes write long and somewhat inelegant sentences, which are not easy to digest. But he is quite unlike other philosophers of his day in his desire for clarity, in the simplicity of his phraseology and imagery, the almost complete absence of specialised words, and above all for the fact that, far from appealing to other philosophers or disputing their arguments, he does not even mention them except for one brief comment on Aristotle and the Aristotelians. He is writing the language of the *honnête homme* and not of the 'specialist'. Nor is he strictly speaking writing philosophy, but rather describing the intellectual adventure that is leading him to the 'New Philosophy'—'les chemins que j'ai suivis' (p. 5). The six sections of the *Discours* were written over a period of time and probably not in order, but though they appear somewhat disparate, each section contains at least one seminal idea which will have an important meaning in the total Cartesian system, and it is to these ideas that we shall give our particular attention.

We have already seen the significance of the autobiographical elements in part I of the *Discours*, but we have yet to examine the striking aphorism which opens it: 'Le bon sens est la chose du monde la mieux partagée' (p. 3). He adduces as evidence the fact that everyone thinks he has his fair share of it. Montaigne had said almost the same in 'De la présomption', and said it ironically. But Descartes is not being ironical[16] (even though we have heard him say that 'la pluralité des voix n'est pas une preuve qui vaille'); for he takes this observation as evidence that 'ce qu'on nomme le bon sens ou la raison, est naturellement égal en tous les hommes'. From this he deduces that conflicting views arise not from a greater or lesser degree of reasonableness but from differing methods of reasoning. He thus clearly implies from the outset that what is needed is one universal method or 'voie', and the veiled implication is that Aristotle and Aquinas lacked the method.

We cannot at this point get very far in enquiring what Descartes means by 'bon sens ou raison'. He says that it is 'la puissance de bien juger et distinguer le vrai d'avec le faux' and this must mean at least two things: 'bon sens' tells us whether or not a first premise is true, and it tells us whether a deduction follows necessarily or not from a premise. However, we shall understand much more of Descartes' meaning when we arrive at the concept of 'clear and distinct ideas' in part II of the *Discours*.

Part II expounds the method. It opens with Descartes speaking briefly of his stay in Neuburg in 1619 (the time of his dream) and stating as one of the ideas that struck him most forcibly at that time the beauty of the *tabula rasa* and the merits of the work of a single mind, for which he uses one of his favourite images, that of the single architect (p. 12). Here we may reflect that the French seem to have been of Descartes' mind in commissioning Haussman in the nineteenth century to re-design the boulevards of Paris.

Why did Sparta flourish? Not because her laws were necessarily good, but because they were *coherent:* ' . . . à cause que, n'ayant été inventées que par un seul, elles tendaient toutes à même fin' (p. 13). One thinks here of nineteenth-century France and the *Code Napoléon*. One also thinks, a little wryly, of Voltaire's comment on Descartes in the *Lettres philosophi-*

ques: '[Descartes] se trompa, mais ce fut au moins avec méthode et avec un esprit conséquent'—an argument that perhaps only a Frenchman can fully appreciate. All in all, man's accumulations of knowledge 'ne sont point si approchantes de la vérité que les simples raisonnements que peut faire naturellement un homme de bon sens touchant les choses qui se présentent' (p. 13).

Are we then to knock down our entire citadel of knowledge? Even cities must sometimes be razed *if the foundations are unsure* (p. 14). So, after rather illogically murmuring a disavowal of any grand ambition on his part to 'réformer le corps des sciences', Descartes concludes that this is in effect exactly what he intends to do, though at a personal level:

> . . . je me persuadai . . . que, pour toutes les opinions que j'avais reçues jusques alors en ma créance, je ne pouvais mieux faire que d'entreprendre une fois de les en ôter, afin d'y remettre par après ou d'autres meilleures, ou bien les mêmes, lorsque je les aurais ajustées au niveau de la raison. Et je crus fermement que par ce moyen je réussirais à conduire ma vie beaucoup mieux que si je ne bâtissais que sur de vieux fondements . . . (p. 14).

An illustration given by Descartes elsewhere for the same procedure is of a man emptying a barrel of apples and then replacing or rejecting them one by one after testing each for soundness.

This is not, says Descartes, attempting to reform things 'qui touchent le public'—in such cases it is better to leave well alone, because in the public domain things 'sont quasi toujours plus supportables que ne serait leur changement'—a nod in the direction of the neophobiacs, who were haunted by the terror of civil war: 'Jamais mon dessein ne s'est étendu plus avant que de tâcher à réformer mes propres pensées, et de bâtir dans un fonds qui est tout à moi' (p. 15), and: 'La seule résolution de se défaire de toutes les opinions qu'on a reçues auparavant en sa créance, n'est pas un exemple que chacun doive suivre' (p. 16). There is surely here an element of chicanery. Descartes' ambition, in starting from a *tabula rasa*, was nothing less than to replace Aristotle as 'le Philosophe', to inaugurate a new philosophy which would be 'pratique' and would oust 'cette philosophie spéculative qu'on enseigne dans les écoles' (p. 59), and which would certainly have a vast impact in the public sector, as Descartes will prophesy with absolute lucidity in part VI.

Now he brings us to the method itself, stating that, as against the multitude of precepts required by traditional logic, four precepts, rigidly observed, will suffice.

What then are these four precepts? 'Le premier était de ne recevoir aucune chose pour vraie que je ne la connusse évidemment être telle . . . ' (p. 18). There are here two key words: *je* and *évidemment*. The first implies the determination to use original and personal judgement as against authority, be it that of Aristotle, Plato or Aquinas. The second presents more difficulty, for how is one to know that a thing is 'evidently' so? Descartes' criterion is 'ce que se présenterait si clairement et si distinctement à mon esprit, que je n'eusse aucune occasion de le mettre en doute'. Descartes illustrates it on numerous occasions.[17] Yet this 'clairement et distinctement' was found unsatisfactory even by many of his contemporaries.

The principle of *personal satisfaction* implicit in this first precept is of great interest for the science of the age in which he lived.[18] Also, when one translates the criterion of personally satisfying evidence from the Scientific Revolution to the Early Enlightenment, one finds it giving rise to a new and much more rigorous concept of what constitutes acceptable evidence in, say, historiography and psychology, and in particular to the rejection of unchallenged authority. Consequently, many long-standing assumptions were re-examined in the 'human' sciences—just as Descartes willed that, in metaphysics, and physics, they should be. The trouble with Descartes as empiricist was that he was not *enough* of one to be rigorous in his observations—he was always ready to theorise rather than to search for fact, being more satisfied with the *clarity* of a theory than with its coherence with empirical data.

Though Descartes' criterion of evidence may have led him into many errors of physics, which were soon to be refuted, we must distinguish here between his use of the *inductive* and the *deductive* modes. When he uses the inductive method to say that we know the heart to be a central-heating machine because of the heat we can feel in it with our fingertips (pp.

47–8) he is making an empirical mistake; his senses are leading him to an incorrect theory. But Descartes well knew that our senses can lead us astray, and nearly always when he talks of 'bon sens', 'raison', 'lumière naturelle', 'idées claires et distinctes', *he is not thinking of sense-data at all.*

We have already implied that his way of thinking was much more deductive than inductive, and in fact, when he speaks of 'clear and distinct' ideas, he is speaking of what most people would be content to call 'axiomatic truths', and not at all of observable facts. In other words, he is a 'rationalist' in the original sense and not an empiricist.[19]

'Bon sens' must not be confused with 'common sense' in so far as 'common sense' comes from our physical experience of the world. For example, 'common sense' would tell us that the sun revolves round earth, because we see it do so. But *'bon sens ou raison'* tells us that the experience could be equally well explained in either of two ways—the sun's revolving round earth, or the sun's remaining still while earth revolves on its own axis.

In fact, 'bon sens' must be understood to mean 'pure reason', even without 'experience', and it is pure reason that gives 'clear and distinct ideas'. The most outstanding illustration of this is the notorious 'premier principe': 'Je pense, donc je suis'. (p. 31). Against all argument, Descartes insisted again and again that this was *not* a deduction, in spite of the apparently deductive 'donc', but an *intuition* of a necessary, firm and assured truth. And *intuition*?

Par *intuition* j'entends, non point le témoignage instable des sens, ni le jugement trompeur de l'imagination qui opère des compositions sans valeur, mais une représentation qui est le fait de l'intelligence pure et attentive, représentation si facile et si distincte qu'il ne subsiste aucun doute sur ce qu'on comprend; ou bien, ce qui revient au même, une représentation inaccessible au doute . . . [20]

What, then, gives 'pure reason' the capacity to have such 'intuitions'? The fact that it is innate, given to us at birth by God. The subject of innate ideas is not in fact raised here but Descartes will come to it in the future almost every time he discusses 'intuition'. And there was to be a violent debate in the seventeenth century between those who believed in innate ideas (*'idées innées'*—a concept much older than Descartes) and those who, like John Locke in his *Essay Concerning Human Understanding* (1690) and like Gassendi in his controversy with Descartes, contended that all ideas come from lived experience. Descartes himself did not in fact argue for 'innate ideas' so much as for an 'innate *potential* for having clear and distinct ideas'. (Contrary to a common view, Locke did not direct his *Essay* specifically against Descartes.)

The concept of 'intuition' as a function of pure reason is involved with 'Cartesian dualism' and with the fundamental differences between 'Classical' and 'Romantic' ways of envisaging 'mind'. We shall therefore enquire further into it when we reach the 'Je pense, donc je suis' in part IV. For the moment let us return to part II and the remaining precepts of the method. The second precept is: ' . . . de diviser chacune des difficultés que j'examinerais, en autant de parcelles qu'il se pourrait, et qu'il serait requis pour les mieux résoudre' (p. 19). This precept at once reminds us of the famous scholastic principle of 'Ockham's razor', which is in purpose the same.[21] The third precept is: ' . . . de conduire par ordre mes pensées, en commençant par les objets les plus simples et les plus aisés à connaître, pour monter peu à peu comme par degrés jusqu'à la connaissance des plus composés, et supposant même de l'ordre entre ceux qui ne se précèdent point naturellement les uns les autres' (p. 19). The precept corresponds exactly with Règles IV and V in the earlier *Règles pour la direction de l'esprit*,[22] and applies more particularly to deduction—by 'objets' we should understand 'objects of understanding', that is, ideas. Yet it clearly could be, and was, appropriated by the followers of the inductive (empirical or Baconian) route, who understood 'objets' to mean 'phenomena'. One notices in the last words of this precept ('et supposant même de l'ordre . . . ') the ascendancy that the order of reason has in Descartes' mind over the order of observable reality.

The last precept is: ' . . . de faire partout des dénombrements si entiers et des revues si générales que je fusse assuré de ne rien omettre' (p. 19). The purpose of constant 'going over' of the chain of reasoning is not only to be sure of omitting nothing. It is also necessary because one may, by the time one has reached the end of the chain, be no longer sure of what the first premise was; that memory can deceive follows from 'universal doubt'; consequently one must learn to hold a whole sequence of reasonings in one's mind simultaneously, and to this even 'bon sens' is not accustomed—only this fourth precept can guarantee success.[22]

In summary, the method consists of only four stages: (1) choice of an evident first premise; (2) division of the problem into manageable parts; (3) proceeding from the most simple to the more complex; (4) recapitulating and reviewing the entire sequence until the whole can be assimilated at once.

The method then is: (*a*) very close to mathematical method; (*b*) very commonsensical; (*c*) very characteristic of the modern mind since the time of Descartes. In (*c*) one may observe the extent to which Cartesian rationalism has influenced the whole cast of French thought, even in subjects that might seem far removed from its field of enquiry—such as, in literary criticism, 'commentaire littéraire' or 'explication de texte'.

Having set out the method, Descartes asks: 'What are the most evident truths?' and the answer is: 'Those of mathematics'. Consequently it was in mathematics that Descartes first worked by the method, and on p. 20 he unemphatically points to some of the important relationships which he discovered between the (at that time) very distinct branches of mathematics. The sense of p. 20 is not entirely clear, but two remarks are worthy of close attention. One is: 'je devais les supposer en des lignes'; the other is: 'il fallait que je les expliquasse par quelques chiffres les plus courts qu'il serait possible.' These remarks seem to refer to the discovery by Descartes of analytical geometry and its important subdivision, co-ordinate geometry; a discovery for which he must share the honour with Fermat, who worked on the problem in 1629. They are merely allusions to the companion tract *La géométrie*, but for those who could see the enormous significance for future mathematics of that deliberately obscure essay, Descartes must have seemed very modest in the claims for the method with which he ends part II (p. 21).

Descartes begins part III by remarking that one does not knock one's house down without ensuring that one has temporary accommodation (p.22). The problem is clear: if one is to invoke the principle of universal doubt ('*de omnibus dubitandum*') as Descartes does in part IV of the *Discours* and in the *Méditations*, it is all very well to say that nothing is certain, that we may be living in a dream, that sense impressions are deceptive—none the less the real world will continue to impose its demands. Therefore Descartes evolves a double standard. A thing may not be proven in philosphy, but it may be prudent to regard it as true in daily life. Therefore he evolves 'une morale par provision' (p. 23), consisting of a few 'realistic' maxims.

The first of these maxims: '. . . était d'obéir aux lois et aux coutumes de mon pays, retenant constamment la religion en laquelle Dieu m'a fait la grâce d'être instruit dès mon enfance, et me gouvernant en toute autre chose suivant les opinions les plus modérées et les plus éloignées de l'excès qui fussent communément reçues en pratique par les mieux sensés de ceux avec lesquels j'aurais à vivre' (p. 23). To obey the laws and customs of his country: this is the principle of Montaigne which Descartes agrees with wholeheartedly, that, though what one has may not be perfect, it is better than change on the national scale. To remain in his religion: this was the attitude one could expect from the Descartes who withheld *Le monde* in 1633, no saint but regarding himself as a good Catholic, and friend to Bérulle, the Oratorians and the Jesuits:[24] '. . . en toute autre chose suivant les opinions les plus modérées et les plus éloignées de l'excès.' Moderation, avoidance of excess, this again is characteristic of the concept of *honnêteté*, and shows very clearly the growing classical love of the golden mean, 'la mesure'. 'Ma seconde maxime était d'être le plus ferme et le plus résolu en mes actions que je pourrais . . . ' (p. 24). This is stoicism, a current trend in the first thirty years of the seventeenth century and characteristic of much of Corneille's dramatic thought. It led Descartes to persevere in certain lines of reasoning even when they were shown to be dubious (tending, we have said, to place clarity and consistency above all else), and shows itself in his adamantine resistance to all criticisms, even those of his friends.[25] 'Ma troisième maxime était de tâcher toujours plutôt à me vaincre que la fortune et à changer mes désirs que l'ordre du monde . . . ' (p. 25). A wise maxim in any philosophy, this is again stoic in essence. Rodrigue, in Corneille's *Le Cid*, does not like having to kill the Count; it is contrary to his dearest wish; but 'l'ordre du monde' (the principle of family honour) requires it, and he does it.

It must be clear that Descartes' interest in such moral issues was not feigned since they arise also in his last work, *Les passions de l'âme*: 'Article 50. Qu'il n'y a point d'âme si faible qu'elle ne puisse, étant bien conduite, acquérir un pouvoir absolu sur ses passions.' And 'Article 148. Que l'exercice de la vertu est un souverain remède contre les passions.'[26]

It is also clear from the discussion with which Descartes follows this maxim that he considers the 'classical' man—who avoids excess and realistically assesses and makes the best of his world—as 'natural man'; one could say that his 'homme naturellement raisonnable' precedes the 'homme naturellement bon' of some eighteenth-century thinkers. Here is an astonishing statement indeed: ' . . . notre volonté ne se portant à suivre ni à fuir aucune chose que selon que notre entendement la lui représente bonne ou mauvaise, *il suffit de bien juger pour bien faire* . . . ' (p. 27, my italics). Here is 'l'homme bon parce que raisonnable'. The view is consistent with the Cartesian 'Omnis peccans est ignorans' ('one sins only through ignorance of the truth', a traditional Christian saying reinterpreted by Descartes so that 'truth' no longer seems to mean 'the truth of revealed religion') and it affirms the triumph of reason over the inclinations of fallen man. But does Descartes indeed have any of the intuition of man's fallen estate that one might expect from a Catholic and which is so strong after 1650? What would he have replied to Saint Paul on the perversity of human nature?—'For the good that I would I do not: but the evil which I would not, that I do.' (Paul to the Romans, 7, 11). Would he have said, as he does in *Méditations*, IV, the following? ' . . . si je connaissais toujours clairement ce qui est vrai et ce qui est bon, je ne serais jamais en peine de délibérer quel jugement et quel choix je devrais faire; et ainsi je serais entièrement libre, sans jamais être indifférent.'[27]

How then does the Old Adam manifest himself to Descartes? Not in sin, for sin is only the consequence of erroneous judgement. He manifests himself, if at all, in man's propensity to false reasoning: through prejudice, haste, lack of distinctness in ideas. It seems implicit that: give man sound judgement, free him from intellectual error, and what need is there of a Saviour?[28] Man's *nature* inclines him to obey sound judgement; and, given sound judgement, it follows, he could work out all by himself a moral code equal to all human experience. For our century, so used to following in Descartes' footsteps, his faith in reason may seem less prodigious than it was. Yet it has, from time to time, been called his 'temptation to angelism', and worried some theologians in his day.

Now we come to part IV, which we may summarise as: 'Metaphysics: the search for and discovery of a basic certainty; proofs of God'.

Descartes begins his metaphysical enquiry from *universal doubt*, sometimes called 'hyperbolic doubt', and this is very important for his *tabula rasa*, since, in causing him to doubt everything, it allows him in one movement to reject and henceforth ignore all previous philosophic teachings. One cannot trust authority, one's own learning. Nor even one's own awareness of the material world: for had not Descartes often vividly dreamed that he was seated by the fire reading when he was really in bed asleep? Therefore, he will doubt all his concepts: '. . . je me résolus de feindre que toutes les choses qui m'étaient jamais entrées en l'esprit n'étaient non plus vraies que les illusions de mes songes' (p. 31). This is not a true nihilism: since the doubt is only a pretence ('feinte') or supposition—thus, 'hyperbolic'—it is an attitude adopted for the purposes of the reasoning. None the less, the lack of a personal sense of reality which can be observed in Descartes' psychological make-up doubtless made such a position easy for him to adopt. In *Méditations*, I, Descartes reinforces this initial position by inventing the famous 'mauvais génie' or 'malin génie' who is capable of deceiving the human mind in all things or happily, as it turns out, in all things but one:

Je supposerai donc qu'il y a, non point un vrai Dieu, qui est la souveraine source de vérité, mais un certain mauvais génie, non moins rusé et trompeur que puissant, qui a employé toute son industrie à me tromper. Je penserai que le ciel, l'air, la terre, les couleurs, les figures, les sons et toutes les choses extérieures, que nous voyons, ne sont que des illusions et tromperies, dont il se sert pour surprendre ma crédulité. Je me considérerai moi-même comme n'ayant point de mains, point d'yeux, point de chair, point de sang, comme n'ayant aucun sens, mais croyant faussement avoir toutes ces choses.[29]

As soon as Descartes has imposed on himself the principle of universal doubt, he sees in a flash ('simplici mentis intuitu') that one thing cannot be doubted: 'Mais aussitôt après je pris garde que, pendant que je voulais ainsi penser que tout était faux, il fallait nécessairement que moi qui le pensais fusse quelque chose . . . ' (p. 31). Doubt is a form of thought, and thought requires a thinker, this is the reasoning.[30] While one is thinking, even to doubt everything, one neccessarily exists as a thinking being; ' . . . et remarquant que cette vérité, *je pense, donc je suis,* était si ferme et si assurée, que toutes les plus extravagantes suppositions des sceptiques n'étaient pas capables de l'ébranler, je jugeai que je pouvais la prendre sans scrupule pour le premier principe de la philosophie que je cherchais' (p. 31). Philosophers have none the less always been sceptical of this intuition. The evidence does not, it is pointed out, entitle Descartes to say: 'I think therefore I am' ('cogito ergo sum') but only 'A thought takes place, therefore something is' ('cogitatur ergo aliquid est'). It is pointed out that the *cogito* is a kind of tautology, born of the tricks language can play: 'Je pense, donc je suis' can be rendered in Latin: 'sum (res cogitans), ergo sum'.

We have seen however that for Descartes 'Je pense, donc je suis' is not a deduction; it is an 'intuition', a 'clear and distinct idea', springing straight from innate reason. It is not, however, an intuition that all must share, since it depends, as Gassendi pointed out indirectly, on the *unspoken* understanding that every action requires a 'self'.[31] Contrast the way two nineteenth-century poets, Rimbaud and Mallarmé, both with tendencies towards mysticism, envisaged the act of thought. Rimbaud, in the famous *Lettre du voyant,* writes: 'Cela m'est évident: j'assiste à l'éclosion de ma pensée: je la regarde, je l'écoute . . . ' 'It is evident to me that I am present to witness the blossoming of my thought'.[32] And he remarks that the poet is like a piece of wood which wakes up to find itself turned into a violin—*not responsible* for its own music, *not* the author of the thought it gives forth.[33]

Mallarmé too seems to have earlier reached a point where he

ceased to envisage himself as actor of his own thoughts: '... ma Pensée s'est pensée...'; 'C'est t'apprendre que je suis maintenant impersonnel et non plus Stéphane que tu as connu,—mais une aptitude qu'a l'Univers spirituel à se voir et à se développer, à travers ce qui fut moi...'.[35]

We see in these contrasts the vast gulf which separates Descartes from the anti-positivist side of nineteenth-century thought, or simply, one could go so far as to say, Classicism from Romanticism. Descartes' *cogito* happens in a mind imbued with scholastic thought. His contemporaries were quick to point out to him the parallel between it and Saint Augustine's 'Si fallor, sum' ('If I can be mistaken, I am'), and Descartes was happy to acknowledge himself in good company with this Father of the Church, generally so important to the seventeenth century.[36]

Descartes' 'intuition' comes, he would have it, from 'pure reason'. It does not come from Pascal's *cœur* or from Romantic 'intuition'—that is, in both cases, from 'existential intuition', involving the whole of human experience (which we shall discuss further in connection with Pascal). Mind, said Descartes, is entirely distinct from the material universe; it does not exist like matter in three dimensions, nor are its thoughts 'given' by experience of three-dimensional existence. At this point in the *Discours*, indeed, such existence is not even proven. Descartes' 'pure mind', it is clear, is not just a concept, it is the way he 'intuited' his very being; and from this arises his vision of man, 'fallen' or not, as intellectually above nature, and therefore destined to be master of the world. This is the 'classical' Descartes, but in fact not classical in the Greek sense, for the Greeks feared *hubris*. It is the Descartes who marks French thought, who de-christianises it, and whose idol of 'rational man' was abhorred by a minority from Pascal to the Romantics and, it would seem, finally thrown down for the majority by Freud and Jung.

Thus far, Descartes' personal existence as mind is evident to himself; he has transcended universal doubt: '... voyant que je pouvais feindre que je n'avais aucun corps et qu'il n'y avait aucun monde ni aucun lieu où je fusse, mais que je ne pouvais pas feindre pour cela que je n'étais point...' (p. 32). How can mind exist if there is 'aucun lieu où je fusse'?—it can exist because the characteristic of the mind-substance is that it is *not extended in space*.[37]

He is thus able to define his own nature: ' . . . je connus de là que j'étais une substance dont toute l'essence ou la nature n'est que de penser, et qui pour être n'a besoin d'aucun lieu ni ne dépend d'aucune chose matérielle, en sorte que ce moi, c'est-à-dire l'âme, par laquelle je suis ce que je suis, est entièrement distincte du corps, et même qu'elle est plus aisée à connaître que lui . . . ' (p. 32).[38]

The *kinds* of thought which belong to 'l'âme raisonnable' are outlined in *Méditations,* II, and could surprise the unwary, for Descartes considers *feeling* as an act of mind: 'Mais qu'est-ce donc que je suis? Une chose qui pense. Qu'est-ce qu'une chose qui pense? C'est-à-dire une chose qui doute, qui conçoit, qui affirme, qui nie, qui veut, qui ne veut pas, qui imagine aussi, et qui sent.'[39]

Descartes is now alone with or as his mind, with no certainty that his body exists or that there is any space in which it *could* exist; a position which can rightly be called solipsism (from *solus ipse*, self alone). Not encouraging. However, he at once finds a way out of this apparent dead end, not by deducing in the first instance the existence of the material world—which would be impossible to do—but by deducing from his own existence as a thinking mind the existence of God. He offers in fact three proofs of God (pp. 33–7), but, though they are to some extent inter-related, we need consider only the first.[40]

Descartes is able, he affirms, to think clearly and distinctly of *perfection*. Could this thought come from within his own mind? No, because he is subject to doubt, therefore imperfect, and perfection cannot come from imperfection (Descartes here fails to acknowledge that he is dealing not with *perfection* but with the *concept of perfection*). Could the thought come out of nothingness ('le néant')? No, because non-existence is by definition less perfect than existence (another scholasic affirmation). So the idea of perfection must originate in some source which exists outside Descartes' mind and is itself perfect—that is , by definition, in God.[41]

This argument will never satisfy everyone, because one may wonder whether it is really possible to have a *clear and distinct* idea of perfection or whether, as Hobbes thought, 'perfection' is merely a word abstracted from a confused notion that some things are better than others and that therefore something must be 'best'. However, the argument pleased Descartes. A worse objection noted by his contemporaries is that, from a 'clear and distinct idea' of perfection he proves the existence of God (p. 33) and only later uses the reality of God who is all truth as guarantee of the rightness of 'clear and distinct ideas' (p. 37). This is the notorious 'Cartesian circle' or 'cycle', which its author defended in a most unsatisfactory way.

Descartes has proved to his own satisfaction his existence as a thinking mind and has escaped the solipsistic trap by proving, again to his own satisfaction, the existence of God. The next step to be taken in his ontology, before metaphysics can give rise to physics, is obviously to prove, by reason, the existence of the extended world (since mind and God, already proven, are unextended).[42] This critical step is taken at the end of this section of the *Discours*, but in the most perfunctory manner, by invoking the veracity of God: ' . . . car la raison ne nous dicte point que ce que nous voyons ou imaginons soit véritable, mais elle nous dicte bien que *toutes nos idées ou notions doivent avoir quelque fondement de vérité*; car il ne serait pas possible que Dieu, qui est tout parfait et tout véritable, les eût mises en nous sans cela . . . ' (p. 38, my italics). In other words, the proof of God has destroyed the hypothesis of the 'mauvais génie'. Therefore, God is our guarantor that our senses do not deceive us *entirely*. This is clearly not enough: we must be sure that our sense-impressions, though not necessarily identical with the reality of phenomena, correspond to it in the essentials; we must be able to distinguish between the dream-state and the waking state, and between sense-impression and imagination (or even hallucination). Descartes is fully aware of these problems, but he offers no answers to them in the *Discours*. To find the complete argument of the reality of the world proved from God one must range widely through his other works.[43]

The further question must arise as to how what exists in the extended world can become part of unextended mind (how 'phenomenon' becomes 'idea of phenomenon'). Descartes never really answers this question, but he does take the notorious step of attributing the transition to the activity of the pineal gland, that mysterious little part of the brain which for Descartes is capable in some unexplained way of converting extension into non-extension, matter into thought.[44] The problem is not touched on in the *Discours*, even in the physiological enquiries of part V. Descartes seems, however, satisfied that he has said enough on p. 38 to allow him to take the existence of the material world as established, and so he passes from metaphysics to 'l'ordre des questions de physique' in part V.

Part V we may summarise as dealing with: 'Some scientific questions, especially on the physiology of the heart and lungs; the difference between man and animal; suggestion of the immortality of the human soul'.

The section opens with Descartes' claim to have discovered immutable laws of nature established by God (pp. 39–40). He then goes on to give a summary of *Le monde*, 'un traité que quelques considérations m'empêchent de publier . . . ' (p. 40). The interest of the exposition is this: Descartes argues that, given certain laws, chaos would necessarily *evolve* into a universe such as we know: 'Après cela je montrai comment la plus grande part de la matière de ce chaos devait, en suite de ces lois, se disposer et s'arranger d'une certaine façon qui la rendait semblable à nos cieux . . . ' (p. 41). Such an explanation flies, of course, in the face of Genesis; but Descartes saves himself by a piece of transparent chicanery: 'Toutefois je ne voulais pas inférer de toutes ces choses que ce monde ait été créé en la façon que je proposas, car il est bien plus vraisemblable que dès le commencement Dieu l'a rendu tel qu'il devait être.' (p. 43). This is nothing but Descartes the diplomat saving the face of the Church with an unconvincing escape-clause. However, he adds, returning to his thesis, it is accepted among theologians that God's action is continuous to conserve the created world, so that one can conceive of the universe's evolving out of chaos 'sans faire tort au miracle de la création'. And he cannot resist taking away from his escape-clause by adding, as a final comment on the nature of things, that it is 'bien plus aisée à concevoir lorsqu' on les voit naître peu à peu en cette sorte, que lorsqu' on ne les considère que toutes faites' (p. 43).

He states that he went on from the description of plants to that of the animal kingdom and of man (in *L'homme*, which belongs with *Le monde*). He goes on to discuss in particular the heart and arteries (pp. 44–50), the lungs (p. 50), the digestive system ('la coction', p. 51) and the nervous system (pp. 51–2). Descartes admired William Harvey and by 1633 knew his *De motu cordis* (1628),[45] but disagrees with him on the cause of the circulation of the blood. While Harvey rightly sees the heart as a muscle serving to pump the blood around, Descartes does not even discuss the possibility, but claims that the heart is a kind of central-heating system causing the blood to rarefy and expand and thus to circulate (p. 46). His view is based on a mechanistic theory.[46] This, though viable in principle, is vitiated by a certain *parti pris*:

Au reste, afin que ceux qui ne connaissent pas la force des démonstrations mathématiques, et ne sont pas accoutumés à distinguer les vraies raisons des vraisemblables, ne se hasardent pas de nier ceci sans l'examiner, je les veux avertir que ce mouvement que je viens d'expliquer suit aussi nécessairement de la seule disposition des organes qu'on peut voir à l'œil dans le cœur, et de la chaleur qu'on y peut sentir avec les doigts, et de la nature du sang qu'on peut connaître par expérience, que fait celui d'un horloge, de la force, de la situation et de la figure de ses contrepoids et de ses roues. (pp. 47–48)

The analogy between physiological action and clockwork,[47] the apparently rigidly scientific approach and absence of metaphysical or mystical elements, these things rightly excited Descartes' contemporaries. It was only a pity that in using the right approach he should have fallen victim to the two weaknesses which he had named as the great threat to 'clear and distinct' ideas—namely: prejudice and haste. Prejudice in seeing only one explanation for the movement of the heart when he knew that Harvey had offered an alternative worthy of consideration and 'scientific' if not 'mechanistic'; haste in being prepared to adopt such dubious criteria as the heat of the heart felt by the fingertips and the evidence of the naked eye when the whole problem of the capillaries was under debate and under the magnifying-glass.[48]

What interests the historian of ideas most in this whole misguided exposition on the heart, besides the affirmation of a mechanistic physiology, is the emphasis put by Descartes on first-hand observation: 'Et, afin qu'on ait moins de difficulté à entendre ce que j'en dirai, je voudrais que ceux qui ne sont point versés en l'anatomie prissent la peine, avant que de lire ceci, de faire couper devant eux le cœur de quelque grand animal qui ait des poumons . . . ' (pp. 44–5). In a climate of opinion where many were accustomed to air views on the metaphysical implications of the most dubious 'scientific information', this insistence that the public should *check the facts* is something new. It is known that Descartes himself frequently visited the abattoirs of Amsterdam and did many dissections.[49]

We may pass rapidly over the discussion of the lungs, which according to Descartes serve to cool the blood vaporised by the heat of the heart back into blood again (p. 50), and of the digestive system. We may however remark on Descartes' description of the nervous system, which became very popular in the later seventeenth century: for him, there are certain 'esprits animaux, qui sont comme un vent très subtil, ou plutôt comme une flamme très pure et très vive . . . ', which rise from the heart to the brain and are then directed around the body through the nerves, envisaged as a network of fine tubes, to activate the muscles. (p. 51) The picture of these 'esprits animaux' as 'un vent' or 'une flamme' may seem naïve, but the principle is *grosso modo* correct.[50]

Descartes next develops at greater length the principle of 'mechanistic' physiology sketched on pp. 47–8. Now, on pp. 52–3, comes the famous theory of 'l'animal-machine': the animal body and the human body are *machines*, differing from man-made automata only in the degree of complexity that God, the supreme clockwork maker, is able to introduce into them.

If man's body is a machine, man himself is not; he is much more than a machine through his union of body with mind. How do we know this? One can imagine, says Descartes, building a machine on the model of a monkey, which would imitate a real monkey so well that real and man-made could not be distinguished. But an automaton built to resemble a man would always be distinguishable from a true man for two reasons: firstly, that it could not use language or only a very little (speech or meaningful gestures) (p. 53); and, secondly, for the reason that although it might manage a certain number of actions in a way that appeared to be directed by intelligence the number of these actions would be so limited, in relation to possible situations, that it would soon betray itself by behaviour that was visibly not rationally suited to the situation.[51]

We may wonder whether there is a true distinction here. Descartes implies that automatic behaviour is *different in kind* from rational behaviour, whereas his actual exposition more rightly leads us to suppose that automatic behaviour, *of a sufficiently complex degree*, would be indistinguishable from rational behaviour.

It is essential to Descartes that we should consider the difference to be one of kind, for he wants us to accept it as distinguishing between mindless and mind-directed behaviour—and he intends to show us that this same difference between man and automaton must hold between man and beast. Lack of speech and lack of variability of behaviour indicate to Descartes not merely that animals are less rational than man but—he jumps to the extreme—that they have no reason at all.

Our century which is paying such close attention to animal behaviour and communication is inevitably antagonised by the 'scientific' pretention of a man who in all probability never once in his life *studied* the behaviour of a living animal, and on the 'animal-machine' his own century was fiercely divided.[52] Descartes does not *specifically* claim here that animals have no feelings (though this was a conclusion many drew) nor indeed does he actually say here that they have no soul; but rather that their soul is of a kind different from man's, since he tells us specifically that there is no error so likely to lead feeble minds to stray from the path of virtue than to imagine: 'que l'âme des bêtes soit de même nature que la nôtre, et que par conséquent nous n'avons rien à craindre ni à espérer après cette vie, non plus que les mouches et les fourmis . . . ' (p. 56).[53] This is at the conclusion of part V, which shows little interest in what happens to flies and ants after death—it merely affirms that nothing of them survives. If they do have a soul of any kind, it is taken for granted that it is not immortal. What does interest Descartes in this conclusion is to relate how in *L'homme* he had shown how very different the human soul is from that of an insect, how independent it is of the body and how, in consequence, it is not subject to death along with the body. Seeing no cause other than death which could destroy the soul, he remarks cautiously: '∵ . . . on est porté naturellement à juger de là qu'elle est immortelle' (p. 56). How very different from most arguments about the immortal soul in his time! Nothing about faith, Providence, God's will and his purpose for man; only 'scientific' observations and inductions therefrom!

Part VI of the *Discours* expresses views on the future rôle of the New Philosophy that are of the profoundest significance but tend to be neglected. After a few discreet words in defence of Galileo (p. 57) Descartes launches into a panegyric of the new science (pp. 58–65) and especially of the Method: ' . . . j'ose bien dire que je n'y ai remarqué aucune chose que je ne pusse assez commodément expliquer par les principes que j'avais trouvés' (p. 61). He now knows that, even given the Method, no one man can deal with the whole of nature (p. 59). He is speaking only of medicine, but the same applies to all aspects of science ('la Vérité'). Therefore he calls for a vast collaboration: exchange of information among *savants*, and between *savants* and the public. He did not take this so far as wanting scientists to work in teams. Given this passing on of information, which saw realisation with the Mersenne and Montmort groups, then with the Royal Society, the Académie royale des sciences and the *Journal des savants*, Descartes foresees an unlimited benefit to be derived from the new science, a veritable 'brave new world'.

There is one particularly significant passage which makes this clear:

Mais sitôt que j'ai eu acquis quelques notions générales touchant la physique, et que, commençant à les éprouver en diverses difficultés particulières, j'ai remarqué jusques où elles peuvent conduire, et *combien elles different des principes dont on s'est servi jusques à présent*, j'ai cru que je ne pouvais les tenir cachées sans pécher grandement contre *la loi qui nous oblige à procurer autant qu'il est en nous le bien général de tous les hommes*: car elles m'ont fait voir qu'il est possible de parvenir à *des connaissances qui soient fort utiles à la vie*; et qu'*au lieu de cette philosophie spéculative qu'on enseigne dans les écoles, on en peut trouver une pratique* . . . et ainsi nous rendre *comme maîtres et possesseurs de la nature*.

Ce qui n'est pas seulement à désirer pour *l'invention d'une infinité d'artifices* qui feraient qu'on jouirait sans peine *des fruits de la terre et de toutes les commodités qui s'y trouvent*, mais principalement aussi pour la *conservation de la santé*, laquelle est sans doute *le premier bien et le fondement de tous les autres biens de cette vie* . . . (pp. 58–9, my italics).

We are to enjoy the benefits of the new science which will be directed towards the welfare of all mankind, through its practical applications in technology ('artifices', 'commodités')[54] and especially medicine, health being classed as the 'highest good';[55] all this because Descartes' newly-found scientific principles have ousted 'speculative' philosophy (scholasticism) and opened the way to materialistic progress. Thus men are to become 'comme maîtres et possesseurs de la nature'. It is true that this grandiose picture of man's future estate is elsewhere discreetly modified by Descartes' ethical preoccupations.[56] Yet it is clear that, in his mind, the concept of material and intellectual progress is closely associated with the concept of man's 'good', and has left little place for the idea of spiritual progress. In this sense, the Scientific Revolution is of a piece with the Early Enlightenment, in which the idea of moral progress is closely bound up with that of the *intellectually-based* improvement of the social structure, in which of course the organised Church was to have its rôle severely circumscribed.

This then is one of the most ambitious statements of the future rôle of science in man's history to be found in seventeenth-century France. It must not, of course, be imagined that it was the first in the field. Sir Thomas More in book 2 of *Utopia* (1516), Bacon in *Of the Advancement of Learning* (1605) and in his story *New Atlantis* (1627) had written in similar vein.[57] As to how man is to *control* science, Bacon says in the *Novum Organum*: 'Only let man regain his right over Nature, which belongs to him by the gift of God; let there be given to him the power: right reason and sound religion will teach him how to apply it', a belief with which Descartes implicitly agreed.

We may notice that More and Bacon were Englishmen, and England was a country where 'sweet reason', pragmatism and a boldly experimental outlook were to become traditional.[58] On the continent, Descartes' voice spoke with a ring which seemed to his public startling and, increasingly, imbued with unthought-of and perhaps dangerous possibilites.

(iii) Descartes as scientist

The purpose of this section is to give a brief *résumé* of the most important aspects of Descartes' scientific work, mentioning those we have not so far touched on, and making short comments on their significance.[59] They fall essentially under the headings of: mathematics, physics, physiology and psychology, and we shall look at them in that order.

The greatest achievements of Descartes as scientist lay in the field of mathematics. His greatest *single* achievement (given the work of Vietà and Fermat) was in the invention of analytical and coordinate geometry, a major step towards the unification of the principles of all branches of mathematics. We have already spoken sufficiently of this in our comments on p. 20 of the *Discours*, but may add the curious point that Descartes did not use it in his own physics. The inventions of Descartes were for a while overshadowed by that of the calculus, but later came into their own. Descartes' greatest *overall* achievement in mathematics was undoubtedly the way in which he affirmed its rôle in physics, showing that physics must be *quantified* by its use, something which Bacon had not grasped.

Our second set of observations is directly concerned with the physics.[60] Descartes ranged widely over a considerable number of topics: cosmology, including comets and sunspots, light, gravity, heat (on which he is quite modern), motion, tides, magnetism, meteorology (especially the rainbow and parhelia),[61] the vacuum, the infinitely divisible structure of matter (a 'corpuscular' or 'continuum' and anti-atomistic theory), optics and dioptrics (refraction through lenses). His physiology was closely connected with his physics, but we shall treat it separately.

There are three general observations to be made about Descartes' physics. One: Voltaire declared that Descartes displayed genius *even in his mistakes*, and physicists still agree with this view. Descartes argued that the cosmos could be explained by two essentials—matter in extension, and a fixed amount of motion given by God *ab origine*. Since the existence of three dimensions where there was *nothing* was, rationally seen, nonsense, the universe must be a *plenum*. Apparent void must in fact be filled with 'matière subtile'.[62] Because extension is nowhere empty, if object A is to move it must displace object B and be replaced by object C. Thus comes into being a set of circular motions called 'tourbillons' (vortices). All motion is transmitted mechanistically, by 'push', and there can be no 'action at a distance'. This was shown to be wrong by Newton. The impossibility of the void ('le vide') was proved wrong by the experiments of Torricelli and Pascal on the vacuum. Descartes' apparent belief in the instantaneous transmission of light (its infinite speed) was disproved by Roemer in 1675.[63] Yet there was genius in Descartes' creation of a total system, consistent with known mechanistic principles, if purely theoretical and lacking any real explanation of transfer of energy.

Two: by his cosmology, Descartes destroyed the mediaeval and Aristotelian view that there were two sets of laws, one for earth (sublunary physics) and another for the heavens (celestial physics). He held that any physical law is universal, and thus opened the way to Newton's synthesis.

Three: he completely eliminated obscurantism from physics. For Descartes a mystery was merely an orderly phenomenon not yet rationally explained. Disobedience to the laws of nature was only apparent, and explicable by man's ignorance or miscalculation.

Now to the third aspect of Descartes' science, physiology, which, just like his physics, he treats as mechanistic.[64] In spite of his errors concerning the heart, the pineal gland (of which the function is still today not properly understood), and other things, Descartes' mechanistic approach to the workings of the human body—which he took so far as to say that a man dies not because the soul leaves the body but because the body breaks down like a watch—was essentially fruitful for science. Gone are astrological influences, gone possession by demons, gone the 'humours'. Every organ functions as part of a machine, such as could be created by man were his fingers sufficiently dextrous. Descartes thus created the modern *rationale* of the 'theoretical model'. One aspect of Descartes' physiology which is worthy of mention in its own right is his excellent treatment of the eye, in *La dioptrique*, following the equally excellent work on lenses and refraction.[65]

It is inevitable that discussion of Descartes' psychological work should overlap with that of his physiology, since one of the most important aspects of his psychology is the emphasis on the physiological nature of the passions (the symptoms *are* the emotion). The seventeenth century is known for the interest it took in human behaviour in society, in the form of maxims and character-studies, or indeed meditations on human passions, such as the *Discours sur les passions de l'amour*, attributed to Pascal. Where the *moralistes* are concerned with wisdom, virtue and the follies of man, Descartes is much more dispassionate and is concerned with man's physiological behaviour, not his social behaviour. Of course he would not have been a philosopher were he not also interested in the question of *controlling* the passions, yet even man's mastery of the passions is to come as much through *bodily* controls—good diet, relaxation, the practice of physical discipline—as through the mental exercise of will.

The locations of Descartes' psychology are difficult to correlate, though one looks first to *Les passions de l'âme*, *L'homme* and the letters to Elizabeth. Robert Lenoble has stepped in with a useful article entitled: 'La psychologie cartésienne'. This article also attempts to *reconcile* the sources, since in some soul and body are considered as totally distinct while in others their interaction is shown to be intense. Lenoble shows that one of Descartes' most basic images for the relation between body and mind is that of the body being like the hydraulic machines so popular in royal gardens, while the brain is its master, turning the taps—'le fontenier' (Modern French: 'fontainier'). He quotes from *L'homme*: 'Et enfin quand l'âme raisonnable sera en cette machine, elle aura son siège principal dans le cerveau, et sera là comme le fontenier, qui doit être dans les regards où se vont rendre tous les tuyaux de ces machines; quand il veut exciter, ou empêcher, ou changer en quelque façon leurs mouvements.'[66]

We may add an explanation here: the soul guides the body from its seat in the brain through the pineal gland. Through this organ it receives messages from the body and transmits instructions. However, its instructions are only sometimes reflexes in man, though they always are in animals; the soul does not *consciously* control the pineal gland, but none the less through an act of will it can make the pineal gland do as it wishes; as Bréhier explains, though the soul can not *add* motion to the constant amount which, according to Descartes' physics, exists in the universe, it *can* change its direction and in consequence dominate the acts of the body.[67] That is, man's cognitive faculty is sometimes passive but often active.[68] Animals, on the other hand, having no proper soul, merely respond to the outer world in a purely reflex manner.

For the theologian, of course, all this leads to the interesting question of free will. This was a topic which Descartes preferred to avoid discussing publicly so long as he could. He did however discuss it in some of his letters.[69] As to when the will is *in conflict with* the passions, Descartes argues that: though each volition is naturally connected with some movement of the pineal gland, it can by effort or habit—a kind of yoga—be connected with others (*Passions*, article 44).

As well as his contention that psychology is essentially a relationship between mind (or soul) and body, Descartes offers a variety of *aperçus* which are quite modern. He holds, for example, that emotion is the overflow of nervous energy not used in action and that essentially it is composed of its physical symptoms; that a child's experience begins in the womb and that his personality begins to be formed there; that man is influenced by the traumas and joys of early childhood, buried in subconscious memory, but actively determining his loves and aversions.[70]

It is true that Descartes was in a sense old-fashioned in holding to the doctrine of innate ideas, much in dispute in the seventeenth and eighteenth centuries. The theologians in particular tended to hold ardently to the doctrine of innate ideas ('les idées innées') because it allowed them to contend that the ability to distinguish between right and wrong was God-given in the womb. The followers of John Locke after 1690 contended that this ability was learned from the child's experience of what won approval or disapproval from its elders, so that 'right' and 'wrong' were concepts relative to a given society. Locke was not truly in dispute with Descartes' innatism, which really claimed that what was given in the womb were abilities such as that of grasping that if $a=b$ and $b=c$ then $a=c$—what we still today sometimes call 'native intelligence' and what behavioural psychologists try to measure as 'learning-ability'. Locke indeed agreed that though there were no innate ideas there *were* self-evident ideas—which implies a particular innate cast of the reasoning faculty.[71]

In discussing Descartes' science, we have left over till last one question, which is important but difficult to answer categorically—the question of his degree of commitment to the experimental method, that is, his empiricism. We know that he admired the great protagonist of the experimental method, Bacon, but rejected him as lacking a metaphysics. We know that he tended to underestimate Galileo, the greatest practising empiricist of the early seventeenth century, and that he either did not acquaint himself with many of Galileo's findings or did not bother to use them. We know that he was not always careful about his facts, was gullible in accepting reports of 'phenomena', and favoured speculation and theoretical models to which he forced observation to conform.

All this is rather puzzling, since we know that he told his readers to check his own reports by observation (*Discours*, pp. 44–5); we know that he did many dissections, which could well have led him to a proper understanding of the heart had he not been blinded by an *a priori* concept; it is evident from his *Dioptrique* that he had done the most painstaking dissections of the eye, that he had verified his theories on lenses and that he was familiar with the practice of lens-grinding. He was used to working with technicians. He may have, as he claimed, suggested to Pascal the great empirical experiment of the Puy-de-Dôme. Bréhier attempts to resolve this dichotomy by asserting that Descartes wrote for the public in a grandly theoretical manner while being in private an empirical scientist.[72] This view is not apparently unreasonable, but not all the evidence has been sifted; and we do know that Descartes did not like the experimental method in so far as it requires one not only to perform experiments that verify but also (like Pascal on the vacuum) to devise experiments to *disprove* other people's alternative hypotheses (*Discours*, p. 61). For Descartes life seemed too short for such activities.

In all, Descartes was probably at heart a rationalist like the scholastics. The kind of proof he liked best was the proof from 'pure reason' as in the 'ontological' proof of God. He did not even believe that a physics was possible without a metaphysics, and it is this that raises him above Galileo and Bacon as a creator of a total 'world-picture', even given that this 'world-picture' is decidedly thin in its spiritual dimension. Yet, on the other hand, there is no difficulty in misinterpreting the first step of Descartes' method in such a way as to be able to transfer the method in its entirety into the empirical realm, and this happened, so that Descartes *as theorist* gave a tremendous impetus to the pragmatic element of the Scientific Revolution.

(iv) The controversy Gassendi–Descartes

Pierre Gassendi (1592–1655) was four years older than Descartes. He was a Southerner and studied at the University of Aix-en-Provence where he obtained his doctorate in 1614 and then taught philosophy from 1616 to 1622. He was ordained in 1616 and was a canon at Digne. He was Professor of Astronomy in the Collège Royal in Paris from 1645 to 1648, and then retired South because of ill health. He knew the intellectual circles of Paris and Aix-en-Provence well, and was well known as an 'Epicurean' long before his *De vita et moribus Epicuri, libri viii* of 1647.

He was not a great original scientist, but very good at experimental verification and a fine observational astronomer. He was in touch with the most recent developments in 'mechanistic' philosophy of which, we shall see, he maintained an 'atomistic' version. He appears to have been a devout 'fideistic' Catholic; it could be maintained that he was not really a *libertin* though he usually has a place in discussions of *libertinage*; but in his day all 'atomists', even clerics like him, were suspected of materialism and atheism. It is noticeable that he professed no metaphysics. In his *Syntagma philosophicum* (posthumously published, 1658), God is discussed in the section on physics. He had a great European reputation in his lifetime among the *savants* but, writing essentially in Latin, was little known in 'le monde', the literate but rarely Latinist circles of Paris, until the *Abrégé de la philosophie de Gassendi* by his disciple François Bernier, first published in 1674 and greatly augmented in 1678. This made his thought widely accessible and influential.

Gassendi's great controversy with Descartes was over the *Meditationes*, in Latin in 1641. Mersenne invited Gassendi along with others to submit his views on this work, and Gassendi offered his 'Doutes'. The 'Réponses' of Descartes were scathing and personal. Gassendi was offended; he had apparently not known that his views were to be published, and he was the only contributor to be named by name. He wrote in reply to Descartes' 'Réponses' his own longer and more detailed 'Instances' ('Rebuttals') in 1642, and they were published in Amsterdam in 1644. Descartes wrote on the 'Instances' in a letter to Clerselier; and, against Gassendi's wishes, the *Cinquièmes Objections* (his 'Doutes'), Descartes' *Réponses* and *Lettre à Clerselier* were published in the French edition of 1647. Gassendi's *Instances* were, on the other hand, not included.[73]

Gassendi's analyses of the *Meditationes* are acute, especially when he goes into detail, in the *Instances*. He brings to light the 'Cartesian circle', which he describes as being more theological than rational in its preoccupation.[74] He shows the semantic weakness of the 'ontological proof' of God,[75] and argues that the 'I think, therefore I am' is not an 'intuition' but the minor premise and conclusion of a syllogism, of which the suppressed major premise must be 'Whoever thinks, is'.[76] He sees that Descartes had not truly shown that we can know the 'inner nature' of things.[77] In fact, he sees all the objections that modern philosophers raise.

Above all, in this controversy, there is division over *epistemology*, the theory of what and how man can know. Whereas on other issues Gassendi and Descartes may be to some extent misunderstanding each other, as 'frères ennemis' as some critics put it, here they are truly at odds. We shall now broaden the discussion to see, firstly, what makes Gassendi and Descartes 'frères', secondly, how they differ in their theory of the knowable and, finally—though this does not concern the *Méditations*—what Gassendi offers as alternatives to Cartesian physics and to Cartesian stoic morality.

What Descartes and Gassendi have in common is, above all,

their antagonism to the Aristotelian stranglehold on thought. As early as 1624 in his *Exercitationes adversus Aristoteleos* Gassendi, who had been obliged to teach Aristotle at Aix, attacked the peripatetic philosophers for the stupidity of their 'disputations', their limited choice or knowledge of Aristotle's works, their ignorance of mathematics (though he himself, being a poor mathematician, failed to appreciate the scope of mathematics in Galileo and Descartes and its rôle in the New Philosophy); he attacked the followers of Aristotle for their refusal to engage in experimental verification—in which, as he rightly said, they were no true disciples of their master—and for the way they preferred argument from authority. He attacked them for their garbled language, though he himself wrote by no means so lucidly as Descartes.

However, and here Gassendi differs from Descartes, he also accused the Aristotelians of ignoring and discouraging a wider humanist culture, including Plato. As against Descartes who, with his *tabula rasa*, drew consciously on no tradition, Gassendi, after 1628 at the latest, was to draw on Epicurus, Democritus and other 'atomists' of antiquity, not, it must be made clear, as unchallengeable authorities, but as valid sources of guidance. Even as regards the syllogistic method Gassendi, having once rejected it, reincorporated it into his system of argument. All in all, the fraternity of Gassendi and Descartes is manifest in at least five respects: they were both against the argument from authority; they both despised the 'mauvaises doctrines' (alchemy, astrology, magic); they both favoured original enquiry; they both implicitly favoured a fideistic religion partitioned off from science; and they both favoured a mechanistic as against a qualitative physics.[78]

The main issue which divides Gassendi and Descartes is, as we have said, clear and fundamental: they part company on their theories of the knowable and how it is known. Gassendi sees the merits of 'systematic' doubt but regards Descartes' 'universal doubt' as *démesuré*, a fault against *bon sens*. Could M Descartes ever really have doubted that 'I am', asks Gassendi.[79] Could he really assert that God's purposes are entirely hidden?[80]

Universal doubt, which Gassendi fails to agree was 'hyperbolic', led Descartes to 'pure reason'. Gassendi, on the other hand, believes all understanding to be from experience: not from the senses alone, rather from the senses reasoned on, but from the senses *in the first instance*. All Descartes' 'pure reason', he argues, is in fact *a priori*. Even in mathematics, one cannot have the 'idea of a triangle' prior to the child's experience, as a sentient being, of existence in three dimensions and of the existence of phenomena.[81] To argue for understanding of existence even while totally doubting the senses Gassendi sees as a fault against 'bon sens' or 'lumière naturelle'. 'Bon sens' must be experiential, 'probabilistic' rather than 'rational' (and in practice Descartes is perhaps closer to this stance than he would have admitted, but not nearly so close as Galileo). Gassendi, from his early days an ardent Epicurean, in fact derives this 'probabilism' from Sextus Empiricus rather than from Epicurus. Descartes was so well aware of this rift between his 'rational' view and his questioner's 'experiential' view that he referred to Gassendi in his 'Replies' as 'flesh' and to himself as 'mind'. Gassendi, though doubtless profoundly offended, gently chided Descartes' 'angelism' by saying that he hoped both of them were both flesh and mind. And he always admitted that there could be a reality beyond the reach of the senses.

To consider now the differences between the physics of Descartes and of Gassendi. Gassendi takes issue with Cartesian physics on two fundamentals. Firstly, movement would not be in 'vortices' in a *plenum*—it would be impossible. Therefore there must be an infinite void in which God, capable of creating atoms to infinity, created and endowed with shape and motion atoms to the finite number required for His purpose (and here Gassendi radically alters Epicurean atomism, with its infinity of atoms). Secondly, atoms are sub-microscopic though not infinitely small, but indivisible in practice if not in theory. Descartes on the other hand, with his 'corpuscular' theory, argues that anything having 'extension' (size) must be divisible. However, Gassendi hints that Descartes' corpuscular theory must inevitably be modified into atomism, and perhaps he is right.[82]

Our final topic is the 'Epicurean' moral philosophy of Gassendi. Since the fifteenth century there had been apologists of a misunderstood Epicurus among Renaissance humanists.

Epicurus is understood by Gassendi as by these predecessors to maintain that life is dominated by the pleasure-principle, *rightly understood*; this does not mean a philosophy condoning licentiousness, for the greatest human pleasure is intellectual—the act of understanding. There is little system in Gassendi's moral philosophy, and there is little that is strictly either Cartesian or anti-Cartesian. Both philosophers put a complexion on 'natural' morality which they hoped would be acceptable to the Church, while treating the question of salvation as supernatural, hence extra-philosophical.

Gassendi's own interpretation of Epicurus is austere. A somewhat more equivocal concept of Epicurean *voluptas* associated with 'divertissement' (the sacrifice of intellect to the pursuit of worldly pleasure) may have come into France from the 'libertinage mondain' of Saint-Evremond (1610–1703, a friend of Gassendi's disciple Bernier), who lived in England after 1661 and poured out his somewhat devious thought in a bewildering assortment of minor works; it is possibly because of his influence that some scholars incline to believe that the *honnête homme* of the late seventeenth century may have considered himself, more probably wrongly than rightly, a 'gassendiste'.

In summary, what Gassendi essentially represents, for all his affinities with Descartes, is something that Descartes never envisaged: the continuation of the humanist tradition within the New Philosophy, and a middle position in the *Querelle des anciens et des modernes*. While the Early Enlightenment certainly learned 'systematic doubt' from Descartes, it may well be that the concept of experiential 'bon sens' offered by Gassendi was more easy to assimilate into other disciplines than the 'rationalism' of Descartes. This is certainly true of historiography, where one may see in Bayle a fusion between methodical doubt learned from the Method and evidence assayed according to a 'probabilism' which derives more easily from Gassendi than from Descartes. When Bayle says: 'Thirty books speak of Julius Caesar while none asserts that there was no such person, therefore I am sure there was a Caesar', he is being 'probabilistic' according to Gassendi's standard of 'bon sens'.

(v) Malebranche: a modified Cartesianism

Of the many disciples of Descartes, Malebranche is the most important. He made no secret of starting not from 'universal doubt' but from Descartes' conclusions, and his conscious intention was to make of his master's philosophy a convincingly Christian system. He led the Cartesians so strongly that Alquié can maintain that eighteenth-century Cartesianism is in reality drawn from Malebranche; but he also points out that, in spite of Malebranche's 'christianising' intention, his philosophy was modified back by the 'siècle des lumières' towards deism or even atheism.[83] Our purpose in this brief section is to set out the essential modifications Malebranche brought to Cartesianism: namely, his 'finalistic' explanation of God's purpose, absent in Descartes, and his theory of 'causes occasionnelles', existing in embryo in Descartes, particularly in the *Méditations*.

Nicolas de Malebranche (1638–1715) was financially independent. He studied under the Aristotelian Rouillard from 1654 to 1656, then read scholastic theology at the Sorbonne from 1656 to 1659. In 1660 he entered the Oratory in Paris and in 1664 became a priest, this at a time when the Oratorians officially disapproved of Descartes' Jesuit schooling and of his popularity with the Jansenists. In spite of this, Malebranche's main formation in 'la philosophie', between 1664 and 1670, was essentially Cartesian. 'Dualism' was from early on an essential part of his creed, and the doctrine of the 'animal-machine' became a basic part of his theology. He read Descartes' *L'homme* when it appeared in 1664 and his *Règles* while they were unpublished. He was led by the infinitesimal calculus to modify some aspects of Descartes' physics, and he grew more committed to the experimental method than his master; but he added to Descartes' metaphysics rather than changing them, and the system of 'causes occasionnelles' was intended to fill a real breach in the physics as well as to christianise them.

His first and most directly Cartesian work, the *Recherche de la vérité* was begun in 1668, published in 1674, and reworked up to 1712. The other two main works, the *Traité de la nature et de la grâce* (1680) and the *Méditations chrétiennes* (1683), are more original, but contain by no means any disavowal of Descartes.

To consider now how Malebranche 'christianises' Descartes (who, of course, maintained that his thought was, at the least, not anti-Christian). Firstly, Malebranche fully accepts 'dualism' (the 'distinction de l'âme et du corps' of *Méditations*, VI). However, he gives it a new dimension by maintaining that we do know God's purpose in this: He made soul and body distinct so that man might learn to love Him by detaching his true self further and further from the flesh and attaching himself to the divinity; and he adduces Saint Augustine.[84] This is the 'fin de Dieu' which Descartes judged unknowable.

The second 'christianising' element, the theory of 'causes occasionnelles', requires greater elucidation. According to Cartesian dualism, mind exists 'not in extension' and body 'in extension'. This theory creates a difficult gap in the explanation of cause and effect. Consider: the mind thinks 'I shall move my arm'; the arm moves; but in the Cartesian situation there appears no way of showing that the mind *causes* the arm to move. In reverse: I touch a chair; my mind thinks 'Here is a chair'—but how can the thought have been *caused* by the action? Malebranche would explain the second example, to deal with only the one, by saying that the action does not cause the thought, but that the moment of the action is the *occasion* for God to give me the thought. My action is the 'occasion' for God to intervene, not by a particular act, but by His general will covering such eventualities. Apparent cause and effect is in fact God willing, as 'cause occasionnelle', a particular sequence which will, except in miraculous conditions, always predictably occur; in so many words, a 'law'.

There is a similar lacuna in Descartes' physics. Object *a* strikes object *b* and object *b* moves. However, lacking a concept of energy let alone transfer of energy, and having only that of a fixed quantity of motion in the universe, Descartes can not show that *a causes b* to move. Malebranche explains: God causes object *b* to move; the collision of *a* with *b* is the 'occasion' for God's general will to come into play, and He is the 'cause occasionnelle' of *b*'s motion. Malebranche agrees with Descartes that such apparent 'transfers of motion' take place only when there is contact; so God does not will action at a distance, and the theory of the *plenum* of 'matière subtile' is thereby sustained.[85]

Thus it is shown how, as Descartes had set out in general terms, the universe is sustained from instant to instant by the active will of God. Cartesian physics is thereby made unequivocally theocentric. But Malebranche goes one step beyond, to make the universe Christocentric, which in Descartes it clearly is not. In the *Traité de la nature et de la grâce* it is argued that Jesus Christ is, through particular desires of his soul, the 'occasional cause' of grace.[86] Thus the question of salvation, not treated by Descartes, is not only firmly related to the person of Jesus by Malebranche, but brought into apparent alignment with both the physics and the metaphysics of the Cartesians.

(vi) Attitudes to Descartes

The influence of Descartes was so wide that we must look beyond Malebranche. In discussing how the thought of Descartes was received, the most obvious question is: What did the Jesuits, his teachers, think of him? The question is not too easy to answer.

Baillet tells us that at least for the years 1641–4 Descartes was well considered by the Jesuits, and since he names names there is good reason to accept his view.[87] From this source and from Descartes' letters one may list Charlet, Dinet, Noël (with whom Pascal was to have the famous debate on the vacuum), Vatier and Scheiner as his friends. In a letter to Huyghens of March 1638, Descartes remarks that he had hoped for fruitful criticism of the *Discours* from La Flèche and the Society of Jesus, but had to his surprise received wholehearted approbation.[88]

Whether the Jesuits *continued* to look favourably on the work of Descartes is a more elusive question, but it is probable that they grew more and more hostile to it. In 1640 Descartes had written to Huyghens: ' . . . Je crois que je m'en vais entrer en guerre avec les Jésuites; car leur mathématicien de Paris a réfuté publiquement ma *Dioptrique* en ses thèses . . . '[89] This appears to have been on questions of physics rather than of theology. Perhaps more significant was the sending of le Père Mesland to Canada in 1645 or 1646. Bridoux notes that this exile was 'sans doute en raison des relations trop étroites qu'il avait avec Descartes et du zèle trop grand qu'il mettait à répandre sa doctrine.'[90]

It is *not* likely that the Jesuits approved of the popularity of Descartes' work with the leaders of the Jansenist movement, to which they were fundamentally opposed (see our Chapter 3, Section (ii)). Cartesianism came into Jansenism through the *Oratoire*, whose influence we have seen on the ambitions of Descartes—where Arnauld and Nicole, both to be closely connected with Port-Royal, became its partisans, as did Malebranche.[91]

None the less a limited condemnation, *donec corrigantur* ('until they shall be corrected') was brought against some of Descartes' metaphysics, thought to introduce a problem concerning transubstantiation in the Eucharist, in 1663 by the *Congrégation de l'Index*, and the instigator of this condemnation was probably Fabri, a Jesuit. The general evidence is that, with a few notable exceptions, the Jesuits were hostile to Cartesianism in the 1670s. It was doubtless after the foundation of the Académie des sciences in 1666, and its acceptance, by and large, of Cartesianism, that the Jesuits felt constrained to use Descartes in their teaching.[92]

Yet even after 1666 the temporal powers as well as some men of the Church attacked Descartes' physics. The teaching of new doctrines had been forbidden by the *parlement* in 1625, and in 1671 Louis XIV gave a verbal order forbidding new opinions in philosophy (directed as much against Descartes as anyone, though his thought was scarcely 'new' at that date). Soon, still in 1671, came the famous episode when the Sorbonne tried to persuade the *Parlement de Paris* to make an 'arrêt' forbidding the teaching of any philosophy other than that of Aristotle. The *parlement* was perhaps disinclined to do this and was thoroughly dissuaded, in part by a report from a magistrate of Cartesian leanings (identity uncertain) and perhaps even more by the famous *Arrêt burlesque* (1671) of Boileau, which showed it to what ridicule it would be laying itself open.

Even after this date, Descartes had a stormy passage with

the University of Paris, which was in this supported by the king, as well as with some Jesuits who accused Descartes of Calvinism.[93] Between 1658 and 1695, old-style (Aristotelian) text-books continued to appear in massive numbers.

In the schools of Holland the teachings of Descartes had good fortune, especially at Leyden and after his death, though not at Louvain; however, he had met with persecution during his lifetime from Voët (Voetius), Rector of the University of Utrecht, who had tried to have Descartes' doctrines, as taught there by Regius, suppressed by law, to the great embarrassment of the philosopher and in spite of his cautionary advice to Regius; and Descartes was saved from having to witness the burning of his books by the public executioner only by the intervention of the French ambassador. This malice of Voët endured from 1635 to Descartes' death in 1650. In 1647, Revius, of the Theological College of Leyden, also attacked Descartes' *Méditations*.[94] Yet in spite of these enmities, Holland became a great seedbed of Cartesian thought.[95]

There were of course throughout Europe a good number of important but lesser thinkers who took up, propagated, modified and developed Descartes' thought. It is beyond our scope to pursue in detail these individuals, who have been studied by others.[96] Of all the many names that can be listed, the two most outstanding are those of Malebranche in philosophy, greatly influenced by Descartes and in his turn influencing Spinoza; and in science Huyghens, less influenced by Descartes but, where he *was* influenced, himself very influential.

To remain for the moment in Europe: Leibniz (1646–1716) cannot be said to have been a Cartesian, though he had originally been moved away from scholasticism by his contact with Cartesianism in Paris; in many spheres he attacked Descartes; but he certainly did not evolve his philosophy without reference, albeit negative, to that of Descartes. Spinoza (Amsterdam, 1632–77) wrote a book expounding Descartes (*Renati Descartes principia philosophiae*) between 1656 and 1677, and this was one of the only two of his works published during his lifetime.

What were Descartes' fortunes in the British Isles? Here

again it is not to our purpose to make a detailed study, which one may piece together from the work of others.[97] Descartes himself was not unfamiliar with English thought. He admired Francis Bacon, Harvey and Thomas White, and was interested in Kenelm Digby. He corresponded with the physician Charles Cavendish and with Henry More of Cambridge. He did not care for Hobbes, who had been in the Mersenne circle about 1636 and who wrote the third set of *Objections* to the *Méditations*. Digby much admired Descartes, but Hobbes sided with Gassendi.

There was much interest in Descartes at Cambridge, especially at Christ's College, about the mid-century, and particularly among certain of the so-called Cambridge Platonists, who were Fellows (that is to say, at that time, in Holy Orders); notably, Henry More, Ralph Cudworth and John Smith, as well as the Puritan Nathaniel Culverwell, who was not strictly a Platonist. In the main, however, the English universities were rather bogged down in a scholasticism which had been adapted to Protestantism. John Locke, who studied at Christ Church, Oxford, between 1652 and 1655 and was depressed by its outmoded teaching, was inspired afresh to study philosophy only by encountering the works of Descartes, in whom he remained interested for the rest of his life. Somewhat later, around 1720, the Cartesian physics of Rohault (disguised in part as Newtonian physics) became a set text for Cambridge students.

The Royal Society, founded in 1660, saw errors in Descartes which caused it to regard him as a great pioneer rather than as a great authority, but was happy to see Cartesian physics replacing scholasticism in teaching even after England had recognised the superiority of Newtonian physics. The English churchmen were on the whole rather antagonistic towards Descartes—though they often knew him only by his reputation among the Dutch Protestant theologians—suspecting him of being something of a Papist. In Scotland, on the other hand, he was equally maligned by the clergy as an atheist.

Newton had early allowed Cartesian geometry to replace Euclid in his thought, though later he wrote on his Descartes: 'Error, error, non est geom'. Yet although he later consistently attacked Descartes' physics (as he also attacked Leibniz, who in turn attacked both him and Descartes), he agreed that if he himself had done better it was by standing on the shoulders of giants; of these Descartes was doubtless the tallest in his estimation. It is ironic that the French universities, at first hostile to Descartes, later established him so thoroughly that they could make no proper room for Newton, even well into the eighteenth century, although Voltaire and D'Alembert were crying aloud the greatness of the English thinker and relegating Descartes to the rôle of great but superseded pioneer.[98]

One of the questions which raised most heat among the public at large was that of Descartes' 'animal-machine'. It is scarcely surprising that it was in England, home of animal-lovers, that the doctrine aroused most opposition, illustrated by some writers with the most hilarious examples of animal sense.[99] In France also the question was much discussed in society, for example in the *salon* of Madame de la Sablière. La Fontaine had access to this *salon*, and at some date after 1675 he wrote the well-known *Discours à Madame de la Sablière (sur l'âme des animaux)* (together with the fable: *Les deux rats, le renard et l'œuf*, book 9 of the *Fables*).[100] La Fontaine's position on the issue is essentially a middle one: for him animals are less intelligent than man, but much more intelligent (therefore endowed with soul) than the Cartesians would have it. Sometimes, however, he expresses himself as though his position were at the extreme from that of Descartes: talking for instance of beaver-colonies (which had interested the *Journal des savants*) he writes:

> La république de Platon
> Ne serait rien que l'apprentie
> De cette famille amphibie.

But while La Fontaine protested, others were taking Descartes' doctrine to an extreme the philosopher had never intended: namely, stating that not only animals but men too were nothing but machines.[101] Bossuet, on the other hand, appears to have made the distinction between Descartes and his followers: while greatly fearing damage to the Church from the New Philosophy, he always approved of Descartes himself and, from the Church's point of view, of the doctrine of the 'animal-machine'.

We may say in summary that the best evidence is that Descartes' influence became in the latter part of the seventeenth century an enormous force in ideas, and remained so till about 1750. In Descartes' own day Nicole of Port-Royal wrote: 'Il s'est élevé dans un coin de la terre un homme qui prétend faire voir que tous ceux qui sont venus avant lui n'ont rien entendu dans les principes de la nature. Et ce ne sont pas de vaines paroles, car il faut avouer que le nouveau venu donne plus de lumière sur la connaissance des choses naturelles que tous les autres ensemble n'en avaient donné.'[102] While it remained difficult or even dangerous to his career throughout the seventeenth century for the professional teacher to favour Descartes, Cartesianism flourished in the eyes of the public and the *amateurs*.

Descartes helped to make the Scientific Revolution take a vast step forward: by popularising the use of experiment (all reserves made for his own hesitancy in this field); by popularising the mathematisation of nature and substituting measurement for theories of 'quality'; by popularising the mechanistic view of the universe; by opening the way to a concept of progress; by destroying the prestige of scholasticism and in general by destroying the argument from appeal to authority or dogma. Without taking up the brave drumbeating stand that Galileo had made in the *Letter to the Grand Duchess Christina*, Descartes, merely by consistently evading the theological implications of his thought, did something to free science from the restrictions of 'Biblical truth'. His enquiring disposition—his 'doute méthodique'—set the tone too for the incredulity—the 'historical Pyrrhonism' as Voltaire called it—of the Early Enlightenment.[103] All these aspects of his work held vast potential for the future of materialism and the sciences, including the 'human' sciences. Fontenelle expressed clearly how he saw the importance of the enquiring disposition, in his *Eloges—Descartes*: 'Poussé par son génie et par la supériorité qu'il se sentait, il quitta les anciens pour ne suivre que cette même raison que les anciens avaient suivie . . . Alors on ouvrit les yeux et l'on s'avisa de penser.'

Yet in the most general terms, we must add a rider:

Descartes also had something of that withering effect on the human psyche which we tend to associate with the word 'materialism' and with the decay of Classicism. For the Pythagorean mind, mathematics had been a means to contemplating and understanding the wonder of the universe. One finds something of this wonder even in Newton. Yet in the hands of the Cartesians, number became a tool for mastery over mere things.

Both literally and metaphorically, a great deal of magic disappeared from the world-picture with Descartes. Without adducing the opinions of modern Catholic philosophers, we may note that even Alquié in his little *Descartes*, quite innocent of theological preoccupations, senses something opposed to 'une vision confiante et poétique du réel', which something he does not hesitate to call 'tragique'.[104] The sense of this tragic 'joylessness' or even 'meaninglessness' has been voiced ever since Descartes.

As for the mathematisation of science, who would today renounce its fruits? Yet we may note a Cartesian passion for mathematical analysis and other 'Idols of the Laboratory'—as Suzanne K. Langer calls them—that today falsifies so much thought into pseudo-rationalism, in disciplines where they may be often so unwisely applied, such as sociology or psychology.[105]

We need pursue these unfortunate consequences of Cartesianism no further at this point, since we shall next examine the man who most clearly in the seventeenth century stands against them: Pascal. To conclude this section, we may more aptly quote the words of his most popular disciple, Fontenelle; words in which we may possibly find an irony quite other than the one he intended: 'Avant Descartes on raisonnait plus commodément; les siècles passés sont bien heureux de n'avoir pas eu cet homme-là.'

CHAPTER THREE
PASCAL

(i) Biographical background and Pascal as scientist

'Descartes inutile et incertain' (78).[1] This was one of the remarks made on Descartes by the other unquestioned genius of seventeenth-century France, Blaise Pascal, late in his rather short life. We shall attempt to arrive at an understanding of what he meant by this and similar judgements. We shall also attempt to assess the significance of this remarkably diverse mind whose products became and remain at the centre of French culture and on whom judgements range between Chateaubriand's: 'Cet effrayant génie, Blaise Pascal' and Voltaire's: 'Hélas, Pascal, on voit bien que vous êtes malade'.

Pascal may be ideally claimed by the history of ideas, for neither the history of science not the history of philosophy can render an adequate account of the whole man. His scientific work ranged from pure mathematics through the building of the first calculating machine to his extensive experiments and theorizing in physics. All or some of these achievements are certainly acknowledged in some histories of science.[2] What was of more profound significance was the way Pascal applied his theory of knowledge to science, and in particular the way he clarified the nature of scientific definition. Fully to understand his influence in this sphere, one is obliged to follow him into his study of the use and abuse of definition in the far-removed area of theological controversy (in the *Provinciales*), and this histories of science cannot do. One of the greater anomalies of inter-disciplinary division is that this man, acknowledged by all as one of France's greatest thinkers, does not appear in some histories of philosophy at all—though 'philosophy' means nothing if not 'love of wisdom'. Though regrettable in its implications for modern lines of study, this is comprehensible. Pascal was a man for whom the material world existed—unlike Descartes he never for a moment thought that physics had to justify its existence through metaphysics, and consequently he had no ontology. He had a complex theory of knowledge, but it was not of the kind that today can comfortably be called an epistemology. Consequently, his rich and extensive thinking can not be put into philosophical categories. Even in the field of ethics he is more of a 'moraliste' in the seventeenth-century sense than what would today be called a 'moral philosopher'.

There are a great many books in French on Pascal. The criticism which French writers level against each other is of writing 'hagiographically', of interpreting every development of Pascal's life essentially as a preparation for ultimate sanctity—and unfortunately this accusation is all too often justified. There are indeed two French books on Pascal as a scientist, and in how few bibliographies they figure![3] Among English writers, even Broome, who writes soundly and in detail of 'the foundations of Pascal's thought' maintains the view that his scientific thought was a *development* towards 'something better'.[4]

Consequently, it remains for the history of ideas to attempt a more equitable synthesis and to remember the Pascal of Voltaire, who could have been 'un grand Géomètre', but 'aima mieux depuis être un assez médiocre Métaphysicien'.[5] Of course, we shall not subscribe to this view, which is an unjust one, but which is, as we shall see, understandable in what it tells us of the values of the Enlightenment and interestingly different from most modern views on this major figure of the Early Enlightenment.

Pascal is in fact mostly a man of the pre-classical era, and even a man of Louis XIII's and Mazarin's world, having lived from 1623 to 1662, a year after Louis XIV assumed power in his own right. However, the first edition of the *Pensées* did not appear until 1670 in French and until 1688 in an English translation.[6] This, combined with the fact that the Jansenist controversy, in which he played a very important and publicly known part with the popular *Provinciales*, continued into the eighteenth century, means that his impetus, even in non-scientific matters, by no means faded after his death.

It is not difficult to give an account of Pascal's life with particular reference to his scientific achievements while leaving for a separate discussion his religious apologetics; this is because his real Christian commitment did not come until the end of 1654, eight years before his death, and even in these last years his scientific activities by no means ceased. Our account will be fairly schematic, since Pascal's biography is well established.[7]

Blaise Pascal (1623–1662) was born in Clermont-Ferrand. His father Etienne was a second-generation magistrate, so that, like Descartes, Pascal belonged to a fairly well-established and reasonably well-off upper-middle-class family. He had a sister three years older than himself, Gilberte, who was to become Madame Périer, under which name she left a good deal of not entirely reliable biographical information about Blaise. Two years after him, his sister Jacqueline was born. There was always loving rivalry between her and Blaise, and it was largely Pascal's sense of desolation after his father died and Jacqueline withdrew to Port-Royal that led him to the psychological crisis of his conversion (referred to sometimes as his 'second conversion') in November 1654.

Pascal's mother died when he was three, and Etienne Pascal, having taken his children to Paris (1631), used his intelligence and his relative leisure to educate his own son. Where erudition failed him, he fell back on basic questions and principles, and thus undoubtedly cultivated in Blaise the searching, testing attitude which shows in his genius for going straight to the fundamentals of a problem. As a very young adolescent Pascal was allowed into the circle of his father's scientific friends and moved in the Mersenne group. For all Mersenne's devotion to Descartes, Pascal here learned that neither Cartesian physics nor Cartesian metaphysics could go entirely unchallenged. Later, he was to hold fast to the importance of mathematical method, while rejecting the whole concept of rational proofs of God (or 'speculative theology'). He also learned about mathematics from several of the best mathematicians in France: Roberval, Fermat, Desargues.

In 1639, Etienne Pascal was appointed 'Intendant et commissaire député par sa Majesté en la Haute Normandie', and in 1640 the family were in Rouen. Rouen was by no means a cultural backwater, and a family friend was Pierre Corneille, at that time famous for half a dozen charming comedies and the passionate love-story of *Le Cid* (1636) rather than for the writing of austere tragedies of patriotism.

At seventeen, Pascal published the brief *Essai pour les coniques*, on conic sections—the parabola, hyperbola, ellipse and other curved figures, now used in ballistics and space rocketry. Descartes sneered at this work, asserting that it was all in Desargues, and, indeed, Desargues was always Pascal's mentor in mathematics;[8] but Desargues himself expressed great admiration for the trenchant manner of this maiden publication, which contains Pascal's Theorem, otherwise known as the Theorem of the Hexagon, which Pascal called the 'Hexagramme mystique' and which his contemporaries called 'la Pascale'.[9]

In 1643, Thomas Boullé was burned in the market-place of Rouen for his connection with Madeleine Bavent and the affair at Louviers, but Pascal took no interest in this sinister event. He was beginning work on the first calculating machine, which was to become known in numerous models built by him as the 'pascalin' or 'pascaline'.[10] The principle came to Pascal easily: there is a series of wheels, each of which turns its neighbour by an appropriate amount—ten revolutions or a tenth of a revolution.[11] However, as a commercial venture the machine was not so easy to develop. The technical achievement of building it stretched the resources of Pascal's workmen and his father's purse, only Pascal's workmen could repair and maintain it, and some of Pascal's prospective buyers claimed not to understand it, simple as it is. A real drawback was that, though it added and subtracted very fast, multiplication and division were slow operations, more reliable but less speedy than mental arithmetic.[12] Another drawback, commercial this time, was that the machine was expensive and clerical labour cheap. However, the principle was brilliant in its simplicity, the design compact and beautiful. Given modern electronics, the binary system of our massive computers is a fairly short step beyond it.

In 1644 began a major episode in Pascal's work in physics. Mersenne spread the word of Torricelli's today classic experiment on the vacuum, involving a forty-inch tube, closed at one end, a bowl, a quantity of mercury, and the experimenter's finger. For technical reasons, mostly the defectiveness of glass tubes or an inadequate quantity of mercury, Mersenne's friends in Paris failed to reproduce the experiment. A friend named Pierre Petit brought word of their efforts to Rouen, and Pascal, with access there to the best glass-works in Europe, did the experiment successfully in 1646. He filled a tube with mercury, covered the open end with his finger, sank it inverted in a bowl of mercury and removed his finger. The mercury in the tube began to run out, but ceased to do so when it stood about thirty inches high in the tube. What was in the space left at the top of the tube? Rarefied air?—possibly. Mercury vapours?—possibly. Torricelli had said—a void or vacuum. Classical physics had said from antiquity: 'Nature abhors a vacuum'—'la Nature a horreur du vide'—an expression which by the seventeenth century had lost its anthropomorphism, and was understood simply to mean that in nature a vacuum is impossible. Pascal was sure Torricelli was right, but he wanted to establish a system of proof by demonstration.

As he was soon to write in his *Préface sur le Traité du vide*, one properly verified exception destroys a rule, and to him Torricelli seemed to have found such an exception. But what is proper verification? The seventeenth century had little idea, once the notion of verification by ancient authority had been found wanting. Pascal conceived verification as a series of different experiments, varying the conditions so as to eliminate all hypotheses but one, and then to affirm that, until proof was available to the contrary, this hypothesis must have the status of fact. This system he proceeded to apply, and reported the results in the *Expériences nouvelles touchant le vide*, an account of eight experiments with tubes, siphons and a syringe.[13] Pascal, conscious of the need to force his scholastic adversaries to his view, did not despise showmanship, and experiment 3 describes the Torricelli experiment performed with a tube forty-six feet long (pivoted on a ship's mast), red wine and barrels of water. There can be little doubt that Pascal actually performed this experiment in public, though it is fairly sure that his description of it 'idealises' the result to some extent, since there is no mention of complications such as air-bubbles rising through the wine. By these experiments,

Pascal proved that the 'rarefied air' and 'vapour' hypotheses were false, and was able to conclude that nature's horror of the vacuum is limited and measurable. He was still showing patience and caution, but he was affirming that a vacuum *can* exist.

He then went on to perform a remarkable experiment (before the summer of 1648)—that of the 'vacuum within a vacuum'. This consists of creating a Torricellian vacuum and then repeating Torricelli's experiment *within this vacuum*— where it no longer works! Pascal deduced from this that Torricelli was right in affirming that it is the *weight of the atmosphere* which caused the mercury not to fall below thirty inches in his tube.[14] Where there is no atmosphere, the mercury falls. This, then, was a much more rational explanation than 'Nature's limited horror of the void'.

Pascal was to go on to devise the experiment which would once for all prove Torricelli right. But before this happened, he was caught up in a major confrontation with scholastic thinking. *Le père* Noël, rector of the Society of Jesus in Paris and a former teacher of Descartes at La Flèche, read Pascal's *Expériences nouvelles touchant le vide* and sent him his objections by letter. Noël was not by any means a stupid man, and his letter is not all the nonsense that is sometimes claimed: but it makes many presuppositions drawn from Aristotelian and Cartesian physics and covers many difficulties by imagining qualities or materials that will explain them away. Likewise, Pascal's reply of 29 October 1647 is not the rude missive it is sometimes described as being; on the contrary it is courteous as regards personalities, it takes the trouble to answer every objection point by point, which is in itself a courtesy; but it is rigorous in affirming new scientific standards of proof.[15]

For example, Noël begins by denying the existence of a vacuum in Torricelli's tube for two reasons, the first of which is that the 'apparent void' transmits light with 'reflections and refractions' and must therefore be a body. Pascal refutes him on a question of fact and on a question of principle. Fact: all the 'reflections and refractions' are accounted for by the glass tube, leaving nothing to be explained by the 'apparent void' in this respect. Principle: neither you nor I nor anyone else, says Pascal, know the true nature of light, so how can we know whether it can or can not pass through a vacuum? Noël had in fact produced a glorious definition of light in his letter: '... la lumière, ou plutôt l'illumination, est un mouvement luminaire des rayons, composés des corps lucides qui remplissent les corps transparents, et ne sont mus luminairement que par d'autres corps lucides...' This sounds rather like a joke, but it is not entirely stupid, since it affirms three things: that light (a) travels (b) in rays (c) consisting of 'bodies'. Pascal has the patience not to remind Noël a second time that these three things are unproven to date. He merely points out that as a *definition* of light, the words are useless, since they include two which are themselves undefined and unknown— 'luminaire' and 'lucide'. Pascal could scarcely have had a more heaven-sent opportunity to show the inadequacy of the scholastic style of definition, and he takes it curtly and with telling effect.[16]

Another argument of Noël's—a complex one based on scholastic physics—is that 'purified' or 'subtilised' air passes into the tube through pores in the glass. Pascal's long and careful answer comes down simply to the injunction: Prove it experimentally. You *presuppose*, he goes on, certain qualities of air, inventing all you need as you go along. If this manner of proof is allowed, we can explain puzzles such as magnetism and tides with very little effort. Some physicists, Pascal says, postulate the existence of things which cannot be discerned by the senses nor by any experimental method. Then they claim that the onus is on others to prove that these things do not exist rather than on themselves to prove that they do. Why do they behave so unreasonably?—to explain certain phenomena; but why do they not first examine alternative explanations which can be tested experimentally?

There are, says Pascal, only three sorts of hypothesis. A manifest absurdity follows from the negation of A—then A must be true. A manifest absurdity follows from the affirmation of B—then B is false. From C, whether affirmed or denied, no absurdities follow—then C is not proven or disproven: it remains 'douteux'. Hypotheses such as C should not be called into use. Finally, we come to one of the most critical arguments of the time. Noël says that a vacuum cannot exist, because it is *philosophically* (and, he adds, *common-sensically*) impossible for *nothing* to *exist*. This is the argument of the 'plénistes' following Descartes, that space is coextensive with matter. Pascal replies that his vacuum is empty space, and this he says is a three-dimensional volume capable of accepting a solid object of similar configuration. Empty space is then not identical with nothingness: '. . . ainsi l'espace vide tient le milieu entre la matière et le néant'. And this, he says, does not even contradict Noël's own authorities, including Aristotle. Since this philosophical argument does not prove the impossibility of empty space, it may be understood that anyone who can *produce* an empty space confutes the whole of Cartesian cosmology—going back to our starting-point: that in physics a *proven* exception destroys a 'rule'.

Noël wrote again to Pascal, who did not reply, excusing himself on the grounds of ill-health.[17] There is little doubt that he could see no future in prolonging the debate against an upholder of 'la physique péripatéticienne'. Instead, he pursued his experiments, and arrived at the greatest and most conclusive (so conclusive that its consequences continue to be drawn today).

There is no reason to believe that Nature abhors a vacuum in one place more than another; but, if Torricelli was right in believing that we live submerged in an ocean of air, then the higher we are off the bottom of this ocean the less should be the weight of air; and this should be reflected in a drop in level of the mercury in Torricelli's tube. This was the reasoning from which Pascal devised the famous experiment of the Puy-de-Dôme, a volcanic mountain four thousand feet high near Clermont. He wrote of his project to his brother-in-law, Florin Périer, on 15 November 1647.[18] Périer dutifully performed the Torricellian experiment several times in one day, at increasing altitudes, in the company of several friends, with a monitoring group repeating the same experiment at the foot of the Puy. He announced to Pascal that his hypothesis was proven in a letter of 22 September 1648, which Pascal incorporated into his *Récit de la Grande Expérience de l'équilibre des liqueurs*.[19] He himself relates performing the same experiment with measurable success on a high building in Paris (the Tour Saint-Jacques-de-la-Boucherie) and in a house with ninety steps.

From his new certainties, Pascal projected the use of the

Torricellian tube as an altimeter, guessed at the relationship between barometric pressure and weather forecasting, and described the principle of the hydraulic press (Pascal's Law).[20] Yet for himself it is clear that what he saw as most important was his vindication of the new principles of reasoning combined with experimentation which he had evolved so carefully and justified so triumphantly. If Descartes had not killed Aristotelian physics, Pascal did in these few years, and opened the way for the experimental attitude of the future Académie des sciences.

In a letter to Monsieur de Ribeyre of 12 July 1651, Pascal speaks of completing a treatise of the vacuum, of which only some fragments and the preface survived to be published posthumously. This *Préface sur le traité du vide* (circa 1647), brief as it is, is a key work for the understanding of Pascal's views on human knowledge and on the authority of experimentation versus the authority of the Ancients. It shows us that even at this time, just about when Descartes died, Pascal felt the respect for ancient authority to be a major obstacle to freedom of scientific thought, and even to be a greater force than at any time before: 'Le respect que l'on porte à l'antiquité étant aujourd'hui à tel point, que l'on se fait des oracles de toutes ses pensées, et des mystères même de ses obscurités; que l'on ne peut plus avancer de nouveautés sans péril, et que le texte d'un auteur [understand: d'un auteur ancien] suffit pour détruire les plus fortes raisons . . .'[21] It is characteristic of Pascal's classical and synthesising mind that he does not set out to banish altogether the authority of the Ancients, but only to relegate it to its proper place. It is here that he makes the distinction, essential in his thought, between those disciplines which are learned from the past exclusively and which do not change and the other disciplines in which knowledge improves and increases throughout history as though the education of the human race was that of a single maturing individual.[22]

Among disciplines to be learned exclusively from the authority of the past Pascal lists history, geography, jurisprudence, languages and—above all—theology.[23] We may smile at this view of geography as a completed discipline, seeing how comparatively poor a state it was in. We may also find Pascal's view of historiography out of step with the spirit of the times, though we may become confused as to what he meant here by authority—that of primary or secondary sources from the past? However, what is really important here is Pascal's view of theology—if one reads the recognised sacred books of the past, one will learn the sum of human knowledge in this sphere without being able to add a single thing to it. In theology, Pascal asserts categorically, ancient authority is identical with truth.[24] He is clearly here on the side of the Church as later represented by Bossuet—Protestantism must be wrong, because it is *novel*, and indeed Pascal often speaks specifically against 'nouveauté'.

On the other hand, disciplines which spring from the past but which must be constantly augmented and improved include geometry, arithmetic, music, physics, medicine, architecture 'et toutes les sciences qui sont soumises à l'expérience et au raisonnement'.[25] In this short work, the right of the Modern to feel free to build on the Ancients or to reject them is justified by every argument that we could think of today, and indeed the fact that these arguments are repeated and explained *ad nauseam* makes us realise how difficult Pascal felt that it must be to convince his contemporaries.

In 1651, Pascal's father died and his sister Jacqueline announced that it was her intention to enter the Jansenist convent of Port-Royal. Jacqueline and Blaise had made their first encounter with Jansenism by accident in 1646, while Pascal was beginning to interest himself in the vacuum. The family had been Catholic in a very lukewarm way; now, Blaise and Jacqueline vied with each other in 'piety', and Pascal promptly proved his fervour in an unedifying way by pursuing an ex-Capuchin and doctor of theology whose views he disapproved of until he had him forced by Archbiship Harley to write a humiliating retraction of his views. This wretched episode is known as the Scandal of Saint-Ange, from the name of the victim. The 1646 'conversion' of Pascal is known as the 'first, or intellectual conversion' to his biographers.

Now, in 1651, he showed unwillingness to agree to his sister's joining the Jansenist sorority, and made financial difficulties. This was rather out of character, for, though intellectually ferocious, he had always shown himself a generous person. His real motive may well have been fear of finding himself virtually alone in the world. None the less, Jacqueline entered Port-Royal in January 1652 and Pascal heightened his activities in the brilliant society of the Duc de Roannez, in what is known as his 'période mondaine' (1651–3).

He was sick (he was to die at thirty-nine, probably of intestinal tuberculosis) and, in the midst of his rich, pleasant and intellectually stimulating friends, he knew he was lonely. Various great ladies are said to have tried matchmaking on his behalf, but he never gave any real evidence of interest—indeed, his must be one of the most sexless biographies of all time. Sometimes the *Discours sur les passions de l'amour* is attributed to him and indeed figures, with all the necessary cautionary remarks, in his *œuvre*. If he did write it, it proves nothing except a very slender and theoretical knowledge of sexual passion.[26]

He did however become engrossed again in pure mathematics. His friends' interest in gambling led him to work on some problems involving stakes and the theoretical outcome of unfinished games of chance ('règle des partis'). Thus he found himself working alongside Fermat on what he calls not the mathematics of chance but 'la géométrie du Hasard' (in Latin he calls it 'aleae Geometria').[27] From Fermat and Pascal was to develop the modern mathematical mastery of calculations of probability, vastly important today not only for insurance companies, football pools promoters and Las Vegas but more especially for all physicists since Heisenberg's Uncertainty Principle, especially those concerned with quantum mechanics. The first physicist to use Pascal in this way was Boyle: in studying gases, the behaviour of a single molecule is found to be unpredictable, but the average behaviour of a large number of molecules can be known through the mathematics of probability. Without this piece of understanding, we could not have the second law of thermodynamics which is at the heart of much modern physics. Pascal's special contribution to this field was the Arithmetical Triangle (or Pascal's Triangle), which is said to have been known since the great Arabs, but which Pascal and Fermat, independently of each other and of Galileo, brought to a new point of elegance and usefulness in 1654.[28]

In this same year, 1654, Pascal was growing more and more depressed (the expression used by his family was 'angoisse'), disgusted with himself and *le monde* and with no spark apparently left alive from his 'first conversion'. His second conversion came like a thunderbolt—*FEU*, he wrote at the head of the sheet of paper on which he recorded it (the *'Mémorial'*), dating it Monday 23 November 1654 from about half past ten in the evening until half past midnight.[29] Descartes' Dream was thus followed by Pascal's Illumination. Where Descartes moved into a crisis probably brought about by intellectual exhaustion and over-excitement, Pascal's mania exploded out of a long period of depression and acute anxiety. Now Pascal had a vision of a God who was ' "Dieu d'Abraham, Dieu d'Isaac, Dieu de Jacob", non des philosophes et des savants'— that is, we may understand, known by revelation and not by speculative theology. From now on, though he was far from abandoning science (witness the work on the cycloid of 1658), his life became theocentric, and we shall study this period in the following sections.

During these last years Pascal wrote the *Provinciales* (1656-7) in defence of Port-Royal and projected a grand *Apologie de la religion chrétienne* which survives unfinished as the *Pensées*. It was long thought that Pascal died virtually pen in hand and left the *Pensées* in disorder. There is good reason to think, however, that he began work on them as soon as he abandoned the *Provinciales* (January 1657) and perhaps that he did very little to them after the end of 1658.[30] In consequence, the 1670 edition of the *Pensées* can by no means be regarded as the extreme mis-representation it was traditionally held to be but was perhaps quite close to Pascal's intentions.

At the same time, in 1658, Pascal did his greatest work in mathematics. From conic sections he moved on to the much more difficult shape of the cycloid (which he calls 'la cycloïde' or 'la Roulette')—the line marked out by a point on the circumference of a circle rolling along a plane. This work, combined with his conclusions on the Arithmetical Triangle, took him to the threshold of the integral calculus, which subsumes the differential calculus and the infinitesimal calculus.[31] Leibniz and Newton are both credited with the invention of the integral calculus, and it is pointless to argue who has priority, for it is in the nature of mathematical evolution that great steps forward may be made in different places at the same time quite independently. What is sure in the case of Leibniz is that he made his discovery of the calculus with Pascal's notes on the cycloid in front of him.

This discovery was one of the two greatest mathematical steps taken in the seventeenth century—the other being Descartes' analytical and projective geometry. Classical physics had always examined static situations. The great step forward made by modern physics is to examine a changing situation—such as acceleration or change of orbital direction. This is impossible without the use of the concept of the infinitesimal, and this was the great tool bequeathed indirectly by Descartes and directly by Pascal to Leibniz and the modern world, in the calculus.

(ii) Pascal and Jansenism: the Lettres provinciales

The controversy between Jesuits and Jansenists was a theological quarrel of which the complexities cannot, in their detail, find a place within the scope of this book, and can be followed in more specialised studies.[32] We are concerned with the controversy for two reasons. One is that Pascal's *Lettres provinciales,* which have a famous place in it, show how his new method of scientific discrimination between definition and reality could be propagated into an apparently alien domain. The other is that the pessimistic view of man's fallen state ('la corruption de la nature') so widespread in the second half of the seventeenth century, when it obscures both the joy of the pre-1650 'Catholic Renaissance' and also the confidence in man's will proclaimed by Descartes, would remain largely inexplicable without the phenomenon of Jansenism.

The essence of the controversy concerned the understanding of predestination and divine grace, a cause for conflict with its roots in patristic times. The problem was as follows: If God *predestines* some men to be saved by the grace of His son, what part in their salvation can free will play? Indeed, can free will exist? If, on the other hand, man can freely choose to approach God, what need is there of a grace-bringing Saviour?

There were two main responses to this dilemma as early as the fourth century. Saint Augustine of Hippo, the 'Master of Grace', formulated the view which may be called Western (or 'Roman'). Since the Fall, man is the slave of sin and cannot work for salvation, for he has no free will. Grace brings free will. Yet it would be justice for God to allow the damnation of all men; so man has no claim on grace, which remains an arbitrary gift of God drawing some ('vessels of mercy') to Himself through Christ. The rest remain 'vessels of wrath'. Augustine was forced perhaps to this extreme position by the existence of an alternative, Eastern (or 'Greek') view, formulated by his contemporary, Pelagius. This Irish monk, nurtured on Greek humanism, put the emphasis on the freedom of man. His will was weakened by the Fall, but not to such a degree that he could not freely choose the good. Grace was a universal gift, not arbitrarily bestowed, but God-given to every man in sufficient measure to allow him to win salvation.

Pelagius' view seemed to throw doubt on the need for Atonement by a Saviour, and he was anathematised as a heresiarch. Yet his influence was strong, and in the thirteenth century the modified Augustinism of Aquinas was countered by the 'semi-Pelagianism' of John Duns Scotus. The Council of Trent, anxious to satisfy all elements within Catholicism in order to achieve unity against the Reformed church, while largely favouring Augustine, succeeded in leaving plenty of room for further controversy. Latter-day Augustinism, deriving from Aquinas and called 'Thomism', was largely the prerogative of the Dominicans. A Jesuit General, Aquaviva, openly gave his Society the right to disagree with Saint Thomas, their champion in philosophy, on this one issue of grace, in 1586. The Spanish Jesuit Molina invented 'Molinism', which was almost pure Pelagianism, with his *Concord of Free Will with the Gifts of Grace*, in 1588; and the Jesuits rallied to Molinism against Dominican Thomism. A further complication for Thomist Catholics was that Calvin, too, claimed Augustine as his theological ancestor. Multiple antagonisms reigned, against all papal injunctions, with the passing years.

Then on to the scene emerged an entirely new faction, and the story, which we shall summarise very briefly, is a curious one. A 'new reading' of Augustine was expounded by Jansen (Jansenius, Flemish, 1585–1638), who had been Bishop of Ypres for three years, in his posthumous *Augustinus* (1640). Jansen and his Basque friend, Jean du Vergier de Hauranne, abbé de Saint-Cyran (1581–1643), had followed up their studies at Louvain by coming together in 1619 to restore the primitive meaning of Augustinism, which they felt had been badly eroded. Jansen was the peace-loving philosopher, Saint-Cyran the militant who nearly succeeded in winning Bérulle and the Oratory to the new cause, and who, for a while admired by Richelieu, provoked his enmity, and spent some time in prison; while Bérulle, an ardent Augustinian and enemy of the Jesuits, was more or less disgraced in the last two years of his life (1628–9).

In 1636 Saint-Cyran had become spiritual director of Port-Royal, a Cistercian convent whose worldliness had been radically reformed by its Mother Superior, Angélique Arnauld (in 1609 when she was seventeen), and which had become a shining light of the Counter-Reformation and the 'Catholic Renaissance', a focus of the life of renunciation in that era of high spiritual aspiration, and deeply admired by most Catholics. When Saint-Cyran confronted Angélique Arnauld (and he refused a bishopric offered by Richelieu to remain at Port-Royal) the convent became the bastion of defence for the *Augustinus* and a formidable intellectual centre. The men of the powerful Arnauld family, mostly lawyers, rallied to it, founded the school that formed Racine and favoured Cartesianism, and became the nucleus of the famous 'messieurs de Port-Royal'.

The Jesuits hated the views of Jansen. Jansenism was a major rival to their Molinism, it challenged their hard-won influence, it savoured of Calvinism, and, above all, they thought its terrifying austerity such that it would drive souls from the Church. The controversy simmered, and boiled in 1649 when seven propositions supposed to have been drawn from the *Augustinus* were debated by the Sorbonne. The Jansenists' leader, Antoine Arnauld the younger, did not handle the situation well. His legalistic mind was obsessed with being in the right. He alienated the Sorbonne, then the Pope, then the *parlement* of Paris. By 1656 the situation looked very black for the Jansenists. Arnauld wanted to appeal to public opinion, but recognised that his legalistic style was not appropriate.

But there was the brilliant thirty-three-year-old Pascal, who since his 'Illumination' of 1654 had seemed to forgo his tremendous reputation in scientific controversy and had grown close enough to Port-Royal to accept a Jansenist confessor. Pascal was urged to take up the defence of Port-Royal, and he did. He did more, he produced a devastating attack on the Jesuits in his eighteen *Lettres provinciales* (1656–7).[33] Arnauld and his friend Nicole supplied the theological documentation.[34] Pascal, under the pseudonym of 'Louis de Montalte', supplied the stylish argument. His geometrical training and his meditations on definition in *De l'esprit géométrique* allowed him to cut through the verbiage under which the true issues were buried and to make his work appear the triumph of good sense over bombast and pedantry.[35] His scorn of the world of the 'specialist' caused the same widespread delight as Descartes' had done.

In the *Provinciales*, unlike the *Pensées*, Pascal's commitment to Jansenism goes without question. He is more honest than most writers in the controversy, but there is an unmistakeable element of special pleading, for example in the proof that Jansenism has nothing in common with Calvinism.[36] The letters that truly delighted the public were numbers 5 to 16, a devastating attack on what Pascal regarded as moral flabbiness and hypocrisy in the Jesuits. The satire in these letters is brilliant. Voltaire, who was fundamentally opposed to Pascal's philosophy, extravagantly called the *Provinciales* the first book of genius to have been seen in France; but this immoderate praise is understandable, for Voltaire was acknowledging that Pascal had invented the style of satire that was to be his own and to serve as the main polemical weapon of the Enlightenment. Pascal's pseudo-ingenuous, commonsense approach to questions of dogma made the Jesuits look deceitful and ridiculous, and gave the word 'casuistry' pejorative connotations that had not previously existed, and which have never ceased to be associated with the Jesuits.

The irony is that Pascal's brilliant polemical triumph meant that there could be no stepping back from total war. With Louis XIV convinced that the Jansenists were undesirable, the war was inevitably lost for them, though not till Pascal was in the grave. Systematic persecution ended in the dissolution of Port-Royal before the century was out, and eighteenth-century Jansenism was, except briefly about 1710, little more than a parliamentary alliance with the Gallicans. The triumphant Jesuits were to have their own misfortunes after 1715, but that story cannot concern us here.

Yet though the Jesuits triumphed in the theologico-political sphere, they did not dominate the psychology of late seventeenth-century Catholicism. The prestige of Port-Royal could not be destroyed so easily as its buildings. The gloomy sense of man's destiny in his helpless 'fallen' state that Pascal championed along with Jansenism was a shadow on the spirit of the nation during the 'pious' later years of Louis XIV. Perhaps the savagely cynical La Rochefoucauld was a freakish product of that era, as some of his lady readers asserted in their letters, but *Phèdre*, with its heroine damned in the blood by her heritage and by a vengeful divinity, remains probably the most powerful expression of the innermost mind of its age. And others, unlike Racine not directly touched by Jansenist teaching, even Bayle and Fontenelle, show very little enthusiasm for humanity and its potential for good.

Theological controversy was perhaps in any case unworthy of a man with Pascal's mind. One is inclined to agree with Diderot: 'Qu'il serait à souhaiter que [Pascal] eût laissé aux Théologiens de son temps le soin de vider leurs querelles . . . et surtout qu'il eût refusé pour maîtres des hommes qui n'étaient pas dignes d'être ses disciples . . . ' (*Pensées philosophiques*, XIV). What is certain is that Jansenism fed in Pascal the disgust with life of a sick body and, as we shall see, drove love out of the *Pensées*, even in the projected hymn to the 'félicité de l'homme avec Dieu'.[37]

(iii) The Pensées: *Pascal on reason, man and God*

The Pascal of the *Pensées* as left at his death—or abandoned earlier—is the only Pascal we can be entirely sure of, but the work was clearly never intended to be considered complete as it stood. The Pascal as presented to the world by Port-Royal in 1670 is of great interest, for, in so far as the work was a seminal one for the thought of others, it was in the Port-Royal edition and others pirated from it that the seeds were sown. Yet to study the *Pensées* in this way would be to use an approach too specialised for the present work. Important as it is to try to judge what Pascal meant to his era, it is more important here to get as close as we may to the mind of Pascal himself. We are thus led inescapably to consider the *Pensées* as twentieth-century scholarship has constructed them from the copies which the Port-Royal committee made before they attempted to make their own edition.[38]

Using the text established by Brunschvicg, let us begin our examination by putting together two *pensées* whose juxtaposition can appear to present a puzzle. In trying to solve the puzzle, we may hope at the same time to answer the question with which we opened this chapter: why did Pascal consider Descartes to be 'inutile et incertain'?

The two *pensées* in question are: 'Pensée fait la grandeur de l'homme' (346) and 'Le cœur a ses raisons que la raison ne connaît point . . . ' (277). A superficial reading of these two affirmations can make one believe that in the first Pascal is making the greatest of claims for man's ability to think and that in the second he is denying the same claim in favour of a different human aptitude, namely, the ability to be guided by emotion or sentiment. This is not in the least what Pascal intended; but the misunderstanding has been reinforced over generations by writers who have not specifically meditated on Pascal but have taken 'Le cœur a ses raisons . . . ' out of the context of Pascal's work in order to support a particular view of their own concerning the merits of man's emotional self.

To understand what Pascal actually meant, one must first understand that both 'raison' and 'cœur' are subsumed by the word 'pensée'—that both reason and whatever is meant by 'cœur' are aspects of man's power of thought.

We soon discover this to be true when we explore Pascal on the subject of 'le cœur'. Firstly we find what 'le cœur' is not. 'Les hommes prennent souvent leur imagination pour leur cœur; et ils croient être convertis dès qu'ils pensent à se convertir.' (275) 'Cœur' then is not wishful thinking, nor is it being swayed by emotion. As to what 'le cœur' *is*, Pascal nowhere defines it, but he does tell us something about it, and from this we may arrive at a definition:

> Nous connaissons la vérité non seulement par la raison, mais encore par le cœur; c'est de cette sorte que nous connaissons les premiers principes . . . Car la connaissance des premiers principes, comme qu'il y a espace, temps, mouvements, nombres, [est] aussi ferme qu'aucune de celles que nos raisonnements nous donnent. Et c'est sur ces connaissances du cœur et de l'instinct qu'il faut que la raison s'appuie, et qu'elle y fonde tout son discours. (Le cœur sent qu'il y a trois dimensions dans l'espace et que les nombres sont infinis . . . Les principes se sentent, les propositions se concluent et le tout avec certitude, quoique par différentes voies.) (282)

From this quotation it is clear that 'cœur' or 'instinct' is what gives us knowledge of first principles, and that these first principles concern the basic nature of what we call reality—for example, that we live in three-dimensional space. Thus, 'le cœur' is that which provides us with our first premises or certainties from which 'raison' must make *all* its deductions.

Thus, the activity of 'le cœur' is precisely the same here as that 'intuition' which gave Descartes his first certainty, 'Je pense, donc je suis'. The reader will remember that the *cogito* was arrived at, to use Descartes' own words, 'simplici mentis intuitu'—in a single flash of insight or intuition.

The place of 'intuitus' in Descartes' thinking can not be more clearly shown than it has been by Keeling:

> Our actual thinking when brought into compliance with the Method consists in employing three kinds of intellectual operation, those Descartes names *enumeratio*, *deductio*, and *intuitus*—the first of which depends upon the second, and this upon the third.
> *Intuitus*, the most fundamental operation, is a non-discursive or direct act of prehension, single and momentary and infallible . . . *Deductio* is itself but *intuitus* extended; it is intuition of connexion between intuitions.[39]

Keeling here points to two things in Descartes. Firstly, that the intuition of primary truths is a direct act not consciously reasoned but sure of its own rightness. Secondly, he shows, in an extended contrast between Cartesian and more modern philosophy which we have dropped from the quotation, that the knowledge that *b* follows from *a*—the 'deductive' process—depends on a further intuition; the rules of logic themselves can be known to be correct and to have been correctly applied only by the intuitive grasp we have of them.

Let us consider these two affirmations now in respect of Pascal. On the first, when Pascal tells us that one knows first principles through 'le cœur' he clearly means something very close to what Descartes meant by *intuitus*. Neither could analyse what intuition is, nor how it works. Yet they clearly each had a notion about it, and their notions differ profoundly. Since Descartes' first intuition, the *Je pense, donc je suis*, takes place in a situation of 'hyperbolic doubt' in which *nothing* except the thinking mind as self can be intuited, the act of thought must be held, if only hyperbolically (that is, by pretence), to take place in the void. Thus Descartes is forced by his own hyperbolic doubt to present intuition as what we may call, for want of another expression, an act of 'pure intellect'. Pascal, on the other hand, starts from no such hyperbolic doubt. He takes the real existence of the universe to be self-evident, and so intuition as he conceives it does not take place in a void—it springs directly from his own existence as a sentient being in a real universe; instead of being an act of 'pure intellect', his intuition involves his whole person, his whole reality as common sense understands it.

This difference can be underlined by contrasting the approach of the two thinkers to the question: What am I? In Descartes' dialogue *La recherche de la vérité* the pupil is taught by the master not to speak of himself as a man, that is, a creature with arms, legs and a head, but only as 'a thinking substance'. Pascal cuts straight across the problem by asserting: I know myself *naturally* to be a man: '. . . Il n'y a rien de plus faible que le discours de ceux qui veulent définir ces mots primitifs. Quelle nécessité y a-t-il d'expliquer ce qu'on entend par le mot *homme*?'[40] Pascal goes on to state that the intuition of one's own being comes 'naturellement' and does not even have to be formulated in words. What does 'naturellement' imply? In discussing *le cœur*, Cruickshank writes:

No doubt it is most obviously in the Old Testament that the term 'heart' is used to indicate the whole personality of a man and, more particularly, that focal point of personality which holds together thought, feeling and will in such a combination that they can provide knowledge which is direct, concrete and, to that extent, intuitive . . . It follows, in more secular contexts, that the 'heart' can be a shortened term for what we now call existential, as distinct from *a priori* apprehension of reality. It is in something like this sense—and it certainly cannot be in the sense of irrational emotionalism—that Pascal uses the term when he writes: 'Le cœur a son ordre, l'esprit a le sien qui est par principe et démonstration. Le cœur en a un autre . . .'[41]

'Naturellement' can thus be held to mean 'by an existential . . . apprehension of reality'.

This difference in envisaging *intuition*, on the one hand as an act of 'pure intellect', on the other as 'instantaneous knowledge drawn from the whole personality', is perhaps not real. No doubt Descartes' *Je pense, donc je suis* was an insight that in reality involved his whole personality; but his hyperbolic doubt forced him as part of his 'feinte' to pretend that it came not from a whole personality but from pure mind.

This pretence was the root cause of the vast amount of damage the Romantics held Descartes to have caused to the human psyche throughout the seventeenth and eighteenth centuries. The history of ideas has shown their belief not to have been idle. The long fight of the Romantics to convince their own nineteenth century that man's Cartesian 'intellect' is only the tip of the iceberg as regards what and how man can *know* was quite justified in view of the aridity they found in the post–1789 and post-Napoleonic psyche of the French. The best of twentieth-century thought shows that the instinct of the Romantics to believe that Pascal's view could enrich their understanding was right and that indeed there cannot be today a study of 'mind' that remains within the confines of pure philosophy and does not draw heavily on other disciplines involving the 'whole man'—psychology, physiology, biology and bio-chemistry, to name only the most obvious.[42]

Now we come to Keeling's second affirmation concerning Descartes, namely that, in the Method, not only first principles but the deductive process depend upon intuition. Does this affirmation apply also to Pascal? The answer is that it does—Pascal believes that one arrives at *conclusions*, in the best kind of thinking, by a series of rapid deductions which are intuitively known to be sound; but again his vision of the mind's working differs fundamentally from that of Descartes.

To understand how this is so, we must consider now not the key-word 'cœur' but two other key-words which occur less often but in very famous passages. The key-words are 'justesse' and 'finesse' and are interchangeable; and they occur particularly in the well-known meditation on 'l'esprit de géométrie et l'esprit de finesse' (1–4). The substance of this meditation is as follows.

There are at least two fields of understanding in which the human mind can operate, and each requires its own kind of 'esprit': 'Diverses sortes de sens droit; les uns dans un certain ordre de choses, et non dans les autres ordres, où ils extravaguent' (2). One order of things is the field of mathematical problems in the most general sense. In this 'ordre de choses' the mind reasons in a methodical way according to a limited number of principles. These principles are not commonplace, but, once one has given them one's attention, it is almost impossible to make a mistake: ' . . . il faudrait avoir tout à fait l'esprit faux pour mal raisonner sur des principes si gros qu'il est presque impossible qu'ils échappent' (1). The kind of mind which can do well in this order of things is what Pascal calls 'l'esprit de géométrie', and, in describing it, it is quite clear that Descartes is not far from his thoughts. Descartes, the reader will remember, had said that, given the principles, a child 'instructed in mathematics' could have formed his long chains of reasoning as well as he himself had done.

The other 'ordre de choses' is not specified, except that we are told that it is concerned not with knowledge ('science') but with judgement ('jugement') (4). We are also told that it is a commonplace order of things, what everyone meets every day, and it is clear that this is what we call the 'existential' order or the order of 'reality'. In this order of things what is required is 'l'esprit de finesse', and the operations of 'l'esprit de finesse' are far more complex than those of 'l'esprit de géométrie' even though they may appear more familiar to us (because they involve the 'whole man'). 'Mais dans l'esprit de finesse, les principes sont dans l'usage commun et devant les yeux de tout le monde. On n'a que faire de tourner la tête, ni de se faire violence; il n'est question que d'avoir bonne vue, mais il faut l'avoir bonne: car les principes sont si déliés et en si grand nombre, qu'il est presque impossible qu'il n'en échappe' (1). These principles are sensed rather than known.

Perhaps to put the two concepts into our own imagery will not be misleading. The 'esprit de géometrie', involved in 'science', faces the problem of adding link after link to a chain, testing it at every stage, until it adds the last link which is the solution. The 'esprit de finesse', involved in 'reality', faces an entirely different problem—that of the juggler for whom the 'solution' is to keep a number of balls in the air at once—an 'aesthetic' problem in a sense. The 'esprit de finesse' makes so many fine judgements at once and so rapidly that the Method of Descartes cannot be used—there can be no dividing up of the problem, no recapitulation of steps taken, no analysis of the principles applied to see whether they are 'evident'. When the 'esprit de finesse' has made a judgement, so many things have gone into the making of it that the thinker cannot say, or perhaps even know, how the final judgement was made. Yet he knows when it is a correct judgement and that it has not been reached haphazardly, just as the juggler knows that if the six balls are there in the air in front of him there is no accident involved and everything is 'just right'.

Pascal did not despise the 'esprit de géométrie', having himself used it in mathematics, but he grew to despise the 'ordre de choses' to which it applies itself. It is perhaps implicit that he considered the best mind as that which was capable of 'esprit de géométrie' and 'esprit de finesse' at the right moment, and that he himself was one such mind. Of course, when the juggler has reached his 'solution', his success is self-evident. There is no such evident criterion for the thinker; the 'esprit de finesse' knows it is right only through *le cœur*, intuitively, and it is clear that the quality of the intuition depends on the quality of the whole personality that has that intuition. When we have completed our examination of Pascal's thought, we shall be faced with the difficult and perhaps arrogant task of judging it in the light of his whole personality.

Now we see the explanation of the first of two things for which Pascal rejects Descartes, and this is that Descartes' faith in 'pure intellect' prevented him from trusting in a higher and wiser process of mind—thinking with the whole man (*le cœur*). Pascal insists again and again that 'pure intellect' (*raison*) is unreliable and inadequate:

... Il faudrait avoir une règle. La raison s'offre, mais elle est ployable à tous sens; et ainsi il n'y en a point. (274)

... Il ne faut pas se méconnaître, nous sommes automates autant qu'esprit ... La coutume fait nos preuves les plus fortes et les plus crues; elle incline l'automate, qui entraîne l'esprit sans qu'il y pense. (252)

Imagination.—C'est cette partie dominante dans l'homme, cette maîtresse d'erreur et de fausseté, et d'autant plus fourbe qu'elle ne l'est pas toujours . . .

Cette superbe puissance, ennemie de la raison, qui se plaît à la contrôler et à la dominer, pour montrer combien elle peut en toutes choses, a établi dans l'homme une seconde nature . . .

Qui dispense la réputation? qui donne le respect et la vénération aux personnes, aux ouvrages, aux lois, aux grands, sinon cette faculté imaginative? . . .

L'imagination dispose de tout; elle fait la beauté, la justice, et le bonheur, qui est le tout du monde.

Les impressions anciennes ne sont pas les seules capables de nous abuser: les charmes de la nouveauté ont le même pouvoir.

Nous avons un autre principe d'erreur, les maladies. Elles nous gâtent le jugement et le sens . . .

Notre propre intérêt est encore un merveilleux instrument pour nous crever les yeux agréablement . . . (82)

Ces deux principes de vérités, la raison et les sens, outre qu'ils manquent chacun de sincérité, s'abusent réciproquement l'un l'autre . . . (83)

All these 'puissances trompeuses'—conditioning ('coutume', 'automate'), imagination, the appeal of novelty, illness, self-interest, confusion between mind and sense-impression—all of them, one might say, could affect 'le cœur' just as much as 'la raison'. However, the man who relies on 'le cœur' has this advantage: he is aware that his whole personality is involved, and can guard against self-deception; while the man who relies on 'pure intellect', something which probably cannot exist, is deluded into believing that his thought is unconditioned. We have seen a little of how Descartes' thinking is moulded, without his being aware of it, by the very scholastic patterns he wanted to 'exterminate'.[43]

Not only is pure intellection beset by all these dangers, but it has the limitation of 'l'esprit de géometrie'—it can cope with only 'un certain ordre de choses':

La dernière démarche de la raison est de reconnaître qu'il y a une infinité de choses qui la surpassent; elle n'est que faible, si elle ne va jusqu'à connaître cela. (267)

Il n'y a rien de si conforme à la raison que ce désaveu de la raison. (272)

La nature confond les pyrrhoniens, et la raison confond les dogmatiques. Que deviendrez-vous donc, ô hommes qui cherchez quelle est votre véritable condition par votre raison naturelle? Vous ne pouvez fuir une de ces sectes, ni subsister dans aucune.

Connaissez donc, superbe, quel paradoxe vous êtes à vous-même. Humiliez-vous, raison impuissante; taisez-vous, nature imbécile . . . (434)

If these preceding fragments seem to suggest that Pascal is moving into outright fideism, we must pause to observe that he does not go so far. The Christian is not invited to abdicate reason, but to recognise its limits: 'Soumission et usage de la raison, en quoi consiste le vrai christianisme' (269). 'Deux excès: exclure la raison, n'admettre que la raison' (253). We shall shortly see that Pascal believes human experience and the Bible to offer rational certainties of God: for example, that human experience proves the reality of the Fall and that it is unreasonable not to believe in miracles.

These famous quotations on the limits of reason show us quite clearly Pascal as a bastion against the 'scientific angelism' which we found in Descartes; a voice speaking against the temptation of allowing 'la raison raisonnable' to become 'la raison raisonnante'. In this voice that speaks against excess in either of two directions, we hear unmistakably the tone of seventeenth-century classicism, sounding with an authenticity never to be heard in Descartes' advocating of the middle way and frequently belied by his prophecies of mankind's triumph through reason. Which voice speaks more truly for seventeenth-century France? This is a question that must remain undecided.

So far we have followed Pascal in his attack on Descartes' *theory of knowledge* or of mind. Now, however, we come to the second cause for which Pascal rejects Descartes. If the first was that Descartes had a false theory of knowledge, and so remains essentially an issue of epistemology on which any philosopher can listen patiently to Pascal, the second brings us directly to Pascal as Christian apologist; at which point he may well leave behind the non-believer, for the second and total rejection of Descartes is on the ground that he *applied thought to the wrong object and for the wrong end.*

In following Pascal here, we come to some of his most sensational statements:

Descartes.—Il faut dire en gros: 'Cela se fait par figure et mouvement', car cela est vrai. Mais de dire quels et composer la machine, cela est ridicule. Car cela est inutile et incertain et pénible. Et quand cela serait vrai, nous n'estimons pas que toute la philosophie vaille une heure de peine. (79)[44]

Ordre. —J'aurais bien pris ce discours d'ordre comme celui-ci: pour montrer la vanité de toutes sortes de conditions, montrer la vanité des vies communes, et puis la vanité des vies philosophiques pyrrhoniennes, stoïques; mais l'ordre ne serait pas gardé . . . Nulle science humaine ne le peut garder. Saint Thomas ne l'a pas gardé. La mathématique le garde, mais elle est inutile en sa profondeur. (61)

In these violent rejections of scientific enquiry, Pascal tries to appeal to the current concept of the *honnête homme*. It is more important to be a well-balanced person than to be a philosopher: 'On ne s'imagine Platon et Aristote qu'avec de grandes robes de pédants. C'étaient des gens honnêtes et, comme les autres, riant avec leurs amis, et, quand ils se sont divertis à faire leurs *Lois* et leurs *Politiques,* ils l'ont fait en se jouant; c'était la partie la moins philosophe et la moins sérieuse de leur vie, la plus philosophe était de vivre simplement et tranquillement' (331). This is simply the comment of a humanist. However, the darker preoccupations of the Jansenist mind strike a more troubled and fundamental note: 'Les trois concupiscences ont fait trois sectes, et les philosophes n'ont fait autre chose que suivre une des trois concupiscences' (461). The three concupiscences are the lust for knowledge, the lust for enjoyment and the lust for power. It is clear enough that Pascal, though not referring specifically to Descartes,[45] must have seen these three lusts as guiding the other man at least in his hopes for mankind. Descartes, we remember, promised men that they should solve all problems, enjoy the fruits of the earth and master both their own passions and the natural kingdom. But after his 'Illumination', Pascal, we must guess, felt himself to have been mastered, like Descartes, by at least one of these lusts, the lust for knowledge. And, in the gloomy Jansenist way, he appears to prefer to regard his scientific genius as a temptation (which was still besetting him) and a curse rather than a gift.

Now he prefers to believe that the only merit of philosophy is that it leads one from childish ignorance to learned ignorance (327). He attacks Pyrrhonists (434) and Stoics (360), as he attacked the Stoics in the person of Epictetus as well as the Epicureans in the person of Montaigne in the *Entretien avec Monsieur de Saci.*[46]

But most ferociously of all he attacks Descartes: 'Je ne puis pardonner à Descartes: il aurait bien voulu, dans toute sa philosophie, pouvoir se passer de Dieu; mais il n'a pu s'empêcher de lui faire donner une chiquenaude pour mettre le monde en mouvement; après cela, il n'a plus que faire de Dieu' (77). Descartes had indeed devoted himself to proving the existence of God. But, says Pascal above, for the wrong reason, and, elsewhere, by the wrong method. Descartes had used the ontological argument in the manner of Saint Anselm, in other words he had engaged in rational theology just like the scholastic philosophers. But this, says Pascal, is pure intellect applied to an order of things where it is useless: 'C'est le cœur qui sent Dieu et non la raison' (278). For proof is not faith: 'Voilà ce que c'est que la foi: Dieu sensible au cœur, non à la raison' (ibid.).

Pascal uses the very concepts of Descartes to show the impossibility of rational knowledge of God: because we exist in extension and have boundaries, we cannot intellectualise concerning God, who is not in extension and has no boundaries.[47] Intellectual argument drawn from 'geometric' truths can perhaps give an abstract concept of 'une première vérité ... qu'on appelle Dieu'; but such a concept would move no atheist, and is more appropriate to deism (which Pascal abhors almost as much as atheism) than to Christianity (556; 279; 561). Nor will he use the so-called 'argument from design', the argument we shall examine in Fénelon, that the providential disposition and the beauty of the natural world prove a benign creator:

Le Dieu des chrétiens ne consiste pas en un Dieu simplement auteur des vérités géométriques et de l'ordre des éléments; c'est la part des païens et des épicuriens. Il ne consiste pas seulement en un Dieu qui exerce sa providence sur la vie et sur les biens des hommes, pour donner une heureuse suite d'années à ceux qui l'adorent; c'est la portion des Juifs. Mais ... le Dieu des chrétiens ... c'est un Dieu qui leur fait sentir intérieurement leur misère et sa miséricorde infinie; ... que les rend incapables d'autre fin qui lui-même. (556)

Man, the fragile reed that can think, differs from the mindless universe that can destroy him in that he alone can comprehend his own situation in that universe (347). But this *roseau pensant* must be careful to apply himself to what counts. This is the ultimate reason why science ('philosophie') is rejected: 'Je trouve bon qu'on n'approfondisse pas l'opinion de Copernic: mais ceci . . . Il importe à toute la vie de savoir si l'âme est mortelle ou immortelle' (218; see also 194). Man has been given thought so that he can recognise his own misery in his present state: 'La grandeur de l'homme est grande en ce qu'il *se connaît* misérable. Un arbre ne se connaît pas misérable' (397, my italics; see also 416). Here we have come finally to the explanation of why 'Pensée fait la grandeur de l'homme'; thought is great when it applies itself, not to explaining the universe or proving God, but to recognising its own misery. It is this recognition which leads it directly to desire immortality in God.

This is why a very large part of the work is devoted to evoking the misery of man without God. Why is man miserable? Because he was in a better state before the Fall, and he remembers that state:

La grandeur de l'homme. —La grandeur de l'homme est si visible, qu'elle se tire même de sa misère. Car ce qui est nature aux animaux, nous l'appelons misère en l'homme; par où nous reconnaissons que sa nature étant pareille à celle des animaux, il est déchu d'une meilleure nature, qui lui était propre autrefois.

Car qui se trouve malheureux de n'être pas roi, sinon un roi dépossédé? . . . (409)

This argument of the psychological evidence that man knows himself to be 'dispossessed' was not invented by Pascal; it is a commonplace of mediaeval theology; none the less, it is almost certainly the central thought in the projected *Apologie*. It is man's knowledge that he is dispossessed that shapes his whole existence, and faces him at every turn:

Nous ne concevons ni l'état glorieux d'Adam, ni la nature de son péché, ni la transmission qui s'en est faite en nous. Ce sont choses qui se sont passées dans l'état d'une nature toute différente de la nôtre, et qui passent l'état de notre capacité présente.

Tout cela est inutile à savoir pour en sortir; et tout ce qu'il nous importe de connaître est que nous sommes misérables, corrompus, séparés de Dieu, mais rachetés par Jésus-Christ; et c'est de quoi nous avons des preuves admirables sur la terre. (500; see also 560 bis)[48]

The few who recognise their misery hunger to be raised out of it; the rest are bored with everything except their earthly appetites which require constant feeding (264). So man throws himself into the world to hide from himself the fact that he does not really want it. He seeks tumult, agitation, the multitude, the satisfaction of worldly ambitions; and these things, from the most tireless work to the most innocent play, are only escapism: 'Divertissement—Les hommes n'ayant pu guérir la mort, la misère, l'ignorance, ils se sont avisés, pour se rendre heureux, de n'y point penser' (168). There is a whole section on *Divertissement* with many famous lines in it (164–171), but we can content ourselves with the brief quotation in which Pascal disposes of the whole of earthly endeavour, whether for good or for evil: 'Sans examiner toutes les occupations particulières, il suffit de les comprendre sous le divertissement' (137).

Pascal's endeavour is to turn his reader away from *divertissement* towards the consideration of what earthly life is really like, and he produces many lines of a powerful and terrifying blackness, of which we here quote only a few. 'Le silence éternel de ces espaces infinis m'effraie'(206); 'Le dernier acte est sanglant, quelque belle que soit la comédie en tout le reste: on jette enfin de la terre sur la tête, et en voilà pour jamais' (210). And the most famous of all, which inspired the very specific imagery of the close of Malraux's *La condition humaine*: 'Qu'on s'imagine un nombre d'hommes dans les chaînes, et tous condamnés à la mort, dont les uns étant chaque jour égorgés à la vue des autres, ceux qui restent voient leur propre condition dans celle de leurs semblables, et, se regardant les uns et les autres avec douleur et sans espérance, attendent à leur tour. C'est l'image de la condition des hommes' (199).

We can probably now see what Pascal's plan was likely to be: firstly to make man face the ultimate question of the destiny of the soul by showing him that nothing existed in this world to which he could escape from the question except into misery ending in annihilation; then to answer in favour of immortality guaranteed by Christ. This plan seems fairly clearly set out in *pensée* 60:

Première partie: Misère de l'homme sans Dieu.
Seconde partie: Félicité de l'homme avec Dieu.

Autrement:
Première partie: Que la nature est corrompue. Par la nature même.
Seconde partie: Qu'il y a un réparateur. Par l'Ecriture.

'Par la nature même' means: drawing proofs of nature's corruption from the examination of nature itself.

In another fragment on *ordre* (187), Pascal asserts that 'Il faut commencer par montrer que la religion n'est point contraire à la raison'. We have seen Pascal's conviction that the existence of God cannot and should not be proved by reason. Yet he is also convinced that to believe in God is not irrational or unreasonable. Let us now consider what justifications Pascal proposes for this view.

Essentially, his whole attitude turns on the question of *authority*, and is at the opposite pole from Descartes'. In rejecting the power of reason as a way to convince the non-believer, Pascal puts in its place what he considers a higher power—'l'autorité de celui qui parle'. People do not say, but they ought to say: 'Il faut croire cela; car l'Ecriture qui le dit est divine' (561). Everything depends then from the outset on whether one is prepared to agree that the Bible is divinely inspired. At this point, the modern non-believer is likely to lose interest altogether; but we must remember that we are dealing with a work of which the first version was published in 1670. That was before Richard Simon's critical histories of the Old and New Testaments of which the textual analysis, quite against poor Simon's intention, shattered the faith of many in the divine origin of the Bible. It was also before Bayle's attack on the morality of the Bible, and in particular of the story of David. Pascal turns out to be, in the sphere of religion, simply a neophobiac, a man of the authoritarian school. This is a rather desperate stance for a scientist of his astonishingly penetrating kind.

It is true that he affirms the sense of the Old Testament to be figurative, in particular that the prophets announced that their own sayings which appear to be quite clear were in fact obscure, so that we must deduce a secret (spiritual) sense to be hidden under the temporal (carnal) sense (659). However, he takes as literal the creation of Adam, the Flood and the longevity of Noah and other patriarchs (644)—all things which will likewise appear as events in Bossuet's *Discours sur l'histoire universelle*; like Bossuet too, Pascal believed that Providence, the subtle logic of God, proves itself in history (560 bis, 750, 701); but Bossuet was a priest and nothing of a scientist. Further, Pascal is determined that his reader should accept miracles as reasonable: 'Il n'est pas possible de croire raisonnablement contre les miracles' (815); though it would be right to disbelieve altogether had there been no miracles (811–812). The miracles of the Flood, of Jesus, of the Apostles and the early Saints are necessary to the logic of God's purpose (838, 644). Any man could do as Mohammed did; his coming was not prophesied and he performed no miracles (600).

If one could justly disbelieve in Jesus without the miracles (811), then the reality of the miracles is a *sine qua non* of Christianity. Growing scientific knowledge had paradoxically not only fostered scepticism and caution but had shown that there seemed to be no limit to what was possible. Is this sufficient explanation of why a scientist like Pascal could write: 'La foi dit bien ce que les sens ne disent pas, mais non pas le contraire de ce qu'ils voient. Elle est au-dessus, et non pas contre' (265)? Almost certainly not. There is only one sufficient explanation of Pascal's attitude, and it is that he believed himself to have been party to a miracle, Port-Royal's own miracle, the so-called miracle of the Holy Thorn.

Pascal's niece, Marguerite Périer, was suffering from a disorder of the eye (usually held to have been a lachrymal fistula), and it appeared that if she did not die of the illness she would die of the proposed cure (cauterisation with a hot iron). On 24 March 1656 the fistula was touched with one of Port-Royal's relics, supposed to be a thorn from the crown of Jesus at Calvary. Within hours she was cured. Pascal did not personally witness the event, but he wrote his official testimony ('déposition') concerning what he knew of it, and attested its truth. He also wrote other short texts, which he apparently intended to develop, and which are mainly inspired by this event.[49] We can hardly doubt that this bachelor, who found himself lost in 1652 when his favourite sister Jacqueline went into Port-Royal and who was to lose her altogether in 1661, never forgot the marvellous recovery of his little niece; nor should we forget that, in that day, to believe in miracles was the norm, while to deny them was to flirt with heresy. Since science in that day found no explanation for Marguerite's sudden and dramatic recovery, who are we to blame Pascal for saying that belief in miracles is 'not contrary to reason'?

Still, the tally of Pascal's arguments in favour of believing the Scriptures not contrary to reason is not impressive. More deeply convincing for him, perhaps, was the sense of almost aesthetic satisfaction he got from the God-story. He found a satisfying logic in the prophecies, their fulfilment in Jesus even to the necessity of his being killed by the Jews (761); above all he found the choice of the Jews as God's people—that Jewish race which he considered unique in being sprung from one man, genetically unmixed, monotheistic—as having a specially satisfying logic: 'La rencontre de ce peuple m'étonne et me semble digne de l'attention' (619). He also found a logical pattern in their entire history both before and after the Crucifixion. In the same way, and in the same fragment, he marvels at the fact that the Jewish law, which the Jews claim to have from God, should be (in his estimation) both the first law in the world and the most perfect.

Before we leave the discussion of God and reason, we must remark on the famous, or notorious, argument of 'The Wager' (233, called *Infini Rien*). In this *pensée* Pascal attacks the atheists with their own arms. He shows, with sound mathematical logic as one would expect, that a study of the odds, the amount of the stake and the amount of the possible gain, proves unmistakably that to bet on the existence of God is more favourable than to bet against it. However, the argument relies on our accepting that in losing the 'stake'—our time in this world—we lose nothing of value; and, as has often been pointed out, this condition applies only to those who have already been convinced that human life without God is nothing but 'misère'. Thus it is an argument that can appeal only to those who are *already* prepared to renounce the world, and has no appeal to atheistic humanism.

We are far from having exhausted the *Pensées*, but we are in a position, if not to judge categorically, at least to meditate on some of the judgements which have been made by others. Voltaire, the reader will remember, lamented that it was easy to see that Pascal was sick. Pascal, once he begins discussing the Bible (that is, throughout nearly half the total work) carries true conviction only for those who already believe. For the non-believer, everything turns on whether Pascal's picture of the misery of man without God and his felicity with God has power to move him. It is as he contemplates Pascal's picture of man without God that Voltaire pronounces him sick.

Voltaire, thirty-eight years old and full of fight when he published the *Lettres philosophiques* (1734) and added his commentary on the Port-Royal edition of the *Pensées*, simply did not accept, and indeed directly contradicted, Pascal's view (in 693) that this Earth is a desert island where man wakes to find himself lost. Pascal had in fact gone to a greater extreme in another fragment, writing that without Christ the world would be destroyed or it would be like hell (556). Twenty-five years later and sixty-three years old, Voltaire published *Candide* (1759), which is so pessimistic that it has probably sent many a reader to pray in church. Yet Voltaire never lost his fighting spirit (*Candide* itself is largely a militant work against the Inquisition, the slave trade, the Jesuits); he never, for all his inner disquiet, ceased to believe that there was good one can do in this world. The sense of his criticism of Pascal is made quite clear from its place in Voltaire's work. The *Lettres philosophiques* are a panegyric of intellectual freedom and social progress in England. At the last comes the letter on Pascal; but this is no change of subject; it is there—and this is clear from much of what is said in it—because Voltaire saw Pascal as the arch-nihilist who would prevent human endeavour. All our activities are *divertissement*, Pascal proclaims. But Voltaire's life-style answers, is it *divertissement* to try to dissuade men from burning their fellows or breaking them on the wheel? Perhaps we are all evil judged absolutely. Yet there are degrees of evil—and there are also compassion and self-sacrifice and sweet reason in conduct, which Pascal fails to notice as a human possibility.

Aldous Huxley has condemned Pascal harshly for this failure of balance, and like Voltaire attributes it partly to the sickness of the body: 'Pascal was wise, but wise too consciously, with too consistent a spirituality . . . In his excess of conscious wisdom he was mad; for he sacrificed life to principles, to metaphysical abstractions, to the overmuch spirituality which is the negation of existence. He preferred death to life . . . and I, for one, have more confidence in the rightness of life than in any individual man, even if the man be Pascal.'[50] There is much to criticise in the answers Huxley gives to Pascal in the essays on him. If Pascal says No to life, Huxley says Yes a little hysterically. Yet it is true that Pascal has a blind spot concerning, not what life has to offer man as Huxley tends to over-insist, but what man can put into living. Huxley is right in accusing Pascal of saying No not merely to 'the empty fooleries and sordidness of average human existence' but to the gift of life.

Pascal contemplated writing not only on man's misery without God but on his felicity with God. While he wrote in terrifying words on the first subject, the second is signally absent from his work. We are told briefly that the Christian God is a God of compassion and love; but we are invited to believe that the worst torment of purgatory is—even for the martyrs—the uncertainty as to whether this God's final judgement will be heaven or hell. When the *Deus absconditus* (194) finally shows His face, what a baleful face Pascal expects it to be! Pascal tells us, with profound wisdom, that the order of charity (love) exceeds immeasurably the order of thought. Yet in the work there is much thought, while the sense of love seems to be non-existent. Pascal does indeed seem to be deeply attracted to the feeling of panic (*effroi*) and to glory in the terror of the 'eschatological problem'—death, judgement, heaven and hell. Surely the heart which has known Christ would try to live with love and trust the immortality of the soul to Him who knows about it? Yet we are told that only one question is worthy of the human mind: 'Il importe à toute la vie de savoir si l'âme est mortelle ou immortelle' (218). One must give thought to Huxley's judgement:

[Pascal] perceived that the basis of reason is unreasonable; first principles come from 'the heart', not from the mind. The discovery would have been of the first importance if Pascal had only made it with the right organ. But instead of discovering the heart with the heart, he discovered it with the head. It was abstractly that he rejected abstractions, and with the reason that he discovered unreason. His realism was only theoretical; he never lived it.[51]

Such a judgement appears tragically just. Pascal never lets the heart speak, he never puts his faith in it as, for example, Camus does.

The optimism of Descartes is largely contradicted in French writings between 1670 and 1700. Racine, La Rochefoucauld, La Bruyère, Bayle, all give us a picture of man as the undignified slave of his passions—La Rochefoucauld does it with considerable relish. Even Fontenelle is claimed by one critic to hide a desperate nihilism behind the smile of reason.[52] But not even Racine, like Pascal influenced by Jansenism, is obsessed by the ultimate indignity of total annihilation as is this Christian apologist. In our century, Camus reasoned that annihilation in death rendered life meaningless, void, non-existent, 'absurd'. His head told him so; but his heart spoke louder and told him more clearly still that there are ways and ways of living, and that love, even man's limited capacity to love his fellow-men, cannot be negated.[53]

CHAPTER FOUR

BOSSUET

(i) The classical Catholic

Jacques-Bénigne Bossuet is the perfect example of those educated minds of his era that stood for conservatism. He was Catholic, Absolutist and, loosely speaking, classical in all his thought, and these three aspects of his psychology may be reduced to one: the authoritarian's horror of the dangers inherent in freedom of thought: ' . . . Je suis catholique, aussi soumis qu'aucun autre aux décisions de l'Eglise, et tellement disposé que personne ne craint davantage de préférer son sentiment particulier au sentiment universel.'[1] Yet he was not limited by ignorance of the new. He admired the work of Descartes (the description of the human body in the *Traité de la connaissance de Dieu et de soi-même* is entirely Cartesian),[2] regretting only that the work of the philosopher's disciples was bound to render Descartes himself suspect in the eyes of the Church.[3] In 1691, he sustained an important correspondence with Leibniz, which has been studied by Orcibal.[4]

His defence of conservatism is ambiguous: often insisting on the need for gentleness and moderation; suddenly reverting to demands for stern, 'reasoned' authoritarianism. He was certainly not open-minded; sometimes he was neophobiac in the extreme; and deep inside there was a hard core, which betrays itself most clearly in his *Maximes et réflexions sur la comédie* (1694), unashamedly dictatorial in their 'pious' declamations against the theatre.[5] Some apologists like to believe that this work is not the 'real' Bossuet, but there is much other evidence to support Antoine Adam's view that he was basically a hard man and Martimort's penetrating judgement that he lacked the sense of human reality.[6] These, in a man of such vast moral influence, are important facts: for Bossuet was one of the few members of the Catholic hierarchy who could obtain a hearing from the Protestants, who could remain in good odour with Rome while working for the Gallican Church, and who could be accepted as a father-figure by a vast multitude of Catholics without ever becoming archbishop or cardinal.[7]

His biography can be presented quite schematically. Bossuet (1627–1704) was born in Dijon into a family belonging to the magistrature. Early destined for the Catholic priesthood, he was received *bachelier* in theology in 1648 and in his statutory Latin discourse showed what his lifelong stand would be by choosing as text: 'Fear God, honour the King'. From 1652 to 1659 he was Archdeacon of Metz. Then from 1659 to 1669 came the ten-year period which established his fame, when he was one of the 'grands prédicateurs' in Paris and gave the wildly acclaimed sermons and orations of which the drafts yielded the published *Sermons* and *Oraisons funèbres*. Long held to be the apogee of French prose, they are now recognised by some French critics as what many generations of English readers must have suspected, that is, bombastic and inflated and, in print, devoid of the admirable vigour and economy of the *Histoire universelle*.

In 1669 Bossuet was made Bishop of Condom, but within two years he exchanged this appointment for the key post of preceptor to 'Monseigneur', the Dauphin, and this position he held from 1670 to 1680. As tutor to the first-in-line to the throne, Bossuet might have proved extremely influential on the future, but his pupil did not live to be king. Fruits of these years of teaching were the *Histoire universelle* and the *Politique*, which we shall study hereafter. Finally, Bossuet was named Bishop of Meaux in 1681, thus remaining near Paris and the king, and till his death in 1704 the holding of this bishopric was the period of his main endeavours against strife within the Catholic Church and towards dealing in one way or another with Protestantism.

These endeavours of 'l'aigle de Meaux' deserve some attention. As regards the Jesuit–Jansenist conflict, he always managed to remain relatively uninvolved, even though the conflict was strong at the time of 'Bossuet prédicateur' and though he had been a pupil of Nicholas Cornet, the major Jesuit advocate in the Sorbonne's debate on Jansenius. In contrast, he played the major rôle against Fénelon in the controversy over the newer threat to Catholic orthodoxy, Quietism. This however we shall discuss in our next chapter. He also played a considerable rôle in the perennial conflict between Catholic Ultramontanes and Catholic Gallicans, which reached proportions of crisis at the time when he was appointed to Meaux. At that time Louis XIV, far from having entered his late 'pious' phase, was hostile to Pope Innocent XI. The king, supported by Colbert and Harlay de Champvallon, Archbishop of Paris, chose the *Régale*, a disputed royal prerogative with significant financial implications, on which to take issue with Innocent XI and to force emotions to the point where schism between the Gallican Church and Rome was whispered of.

In November 1681, before entering into possession of his bishopric, Bossuet had the extremely embarrassing honour of preaching the opening sermon to an extraordinary assembly of the French clergy, including ten archbishops. Highly regarded by Rome, personally devoted to Louis XIV, horrified by the threat of schism, Bossuet preached in a tone of conciliation on 'l'Unité de l'Eglise'. In practical terms he gained the right to draft the much-demanded statement of policy which became the *Déclaration des quatre articles*, called the 'Charte gallicane' because it asserted several forms of French Catholic independence from Rome. Bossuet's endeavour was to keep the Declaration as moderate as possible. The Pope read it differently, and controversy continued for eleven years. In fact, Louis XIV was glad enough in the light of the sanctions Rome applied to allow the Declaration quietly to become a dead letter, though Gallicanism did not die with it. At least, schism was avoided and so Bossuet could feel he had done as well as was possible, while becoming a major figure in Church politics.[8] The real test of Bossuet as Christian, thinker and man was in his long-term dealings with the Protestants. He hated the memory of the sixteenth-century Protestants, who, he said, had not reformed religion but 'subverted' it through arrogant individualism.[9] Of the Protestants of his own day he sometimes spoke as though they were 'dear brethren walking in darkness' and on other occasions in tones of anathema.

Bossuet's most basic and constantly reiterated conviction (an essential argument of the Counter-Reformation) was that there was a continuity of religion from Moses—even from Adam—to his own day, and that the Catholic Church stood for that original faith; thus, 'variation' was by definition a sure sign of heresy.[10] Because he demanded no more than minimal consent to Catholic doctrine from the Protestants, they simply could not believe that the real attitudes of the Catholics were represented by his *Exposition de la doctrine catholique sur les matières de controverse* (1671). Innocent XI twice publicly congratulated Bossuet on this work eight years after it was published, but even before it was in print it led to numerous notable conversions, especially that of the king's great general Turenne. The interest of Turenne's niece, Mademoiselle de Duras, led Bossuet into public debate on doctrine with the Protestant pastor Claude in 1678, and the results were published in the *Relation de la conférence avec M. Claude* (1682). Fénelon called this Bossuet's most famous work, a surprising assessment; but the *Relation* certainly did cause an explosion of controversy in England for two years before Bossuet published his *Histoire des variations des églises protestantes* (1688).[11] But between the *Relation* and the *Histoire des variations* occurred many a shameful conversion, for 1685 saw the Revocation of the Edict of Nantes, a catastrophe for France and for Christianity, which gave Louis XIV the name of 'anti-Christ' as far away as America. As to why and how the Edict was revoked, after being eroded piecemeal over several years, that is still today a complex question which, though historically fascinating, cannot concern us here.[12]

The Edict of Nantes, promulgated by Henri IV in 1598, had given rights and privileges to the Protestants. The privileges were soon lost but the relative security of the Protestants in France was sustained, from the fall of La Rochelle to about the death of Mazarin. That the extreme Catholic faction or Church party ('le parti des dévots') thereafter became tireless in demanding of Louis XIV withdrawal of rights from the Protestants is irrefutable.[13] And as early as Palm Sunday, 1662, Bossuet had added his voice, in a sermon before the court on the *duties of kings*, demanding the overthrow of 'the party that heresy had formed'. The attack opens against the Jansenists but then clearly—if unexplicitly—is directed against the Protestants.[14]

Other nations and the moderate Catholics watched aghast as the tragedy developed and the Church party at last persuaded Louis XIV to use the 'secular arm' before and during the Revocation. It was not merely that the terms of the Revocation were grotesque (e.g., that Protestant 'temples' built near Catholic churches be 'transferred elsewhere'); the fact was that the use of the secular arm meant in reality 'conversion' by the 'missionnaires bottés', the king's dragoons. For example, a company, say one hundred and fifty men, would be billeted on a Protestant farmer. He would quickly be financially destroyed, see his wife and daughters raped, and would be lucky if he did not end at the bottom of his own well. Madame de Sévigné remarked smugly; 'Les dragons sont de fort bons missionnaires'. We shall not dwell on the multitude of accounts of cruel persecution, but have touched on them, firstly to indicate the trauma that 1685 was for France, and secondly to ask: What sort of man did Bossuet show himself to be at this time? Several monographs on Bossuet are silent or evasive on this period. Happily, at least three studies examine it in a scholarly way, though a definitive study is perhaps still to come.[15]

Firstly, there is reasonable evidence that Bossuet's voice, both privately and publicly, had a part in bringing about the Revocation, though he may not have had a say in its precise formulation. Secondly, once it had happened, he spoke out in a manner that, all agree, was discreditable. Ten days after sealing the Revocation, the Chancellor Le Tellier died, and on 25 January 1686 Bossuet spoke his funeral oration, praising Louis XIV in glowing language for having 'exterminated the heretics'.[16] To suggest, like Giraud, that Bossuet did not know the facts of the *dragonnades* will not do.[17] A brash letter from the young Fénelon—how he was to change!—callously jokes with his senior about the 'cowardice' of the Protestants in the face of the dragoons. It is true that the letter is dated six weeks after the notorious oration, but Fénelon clearly expects his mentor to share the joke.[18] Bossuet's exchange of letters with the Protestant Pierre de Vrillac from October 1685 to May 1686 (called 'Lettres à un réfugié') shows him visibly wilting before some home truths, such as that the king drew the sword only at the direct instigation of the clergy.[19] In a *mandement* to his rural deans, dated 6 November 1685, Bossuet had invoked the doctrine of *compelle intrare* ('Force them to come in'), about which we shall say more in our Chapter 6.[20]

In his pastoral letter to the 'nouveaux convertis' of his diocese, 24 March 1686, Bossuet asserted, to the outrage of Protestants in Holland and England, that they had not only not suffered 'tourments', but had not even heard of such things.[21] Yet it is known that in early 1686 four companies of dragoons (1500 men, according to a local chronicle) were in Meaux. Whether Bossuet specifically asked for them, and what their activities were, we do not know. We do know that Bossuet was enthusiastic in having Protestant 'temples' demolished; that he was eager in interning children whose parents would not give them a sufficiently Catholic upbringing; that he was especially ferocious towards leaders of Protestant gatherings 'in the wilderness', for whom the penalty was death—though in one case Bossuet got it commuted to the galleys for life, a punishment probably worse than death. He was 'ferme sur le mariage' in his own words, referring to the article of the Revocation that non-Catholic marriage was invalid, so that Protestant children could not inherit; which meant for the Protestants: Become converted, or do not have families.

On the other hand, we know that he tried to avoid bringing to attention cases of 'nouveaux convertis' having died without absolution, knowing that officially their corpses should be dragged on a hurdle; but he did not always succeed in preventing this monstrous practice. Later, in 1703, near death and having seen the start of the Revolt of the Camisards (the Calvinists of the Cévennes, 1702–5), he regretted that France had used too much rigour against the Protestants, instead of 'douceur' and 'insinuation'.[22] This much we can know, then, of what Bossuet's idea of 'firmness' in government could mean in practice, and this may throw some light on the political theory we are now to examine.

(ii) The political theorist

Bossuet is not so interesting a universal political theorist as Hobbes, Spinoza or Locke, but he gives the student of France a fascinating insight into the 'rationalisation' of absolutism. His complete theory is contained in the *Politique tirée des propres paroles de l'Ecriture sainte*, written between 1677 and 1679 and revised later, but published only posthumously, in 1709.[23] Its intent was to codify and justify absolute monarchy almost exactly as Bossuet knew it. Every point of theory is supported by scriptural quotation, but the theoretical edifice is in no sense a reconstruction of old Hebrew political life; it is a French edifice given moral prestige by Biblical injunctions torn from their context, mainly the Old Testament. Bossuet uses the expression 'manier les Ecritures', and he makes fairly indiscriminate but constant use of the method of the '*Anciens*'—argument from authority, with little care for the real sense of the authority.

The contention that Hobbes' *Leviathan* (1654) and other political writings were a 'hidden' source for Bossuet is an interesting one into which further enquiry may one day be made. The contentions in favour of it are acceptable only up to a point.[24] Both men were conservative, both favoured absolutism, but Bossuet must have found the *Leviathan* antipathetic in that it counters point-blank his most cherished theory—that his religion comes in direct lineage from Moses—for Hobbes writes: 'The greatest and main abuse of Scripture . . . is the wresting of it, to prove that the Kingdom of God . . . is the present Church . . . whereas the Kingdom of God was first instituted by the Ministry of Moses, *over the Jews only* . . .'[25] As to whether Hobbes actually had a greater influence on subsequent French political theory than Bossuet, that is another question as yet unanswered.

The argument of Bossuet's *Politique* is easy to follow, set out with 'Cartesian' order, in numbered 'Books' divided into numbered 'Articles' subdivided into numbered 'Propositions'. Where desirable we shall refer to them thus: I, 1, i. The theory of absolutism is bound to appeal to a mind that likes clarity of exposition because it is monolithically simple: there is no subtle balance of powers to be expounded.

The first contention, not seriously challenged till Rousseau, is that man is made to live in society; the second, that God who created him established through Moses the two primary laws: Love God, love thy neighbour. From the outset we sense the weakness of what is to come—its naïveté real or feigned. For Bossuet, differences of estate do not interfere with love, even in a community of men who are 'fallen' and who need government. Bossuet must have known that the willing acceptance of hierarchy had been badly strained for those low down in the pyramid by the century's quota of famines, savage taxes and wars, of which the less privileged always suffered the brunt, and that 'caritas' had little place in his era.

Civic virtues—austerity, frugality, self-control, dedication to the general welfare—are important to Bossuet—Jesus taught patriotism and the apostles and early Christians were good citizens (I, 6, ii–iii)—but it is by no means his intention that civic as opposed to spiritual merit should be most esteemed. The first task of law and the monarch is to promote 'le culte de Dieu': the laws must be financially liberal towards the clergy, must allow their independence, must not tolerate impiety. Political persecution of 'la religion' (Catholicism) would be iniquitous, for good law was born from religion (VII, 2, ii–iv).

It is almost by a tacit bargain that the sovereign is 'sacred, paternal and absolute' (III, 1 and III, 2, ii). Because the sovereign obeys the 'will of God' in protecting 'la religion', 'la religion' guarantees that he will in turn be obeyed. The king is father to his people and is born 'pour le public'. He must protect the weak. Government must be gentle and try to avoid bloodshed (III, 2); it must use wisdom rather than force, and be above all *rational* (V). It is worth recalling at this point that Bossuet praised the 'moderation' of Le Tellier who sealed the Revocation, so that we may understand what he could mean by 'wisdom rather than force' and by 'reason'. The monarch's kindness, incidentally, in no way deprives him of the right of conquest over other nations—an obvious sop to the ambitions of Louis XIV.

In fact the theory lacks 'bon sens', because the benign nature of sovereignty is guaranteed by nothing but the sovereign's mastery over himself. In real terms 'l'autorité royale est absolue'; the king is morally subject to law but not punishable for breaking it, nor can he be made to uphold it, since there is no 'force coactive' against him ('On appelle force coactive une puissance pour contraindre à exécuter ce qui est ordonné légitimement'—IV, 1, iii). What is more, it is necessary and desirable that the prince's authority should be invincible and feared (IV, 1, vi–viii). There is no possible excuse for disobedience, and in fact those who see the interests of the state as different from the sovereign's are, by definition, 'public enemies' (VI, 1, iii). This last proposition is very disturbing, for it means that it is *impossible under any circumstances* to oppose the will of the sovereign without being in the wrong.

There must have been good Catholics who, horrified by the brutality of the *dragonnades* and bitterly observing how the ascendancy of England and Holland was growing in some measure from their relatively tolerant systems, wondered if such theories did not in fact let loose an unstoppable juggernaut. Bossuet, of course, was in the special position of preceptor to the Dauphin when he drafted the *Politique*; he was anti-Machiavellian, probably consciously, and he may fondly have imagined that the moral precepts for the sovereign which take up so much of the later 'Books' had as much appeal for his pupil as his tempting theory of power. In any case, he forgot one of his own teachings: that princes may not live to become kings.

He seems to have been himself a little uneasy. He therefore makes an exception to obedience—when the king commands 'against God'. This opens a very wide field of speculation—for instance, Gallicans and Ultramontanes could rarely have agreed on what is 'against God'. But then Bossuet contradicts himself by asserting that obedience is not to cease 'par aucun prétexte', that even an impious king may be faced only with respectful remonstrance 'sans mutinerie et sans murmure' and prayers to God for his change of heart (VI, 1, iv–vi). As regards the succession, it should be hereditary through the males, preferably the eldest son, and women should be excluded, as under the old Salic law.

The whole work is symptomatic of an almost pathological

clinging to the known. No alterations, let alone alternatives, are even hinted at. On the contrary, Bossuet asserts that it is dangerous to change even non-fundamental laws and that some laws are actually unchangeable. He takes his worship of the known so far as to say that one must accept whatever form of government is in existence, quoting Romans, XIII, 1–2: '... il n'y a point de puissance qui ne soit de Dieu; et toutes celles qui sont, c'est Dieu qui les a établies...' (11, 2, xii). Bossuet's system is itself a Leviathan that was eventually to be stranded by its own monstrosity and rigidity, unadaptable to change from inside or outside. But it gives us a very clear idea of what absolutism and divine right meant to a very influential mind in the latter part of Louis XIV's reign, and a sense of the fear of the unfamiliar that underlay Bossuet's 'immobilité majestueuse'.

(iii) The historian

France offers us no other historian of Bossuet's stature since Pasquier and Bodin in the 1560s, and Bossuet's whole historiography is grounded—in theory—on the premise that history is the working-out of God's providence. This premise puts him, where we would expect to find him, on the 'anti-modern' side of French thought. In England such an attitude to history had grown increasingly unpopular.[26] This seems to be generally true of Europe, as is shown by Peter Burke's interesting study, though he comes to the rather unexpected conclusion that for the seventeenth-century mind the true 'infrastructure' of history is not economy, society, politics or law, but God—and naturally he refers to Bossuet.[27] Among the theorists of history as providence, Bossuet is certainly one of the greatest, and probably the last of any significance. Yet though today many readers may find his theory meaningless, it is of considerable interest for our study to see how it was elaborated and how, despite the theory, a more empirical attitude often shows through.

Bossuet's *Histoire des variations des églises protestantes* (1688) is essentially a polemical work which, though intended as 'un livre de paix', succeeded mostly in enraging the Protestants. It has one merit for the modern historian: since Bossuet openly declared his bias, it was essential that his statements of fact should not be faulted; thus we find a care for fact unknown elsewhere in the religious polemics of the day and comparatively rare in historiography, the more so the further one reads back. Also, dealing with recent events, with Luther and Calvin, Bossuet is too astute to write of the angelic apparitions and miraculous interventions in events so freely adduced in his main work, the *Histoire universelle*.

The *Discours sur l'histoire universelle*, drafted as part of the Dauphin's programme of study and published in 1681, tries to show that all events from the Creation to A.D. 800 (at which point it has already rapidly tailed off) are proof of God's purpose, which is the triumph of Bossuet's 'religion'. But it was also intended to teach a future king some pragmatic lessons.[28] Bossuet does not cross swords with other modern historians. His evidence is drawn entirely from the writers of classical antiquity, in whom he was well read, and naturally from the Bible and the 'sacred authors', such as Aquinas and notably Augustine's *City of God*.[29] Where 'sacred' and 'profane' sources clash, Bossuet prefers the 'sacred'; the reasons for so doing could be charitably described as empirically sound (58, 69).[30] Bossuet gives his sources, though he does not debate their reliability. He gives attention to chronology, dating events both from the Creation (which he maintains, after Archbishop Usher and without hesitation, was in 4004 B.C.) and also B.C. and A.D. (though he believes Jesus was really born about 4 B.C.). Problems of chronology obviously interested him (70-2, 75, 107, 143) but he thought it unimportant for his pupil, who should concern himself with the 'logic' of history, to grapple with them (144). Probably this dubious attitude was quite good enough for the Dauphin.

Much to the work's credit is the general sense of what constitutes anachronism, and Bossuet is fully aware that the Greece of Philip was not the Greece of Themistocles. He makes this one of his opening points (39), and, if the classicists believed in a 'universal', unchanging man, Bossuet, classicist though he was, knew the reality of 'autres temps, autres moeurs'. Also to the work's credit is its style: succinct, elegant, without the rhetoric of the *Oraisons* and *Sermons*, it reminds one of Cocteau's injunction to 'écrire musclé' and somewhat of Pascal.

On the debit side is Bossuet's stubborn credulity for 'le merveilleux', quite out of touch with the spirit of his contemporaries, Bayle and Fontenelle. Jacob and the angel (52) one excuses; Joshua's miracle at Jericho (184) one is less ready to excuse. The immense army of Sennacherib which perished in one night 'by the hand of an angel' (64), the astounding longevity attributed to men before Abraham, and numerous other wonders probably did not discredit Bossuet with most of his contemporaries, who, as we saw in Chapter 1, had almost a craving for 'le merveilleux', but they show that he would have no more truck with the *esprits forts* than La Bruyère. Bossuet is quite clear as to where he stands: he goes out of his way to jibe at 'natural philosophers' who seek a 'scientific' explanation of life on earth, and his categoric adducing of the Scriptures against them (151) must have galled the opponents of authoritarianism. The most significant debit against the *Histoire universelle* is that it is not 'universal'. It deals only with the Western world, and mostly the world of the Bible at that. No India; no China, even though French missionaries were currently there. Even Greece, though favourably contrasted with Asia, gets scant attention by comparison with the heresies against Christianity of Pelagius and others, anathemised at length in predictably loaded terms. And almost two hundred years of Islam are postponed for a later treatment which they were never to get.

Let us now consider the actual structure of the *Histoire universelle*. Part I, 'Les époques, ou la suite des temps', is a general chronological survey based on the Bible and the classical historians. Each of the seven epochs is marked by some great event—the Flood, the bringing of the Mosaic law, the foundation of Rome. Part II is the clearest setting-out one may find of Bossuet's most essential argument, that history is the story of mankind's religion, given *ab origine* and sustained by Providence. It is called 'La suite de la religion', and it is important to understand that this means 'the logical continuity of religion' (or *'the* religion'). It is in the spirit of Augustine's historiography, as Fénelon noticed.[31] It was, as Part II shows, Bossuet's main contention against Protestantism that: 'Toute secte qui ne montre pas sa succession depuis l'origine du monde n'est pas de Dieu' (338).

Bossuet is ferocious against the 'vaine curiosité' of all who are incredulous of history's always happening as it does 'by God's permission' for the furtherance of Catholicism, and blames this incredulity on Satan's fomenting of the 'esprit de révolte. On raisonne sur le précepte, et l'obéissance est mise en doute' (147). Such was the cause of the Fall. Of course, great men often fulfil God's purpose when they think they are fulfilling their own; and God is devious according to men's lights. Thus, the exile of His people (at that time the Jews) in Egypt ensured that they should be eternally thankful to their Deliverer (172). The Romans wanted to humiliate the Syrians, and so protected the Jews—according to God's will (96). Later the Romans tried to eliminate Christianity, and God let them try, for they succeeded only in establishing it more firmly (118). Why did God so often hide himself from man between Adam's 'revolt' and the Incarnation? Because, thinks Bossuet (rather like Pascal), man needed the time to recognise his 'misère sans Dieu' (159). Naturally—like Pascal again—Bossuet sees the prophets and the miracles of Jesus as historical proof of his Godhead. Why were miracles shown to the Israelites before Jesus when God could have worked through 'natural' means? Because the Israelites were not very intelligent, but miracles they could see (178).

A final question to which Bossuet risks an answer is: How long is the Creation to endure? Of two things he is sure. It is not to end before the Jews have become again part of 'le peuple de Dieu' (257). And the Church will last unshaken as long as does the Creation (342). Louis XIV is there, is he not, to 'heal the wounds of the Church' (343)? Bossuet clearly thinks in short spans, and is quite unconcerned with the current speculations on a universe infinite—or 'indefinite'—in space and time.[32]

Part III of the *Histoire* seems to set off on exactly the same lines. It is called 'Les Empires' and begins: 'Les révolutions des empires sont réglées par la Providence . . . ' But we soon realise that Bossuet is discreetly, and without disavowing his theory of Providence, moving towards a more original and empirical position . Human affairs may seem chaotic, but there are 'secrètes dispositions' which prepare changes and there are 'conjonctures' which allow these changes to come about; and these are closely associated with men—nations or individuals. The destiny of men is directly related *to their own nature*, and exceptions to this are not the normal pattern of history. It is *this* infrastructure that Bossuet now tells the Dauphin a prince should especially study: it is 'la vraie science de l'histoire' (354). In the bloody game of empire, the winner is he who has most foresight, most perseverance, most astuteness (355). Even when God inspires a man, He wills him not to neglect 'les moyens humains', and in this last part of the *Histoire* God's interventions are adduced only very infrequently.

Impiety is still a cause of downfall, but the causal emphasis is placed on lack of discipline, brutality, avarice, self-indulgence. The causes again and again invoked for success are the stoic virtues and all that derives from them: frugality, austerity, respect for family and nation, 'natural equity', a good educational system, psychological knowledge of men and, above all, simplicity and coherence in a political system, such as Bossuet's much-admired Egyptians had (357–8). We also see in the cleric a military strategist frequently trying to get out, and he attached great importance to tactics and discipline in war, as against numerical strength, and to success in war in a nation's well-being.

Bossuet is now relying much less on argument from authority, and exploring a theory of causation that his era would have considered observation from 'bon sens'. Nearly all critics see the triumph of the empirical method over the providential (or 'eschatological') view most clearly in his study of the Romans; Bossuet recognised Rome as the centre, first of the ancient, then of the Christian world, and with his study of the greatness and decline of Rome Bossuet reaches the logical conclusion of his discourse, for are we not the successors of Rome 'dont nous respectons encore les lois' (392)? Though the particular causes adduced for the rise and fall of Rome often conflict with or contradict those seen by Montesquieu nearly fifty years later, the *kind* of causes examined are remarkably similar and essentially 'modern': political structure, external pressures, economy and, above all, national character.

Great individuals can shape history, and Rome was 'le plus

fécond en héros', but the number of exceptional men is directly related to the traditions and character of a nation (its 'génie') in a given era, and this genius can mutate from one era to the next. One cannot assert that Bossuet invented this concept of national genius as a shaping force of history. The fact that Saint-Evremond was exploring the same idea at about the same time, without much likelihood of direct contact between the two men, would suggest that the concept was arousing general interest among historians.[33] Yet it is remarkable to see Bossuet the conservative developing a thesis which looks right forward to the nineteenth-century determinism of Taine. The early Roman genius, argues Bossuet, was austere and frugal, born of hard agricultural work, and prized liberty above all worldly goods. Its harshness was tempered by a sense of equity within Rome and towards conquered nations. Patriotism was more valued than personal gain. But this same love of freedom explains the later internal jealousies between people and senate, or plebs and patricians (414). The wars in Asia introduced the Romans to luxury and avarice, generals started the cult of their own personalities, self-interest ruled, the right to citizenship was no longer so carefully guarded. The nation, previously so sagacious, lost its classical balance, 'ne put trouver le milieu' (415).

We have made a fairly long story short. By the end of it Bossuet realises that he needs to remind his pupil of what he as author seems practically to have forgotten, that 'il faut tout rapporter à une Providence'.

CHAPTER FIVE

FENELON

(i) The priest

François de Salignac de la Mothe Fénelon was born in the Périgord in 1651 and died shortly before Louis XIV in 1715. He has been viewed in differing ways: sometimes as a liberal and progressive thinker (especially by the eighteenth century), sometimes as a feudal aristocrat in love with the past fortunes of his own caste. Both these views are still argued. A third view of him as a 'sensibilité frémissante', often to be compared with Rousseau, will not stand examination.

There is, it is true, a puzzle in Fénelon. He had a strong sense of political realities, yet in his spiritual life he moved towards a Quietism divorced from 'action'. This dichotomy need not concern the historian of ideas, for the two aspects of his personality did not impinge one on the other: his politics are markedly Christian, but not in any particular sense Quietist. He was a monarchist, but as regards the actual régime of Louis XIV, he thought it needed radical reform and consistently attacked the realities of absolutism, even while grateful to the King for his years of personal advancement.

His family was of high and ancient Catholic nobility, but poor, and since he was his father's thirteenth child (by his second wife) he had to make a career either in the army or the Church. But he was glad to follow the priesthood, and was ordained, probably in 1675. We must ask the same questions about Fénelon as priest as we did about Bossuet.

As regards the Gallican–Ultramontane controversy, Fénelon considered the affair of the *Régale*, in which he was too unimportant to be involved at the time, as disgraceful; but his loyalties were Gallican, the more so as he aged.[1] This did not antagonise Rome, and indeed, during the quarrel over Quietism, the Holy See showed him all the favour it could. As regards the Jesuit–Jansenist controversy, the facts are simple: Fénelon was not a Jesuit, but he was anti-Jansenist, perhaps before and certainly after 1710, at which date the quarrel was entering a new phase of tension.[2]

Fénelon, though Bossuet's *protégé*, never shared his senior's passionate concern with the Protestant question, even taking into account his *Traité du ministère des pasteurs* and his *Lettres sur l'autorité de l'Eglise*, which naturally show disapproval of the Reformation.[3] Yet one could hardly be a Catholic priest—and ambitious—at that time without being involved in the work of eliminating Calvinism. In 1678 Fénelon was appointed superior of the *Nouvelles catholiques* in Paris, a school or, rather, place of sequestration for Protestant girls who were to be turned into good Catholics. We have referred already to the crass and cruel way he spoke of the Protestants in a letter to Bossuet on the subject of the *dragonnades* in March 1686.[4] At that time, he was on a 'mission of conversion' in the Saintonge area on the Atlantic seabord.[5] His concerns were with reinforcing the blockade to prevent refugees escaping to England or Holland (a great many did escape, though those caught in the attempt were imprisoned for life, the men in the galleys), with showing authority to be 'inflexible', and, a lame third, with suggesting humbly that life in France should be made a little less intolerable for the Calvinists.[6]

Once these episodes were past, Fénelon seems to have avoided taking issue on the Protestant question. Even in the famous *Lettre à Louis XIV*, though he charges the King with ungodliness in no uncertain terms, he does not charge him with persecution of conscience. However, the Revolt of the Camisards (1702–5) seems to have opened his eyes, as it partly did Bossuet's, and made him decide that religious coercion was useless and wrong. If not much concerned with the Counter-Reformation, Fénelon generally took great interest in theology. In 1681 he wrote his *Réfutation du système de Malebranche sur la nature et la grâce* and later produced many small theological treatises, followed by the much larger *Traité de l'existence et des attributs de Dieu* (1705–12, but not published complete—in an inaccurate text—till 1718), in which he returns to acceptance of Malebranche and, through Malebranche, of Descartes.

This *Traité* deserves comment. Though overshadowed by

the earlier *Maximes des Saints* (1697) it was intended to be part of an eventual grand Apology. The *Traité* is in two parts, the first addressed to the layman, the second to the philosopher. Part I concerns proofs of God drawn from 'l'aspect général de la nature' and is a passionate evocation of the majesty, goodness, wisdom and providence of God manifest in the 'marvels of nature'. The argument was by no means new, but had rarely been treated so exhaustively (while both Descartes and Pascal refused to use it)—and doubtless Fénelon's treatment of it influenced many a similar argument in the eighteenth century. Diderot, in his *Lettre sur les aveugles* (1749), found it necessary to combat this kind of argument by asserting that it is 'bien faible' for the blind.

There is in it a certain naïveté, sometimes charming, sometimes ludicrous for us, though we must recall that the 'honnête homme' of Fénelon's day, not given to contemplating nature, may well have had his mind refreshed. Where we think of living creatures adapting themselves to conditions, Fénelon sees the world as marvellously adapted to the needs of life by its providential Maker. Is it not marvellous that the earth is soft enough for growing food yet hard enough to bear man's weight? that we are placed at such a distance from the sun as to be neither too hot nor too cold? And so on. A point of particular note is the praise of regional and seasonal variation, for this fosters trade and thereby the brotherhood of man—an important concept in Fénelon's Christian economic theory. Against the Cartesians who believe in the 'animal-machine', Fénelon asserts that even 'instinctive behaviour' implies mind, and the twentieth-century reader will sympathise with this. He marvels at the perfection of the small world revealed by the microscope and anticipates revelations of a sub-microscopic world, yet shows an ambiguous attitude to the New Philosophy by maintaining without question that the sun moves round the earth.

However, when Fénelon addresses himself in Part II to the philosopher with the 'Démonstration . . . tirée des idées intellectuelles', he follows Descartes' metaphysics (without naming Descartes) with an almost comic doggedness. It is all there: the method, the start from universal doubt (including the 'mauvais génie'), the *cogito*, the position of solipsism leading to the proof of God from the idea of perfection. The train of thought is perfectly methodical, but it differs from Descartes' in being constantly punctuated by explosions of delight, astonishment, or the panic of solipsism. There is a certain fascination with the sheer puzzle of his own mind that makes Fénelon read at this point with a little of the brilliant introspection of Augustine's *Confessions* rather than with the customary coolness of Descartes. Though the *Traité . . . de Dieu* cannot be claimed to be a great work, it deserves more attention than it is usually given; and it certainly shows how in Fénelon, as in Malebranche, Cartesianism could be absorbed into the clerical mind.

We have left till last in this section what is by far the most famous theological work of Fénelon, the *Explication des maximes des Saints sur la vie intérieure* of 1697, which was at the centre of the notorious controversy over Quietism ('la Querelle du quiétisme').

The 'Querelle du quiétisme' held a great deal of public attention over several years, particularly after the *Maximes des saints* had involved the pope and the French court, and had given rise to open war between the two great priests: Fénelon, Archbishop of Cambrai since 1695, preceptor to the Petit Dauphin (the Duc de Bourgogne, eldest son of the Dauphin and second-in-line to the throne) since 1689, and Bossuet, Bishop of Meaux, champion of the Gallican Church and the late Counter-Reformation, one-time preceptor to the Dauphin; both men members of the Académie française. Piquancy was added for the knowledgeable by the erstwhile friendship of the two and particularly by the political implications of the controversy which involved Madame de Maintenon, married to Louis XIV since 1684, and which we shall touch on in dealing with Fénelon's political theory.[7]

Ultimately, the controversy itself, as distinct from Fénelon's Quietism, is for the historian of ideas little more than another intestine scandal of the Catholic Church that rejoiced the hearts of the *esprits forts* (or *libertins*) of the end of the century. It would be of small profit here to examine the embarrassments of Rome, the wrongs of Bossuet's handling of the case and the misrepresentations in his *Relation sur le quiétisme* (1698), the enthusiasm and loss of enthusiasm of Madame de Maintenon, the misfortunes and follies of the eccentric Madame Guyon who had become Fénelon's spiritual partner, or the particularly sordid rôle played by *l'abbé* Bossuet, the bishop's nephew. The story has been told many times.[8]

What remains for us is Quietist thought itself, which gave food for meditation to numerous Catholics in its day and doubtless since, through Madame Guyon's *Moyen court et très facile de faire oraison* (1685), her *Explication du Cantique des Cantiques* (1688), and through Fénelon's *Maximes des Saints*, though this last is not a book to fire the public imagination.

Madame Guyon, born into the 'petite noblesse' in 1648, was a widow whose highly charged emotionalism found an outlet when she learned the way to 'faire oraison'. What is meant by 'faire oraison'?—an act of total self-abandonment to the love of God, in which liturgy, sacrament and good works are superseded and in which the soul must be indifferent to everything including its own salvation. The Church recognised the possibility of such 'oraison' but regarded it as the very rare prerogative of a saintly few and a snare for the multitude—it is no surprise that Bossuet, lacking all mysticism, saw it thus. Madame Guyon presented it as accessible to all. Furthermore, what she presented was very close to 'Molinosism', the propositions of the Spanish priest Molinos (not to be confused with Molina, the source of 'Molinism') condemned by a Bull of Innocent XI in 1687, about a year before Fénelon met Madame Guyon. In spite of the Bull, the formulae of Molinos were translated and found fertile ground in France among many who had a particular devotion to Saint Teresa and Saint John of the Cross, both sixteenth-century mystics, and who loved the memory of Saint François de Sales, whose *Introduction à la vie dévote* of 1608 had a vast readership, with its emphasis on 'le cœur', and 'le repos en Dieu'.[9] But the Church saw in Molinos and Madame Guyon a mysticism of a different and unhealthy kind, in which man's 'quietude' need make no resistance against temptation.

Why did Fénelon allow himself to be captivated by these badly-regarded notions? Not only had Molinos' 'quietude' been condemned before Fénelon met Madame Guyon, but he met her fresh from a sequestration of six months in a Paris convent imposed on her because of the scandals of her travels and activities in the company of the Quietist priest Lacombe. It is true that her release had come from the King through the good offices of Madame de Maintenon, whose enthusiasm for her made her entry into the public life of Paris a triumph. But Fénelon's real motivating force seems to have come from deep within his own nature: for all the goodness of heart apparent in his writing on children he was aware of an aridity in himself which welcomed the flood of mystical exaltation coming from this strange woman, towards whom he was never to lose his loyalty.

The *Maximes des Saints* was Fénelon's attempt to prove that his views and those of Madame Guyon were not against orthodoxy. The arguments are all derived by quotation from the Saints, and Fénelon tries to show that there is nothing in his views that is not part of a tradition of mysticism within Catholicism. He treads with care: the soul filled with pure love is *not* indifferent to its own salvation—but it cares for it only because God Himself does. To no avail. The saints, declared the Church hierarchy, indeed say what Fénelon says they say, but they do not mean what Fénelon thinks they mean. The quarrel became one of interpretation of holy writ, and eventually did little except justify the free-thinkers and the followers of Spinoza in asserting that ancient and sacred authorities were open to critical analysis.

Madame Guyon was in the Bastille in 1698 and stayed there until 1703. Fénelon lost his title and income as preceptor to the Duc de Bourgogne in January 1699, and submitted to a papal brief condemning the *Maximes* in April. That was the official end of the controversy. Fénelon was henceforth disgraced in the eyes of Louis XIV.

This discussion leaves us with not much except the knowledge that even in seventeenth-century France there were those whose religion came less from Church authority than from a deep need within their own psyche, and who regretted that brief pre-Jansenist golden age of the 'Catholic Renaissance'.

(ii) The educationalist

Fénelon's main contribution to educational theory is *De l'éducation des filles*, published in 1687, two years before he was named preceptor to the Duc de Bourgogne.[10] As preceptor, Fénelon wrote an educational treatise for the duke in novel form, the famous *Télémaque*, but we shall consider this work for its political and economic ideas in our next section.

On education for the female sex, Fénelon is disappointing; on methods of teaching the very young of either sex, to which about half *De l'éducation des filles* is devoted, he is excellent. For his time, Fénelon is not an advanced feminist. It is true that before 1650, feminine education in France was not a progressive field. However, between the mid-century and 1687, the advocacy of teaching for girls on terms of parity with boys made itself heard in tones often much more demanding than Fénelon's, by Poulain de la Barre and others.[11]

One might have expected Fénelon to allow the pace to be set by the *savantes* (often, it is true, largely self-educated) who were not lacking in high society—particularly among the 'cartésiennes'—and whom he certainly knew. But he fears the making of 'savantes ridicules' (having perhaps in mind Molière's satire in *Les femmes savantes* of 1672).[12] On the other hand, he cleverly uses the then common view that women are in all ways feebler than men to argue that they should therefore be 'fortified' by education.[13] But why should this be desirable? Because, as wives and mothers, women rule 'les mœurs', and history is largely the record of havoc caused by women without virtue.[14] It would seem then that Fénelon wants women educated not as a natural right but for the benefit of men. One can partly excuse his patronising attitude when one sees how startlingly accurate is his evocation of what we may call the 'Emma Bovary syndrome', and of how bad a bad convent education can be: 'Une pauvre fille, pleine du tendre et du merveilleux qui l'ont charmée dans ses lectures . . . voudrait vivre comme ces princesses imaginaires, qui sont, dans les romans, toujours charmantes, toujours adorées, toujours au-dessus de tous les besoins. Quel dégoût pour elle de descendre de l'héroïsme jusqu'au plus bas détail du ménage!'[15]

The actual syllabus that Fénelon wants to offer girls is disappointingly conservative. This is because it is based on the principle that 'la science des femmes, comme celle des hommes, doit se borner à s'instruire par rapport à leurs fonctions; la différence de leurs emplois doit faire celle de leurs études'. And Fénelon, unlike Poulain de la Barre, cannot imagine that the structure of woman's life could change—thus, her function in life will be: to educate her own sons for a time and her daughters till they marry or become nuns; to direct the lives of her servants both in their service and in their morals; to regulate household expenditure, with honour and economy; often, to deal with income. A curious woman will find these things, says Fénelon, very limiting, but she is mistaken in underestimating their importance. In consequence, a woman needs to know domestic economy, arithmetic, simple common law, seigneurial rights and duties, how to give children a moral education. She may learn international modern history, and Graeco-Roman history will show her 'des prodiges de courage et de désintéressement'. She may read 'les livres profanes qui n'ont rien de dangereux pour les passions'—which do not include novels and drama. Fénelon considers his contemporaries mistaken in believing that a well-educated girl should know Italian and Spanish—a little Church Latin would be more useful, to help her follow the divine office. She may be allowed to read selected books of eloquence and poetry, but not pagan fables which are 'full of impious absurdities'. She may study a little music and painting; God favours art so long as it is in praise of Himself.

None of this contains much merit from a more modern viewpoint. When one looks at *De l'éducation des filles* from the other standpoint, that of teaching-method with small children of either sex, one finds, in contrast, a remarkably enlightened, psychologically sound and forward-looking stance. One could place the work a good deal higher than that much vaunted 'pioneer' work, the *Emile* of Rousseau. Fénelon, unlike Rousseau, obviously knows and loves children, and shows the human understanding that makes his 'letters of spiritual direction' great. His theory here is clearly aimed at the rich—one tutor, one child, or at the most a very small number. Yet it applies equally well on the classroom scale, though Fénelon discusses state education only in a very brief and not very interesting passage of *Télémaque*.[16]

True enough, his attempt at a physiological understanding of the child's brain is laughable. But this does not vitiate the wisdom of his practical approach, which is based on two main premises: that children are fundamentally timid and should not be intimidated; that they enjoy the achievement of learning as much as they do play (indeed, learning is a kind of play for them) and respond not to force but encouragement, from a teacher who *participates* with the child. A very few examples from Fénelon's liberally illustrated theory must serve to show how he considers the child's learning as integrated with his emotional development. Praise is essential to all children, even the vain. Jealousy should not always be thwarted: every child should have his little triumphs. Punishment should consist of withdrawal of affection, but it should be too brief to cause severe distress. Punishment should not invariably follow threat—the modern principle of 'intermittent reinforcement'. The most important lesson, emotional self-control, can only be taught by example, but too much austerity is undesirable: teacher and child can frequently enjoy being silly together.

Naturally, religious instruction is important to Fénelon, but for him religion is historical reality and can be taught as such, through vivid stories and play-acting, not through moral or metaphysical abstractions. The one specific sign of Fénelon's commitment is that he says the child should be warned against the 'trap of (Calvinist) novelty' in religion—Bossuet's 'innovations'.[17] We can see that Fénelon hits hard at the then current image of the 'severe dignity' of the pedagogue. He himself was without pomp, as we see in the agreeable *Fables* he wrote for the young Duc de Bourgogne: 'Il y avait une fois un roi et une reine qui n'avaient point d'enfants. Ils en étaient si fâchés, si fâchés, que personne n'a jamais été plus fâché.'[18]

(iii) The political and economic theorist

In *De l'education des filles*, Fénelon wrote: 'Le monde n'est point un fantôme; c'est l'assemblage de toutes les familles . . .' His Quietism never led him to disregard worldly realities. In Saintonge he showed himself tolerably shrewd, if not in those early years deeply compassionate. Contemporary government and the immediate and future welfare of France were not, he believed, specially attended to by God, and he thought about them in realistic terms. He never produced major works of political theory.[19] But all his life he strove, through circulated memoirs, plans, letters, and written advice to his royal pupil, to be a real influence.[20] He was at the centre of an important group, as we shall see. Most of his projects were thwarted, and were known at the time only to a handful of people, but influential people. They interest us for their underlying concepts.

These concepts are far removed from Bossuet's. Where Bossuet saw a guide to monarchy in the letter of the Scriptures, Fénelon found it in the spirit. Again, he was too much part of the old aristocracy ever to cry with Bossuet: 'Rois . . . vous êtes des dieux'. Fénelon wanted practical controls on absolutism. For instance, in his plan for reviving the Estates General, he seeks specifically to prevent the king from interfering in elections or using subtle bribery.[21] The question of whether Fénelon's desire to see the seigneurial power of the aristocracy revived was retrogressive or progressive has exercised scholars all this century. The *philosophes* admired him, without being influenced by him in any specific way. The recent work of Rothkrug perhaps indicates that if one studies Fénelon's politics he will seem a feudal reactionary whereas his economic theories will seem progressive.[22]

Four threads in Fénelon's worldly life seem to need disentangling: his actual power, his political plans, his economic plans, and finally the purely theoretical politics and economics of *Télémaque*.

To discuss first his real power: he was the centre of a court faction, indeed a cabal, both before and after his disgrace of 1699. It consisted of Madame de Maintenon (up to 1697, when things began to go against the Quietists), the ducs de Beauvillier and de Chevreuse; the marquis de Seignelay, and, on the periphery, perhaps Saint-Simon, famous for his *Mémoires*. Fénelon was one of Madame de Maintenon's spiritual directors. Beauvillier became governor to the Petit Dauphin and to the ducs d'Anjou and de Berry in 1689 and promptly made Fénelon preceptor to all three. Seignelay, Colbert's son, entered the most powerful body under the king, the *Conseil d'en haut*, in the same year. Beauvillier joined him there in 1691. Beauvillier and Chevreuse were also Colbert's sons-in-law, and Chevreuse was one of Louis XIV's most trusted advisers. A formidable group, all dedicated to controls on absolutism.

When Bossuet attacked the *Maximes des saints* in 1697, he was almost certainly given the courage to do it by Pontchartrain, *Contrôleur général* in command of finance, whose interest was not religious: he feared that the liberal economic theories of the Fénelon group would make it difficult to settle with the Dutch in the Treaty of Ryswick in that very year. Both Pontchartrain and Bossuet took advantage of Madame de Maintenon's fear of Louis, who was intensely hostile to Molinosism long before Fénelon became suspect. The crisis of Fénelon's disgrace did not end the activities of the group.[23] By 1701, the Duc de Bourgogne was writing to Fénelon again in affectionate terms. Beauvillier and Chevreuse were still strong at court. In 1711 the three worked together on the *Plans de gouvernement . . . pour être proposés au Duc de Bourgogne*, known as the *Tables de Chaulnes*.[24] In the same year the Grand Dauphin died, and in 1712 both the Petit Dauphin and his wife died. Without knowing which of the two surviving princes would be the next king, Fénelon and Chevreuse at once made plans for their education.[25] But death overtook Beauvillier, Chevreuse and Fénelon before the throne became vacant. Only the theories remained, to be published throughout the eighteenth century.

The theories were essentially as follows: to limit the monarchy and to make it recognise limits for itself; to associate the nation more closely with the government; to re-establish the high and ancient nobility; and to avoid warlike policies. These ideas, associated with ideas on economic reform which, for the sake of clarity, we shall treat separately, recur constantly, and we can see most of them elaborated in detail in the *Examen de conscience sur les devoirs de la royauté*.[26] Louis XIV would have been hard put to it to answer this *Examen*. But Fénelon's fiercest attack against the moral and economic cost of the King's vainglory and warmaking is one that Louis almost certainly never saw, and which was probably written to encourage Madame de Maintenon and Beauvillier to speak frankly to him: the famous *Lettre à Louis XIV* (probably 1694).[27]

It was in the internationally critical and internally disastrous year of 1710 that Fénelon, fearing like many another the actual demise of France, emphasised most clearly the need of a close association between monarch and people, even while fearing that Louis XIV could never be persuaded of it.[28] Fénelon was honestly convinced that old and high aristocracy constituted the natural leadership of a nation, acceptable to all members of that nation. His desire to see the *Etats généraux* convoked again after being long in abeyance was not exactly a democratic move, since a composition for a province of one nobleman, one high cleric and one member of the Third Estate—though all freely elected—was not what we would call proportional representation. In the Revolutionary years, the proportion was to become one nobleman, one high cleric, two members of the Third Estate, which was nearer to the sixteenth-century practice. However, some of Fénelon's other projects, such as an end to the selling by the King of public offices, were more democratic in inspiration, as well as being aimed at limiting the monarch's influence.[29]

Let us consider now the third of our threads, Fénelon's economic plans. Rothkrug sees Fénelon as a key figure in projects for financial reform.[30] His well documented thesis is as follows. Though the term 'mercantilism' was not coined until the eighteenth century by Adam Smith, the economic policies of France had been mercantilist since at least the beginning of the sixteenth century. Mercantilist theory is grounded in several beliefs: that bullion is true wealth, that internal exchanges of wealth are insignificant since they bring no bullion into the economy, that other nations are there only to be exploited ruthlessly by such measures as protective tariffs. It is clear that Fénelon was anti-mercantilist on all these points. He believed that wealth consisted in an abundant population working a limited amount of land efficiently; that internal commerce was very important in re-distributing wealth and keeping the people's lives economically viable; that commerce establishes brotherhood between nations and is essentially godly; and that trade should be unfettered by tariff barriers. These views add up to what Rothkrug calls 'Christian agrarianism'. We may emphasise that stress on internal trade implies a better deal for the bulk of the people and that stress on international free trade is intimately bound up with Fénelon's Christianity and with his pacifism.

At the same time, free trade does not mean for Fénelon the

avoidance of rendering accounts. One of the phenomena of the last twenty years of the seventeenth century in Europe and England was the growing realisation of the importance to economic efficiency of accurate national statistics. There is a clear relationship in France between this trend and the preceding developments in the Scientific Revolution. Colbert in 1664 and Vauban in the 1680s had tried to develop such statistical analyses, without too much success. In 1697, Fénelon's group, under Beauvillier, wrote a letter to all the Intendants in the provinces asking for an economic census of the nation's wealth. The eagerness of the response they received shows perhaps the growing realisation of the power of 'scientific' knowledge as well as of the critical situation of France's economy. It also meant that, had the duc de Bourgogne for whose benefit the enquiry was set in motion lived, he would have been France's best-informed monarch up to that time.

Our discussion of Fénelon's political and economic thought ends with the pure theory contained in *Télémaque*, 1699. This is a novel of adventure with a strong educational bias. It relates the wandering of Telemachus in search of his father Ulysses. The young Telemachus, who bears certain resemblances to Fénelon's own pupil, is accompanied by Minerva, goddess of wisdom, who has taken the form of the youth's elderly tutor, Mentor. Mentor instructs Telemachus in the ways of humanity, teaches him the traps of his own character, and shows him the strengths and shortcomings of the governments they encounter, particularly monarchy. The novel is long but quite readable, though more Virgilian than Homeric; it was immensely popular in the eighteenth century.[31] It does however have a major flaw, in the person of Mentor himself. He has fine qualities and real wisdom; but he is a compulsive talker. Even when he and Telemachus are clinging for their lives to wreckage in a stormy sea the harangue continues. One marvels at the docility of the pupil under this barrage.

Our discussion of the ideas in *Télémaque* must be limited to one famous section, book X, where Mentor guides Idomeneus, driven out from Crete for impiety and inhumanity and now sadder and wiser, in setting up his state in the Sallentine Plain, in the heel of Italy. Mentor undertakes a statistical survey of the land, the workers and commerce, his objectives paralleling those of Beauvillier's enquiry of 1697.

Armed with this survey, he will undertake to bring about complete freedom of trade. Dealing in luxury goods will however be banned as being conducive to 'softness'.[32] There will be seven classes of freemen and one of slaves, all identifiable by their mode of dress, which will be very simple even for those of the most ancient nobility. The general tone will be of 'une noble et frugale simplicité'. The schools will teach fear of the gods, love of honour and country, respect for law. This 'Spartan' attitude of Fénelon was common to most of the 'Anciens'. In two fields, society will invest heavily: there will be large sports stadia and well-stocked arsenals. Readiness for war, says Mentor, is the best way of not being forced into war. There will be mobility of labour—the dream of every economist. Superfluous artisans will be taken from the towns and set to cultivation. Foreigners will be brought in to do the heaviest agricultural work, on the promise of eventual integration and land of their own. Every family, of every class, will own land only in proportion to the number of its members; so there can be no accumulation of land by purchase, and everyone will have to work the soil hard. Thus, the workers will be encouraged to have larger families, so as to have more land and the hands to work it. Neglect of one's property will lead to fines.[33] Finally, Mentor warns the king not to make himself into an idol, for, the more absolute a king, the less his real power, since the State languishes under him as he takes everything and ruins everything—an echo of the *Lettre à Louis XIV*.

What are we to make of all this? It is theory, but very thought-provoking, and amazing for its day, even if in part derived from Plato's *Republic*. Clearly, Fénelon did not envisage introducing a class of slaves into France, though others may have done; he is merely evoking a neo-Minoan State in his fiction. His ideas aim at the economic well-being of all, without the disappearance of a class-structure. However, this welfare, democratic perhaps and certainly humane in intent, is clearly to be achieved somewhat at the expense of what Western democracies would today call individual freedom. What would we say to a society where our music is controlled by law, and magistrates are appointed to watch specific families and control individual morals? None the less, this theory is much less rigid and much less economically ignorant than Bossuet's.

Bossuet, 'l'aigle de Meaux', commanded great respect; but so did Fénelon, 'le cygne de Cambrai', especially among devotees of Saint François de Sales. It was visible that one could be a Catholic archbishop yet not believe absolutism to be the only system a Christian God could conceivably have ordained.

CHAPTER SIX

PIERRE BAYLE

With Bayle and Fontenelle, we are still essentially in the period 1680 to 1715 which largely covers Bossuet and Fénelon. They represent everything that Bossuet opposed, and are the two most important figures in what has long been known as the Pre-Enlightenment, before the term Early Enlightenment was coined. While Fénelon was much admired by the 'philosophes', his actual influence on the Enlightenment does not go beyond a generalised enthusiasm for his largely humanitarian outlook. The influence of Bayle and Fontenelle was, in contrast, formidable and specific on the eighteenth century—which, however, may not have seen them exactly as they were.

This last point is particularly true of Bayle who, among all the main thinkers we are considering, was the only Protestant. We may add that he was the only one who specifically lived by a profession—that of university teacher and journalist, his workaday academic life being very different from the tutorships enjoyed by Bossuet and Fénelon. A further difference was that he had no privilege of birth, wealth or connections. It has long been a commonplace that reading Bayle reveals him as an intellectual chameleon, constantly appearing to change.[1] The truth is that he had so open and searching a mind that he never got as far as making positive assertions except in the ethical field, and his honesty and lack of a rigid system remind us of no one so much as of Diderot.[2] The most suitable way for us to present his thought seems therefore to follow his biography schematically, developing particular ideas at the most appropriate points.

Bayle was born in 1647, second of three sons of a Protestant pastor of good family and culture, and he died in 1706. His

147

upbringing in the village of Foix near the Spanish frontier could seem that of a provincial backwater. Though one should not underestimate the intellectual life of such Protestant enclaves, from first to last he was never in very close personal contact with the mainstream of French culture. This fact was compensated for by his phenomenal reading of Ancients and Moderns, and he became a mine of erudition and a writer of astounding industry.

He was educated in Greek and Latin by his father, attended the Protestant academy in the small town of Puylaurens, then at twenty-two took a degree in arts at the Jesuit college of Toulouse. Shortly after this, he became converted to Catholicism—no small wrench, seeing that his elder brother Jacob was destined to become a pastor like his father. It was an even bolder decision, much meditated, to become reconverted to the Reformed church. By doing so he not only lost his privileged position of 'new convert' but became a 'lapsed Catholic', a category regarded with special malice by the Catholic authorities, who were already showing the militancy which was soon to become outright persecution of the Protestants. These changes in position were no idle whims, but manifest the courage and disinterestedness Bayle always showed in his quest for truth.

Bayle knew the danger he was now in, and fled to Geneva, the main haven of Calvinism, but now less theocratic than formerly. From 1670 to 1672 he earned a modest living as a private tutor, studied Protestant theology, Biblical exegesis—and Cartesianism, not at that time frowned on in Geneva.[3]

At this point, then, we may break off to consider the later influence of Descartes on Bayle. Bayle was to hold that the main obstacles to truth are the authority of great individuals, the traditions of antiquity, and majority opinion. While this stance is not surprising in a Protestant, it is also eminently Cartesian.

However, Bayle does not accept Descartes' criteria of truth without argument. In particular, he will not agree that 'clear and distinct ideas' transcend universal doubt. Descartes, in taking 'extension' as the *sine qua non* of the material world, was trying to show in physics that 'matter co-extensive with space' was a clear and distinct concept, and therefore reliable, while Aristotelian 'qualities' such as colour, sound and smell were not. Late in his career Bayle would reject this argument, by saying that if God could allow a peasant to be deceived as to the reality of colour He could equally allow the scientist to be deceived about the reality of 'extension'. Both peasant and scientist take as realities what are only 'modifications of their own soul'. This argument appears in one of the most controversial and most read articles of his *Dictionnaire historique et critique* (1696), 'Pyrrhon'.[4] The argument is attributed to one priest, generally called the 'abbé pyrrhonien', talking with another, and is so forceful that many readers thought Bayle himself was a Pyrrhonist. Pyrrho, the first of the great Greek sceptics, had proclaimed that truth is unattainable and that one must 'follow the appearances'. As regards the new physics, this is exactly Bayle's stance. He implies that the reality of the physical universe cannot be proven, but states that, since the new physics makes sense of the appearances, there is no practical point in doubting its veracity. Indeed, neither physics nor ethics nor the State, but only theology, need fear the Pyrrhonist.[5]

Descartes was to be of great importance to Bayle in his own main field, his enquiry into the best methods of historiography. Bayle did not write whole histories, but implicit in most of his work is a 'Cartesian' stand on the criteria of reliability of sources. This stand is fairly explicit in three major works: the *Pensées diverses sur la comète* (1681), the *Critique générale de l'Histoire du calvinisme de Monsieur Maimbourg* (1682), and the *Dictionnaire*. Descartes' 'hyperbolic doubt' could have of course dire consequences for the historiographer: if everything is potentially illusion, one could postulate that all memory, all historical records, even the past itself are illusion. Bayle here adopts the Pyrrhonist view: if Caesar's existence is attested only in the world of appearances, it is in the same world of appearances that we move, so that properly tested historical evidence is in practice as reliable as any scientific evidence: '. . . On ne trouvera guère de choses plus inébranlables que cette proposition "César et Pompée ont existé et n'ont pas été une simple modification de l'âme de ceux qui ont écrit leur vie".'[6] It is not then Descartes' 'hyperbolic doubt' that

Bayle adopts, but Descartes' determination to avoid prejudice and haste and not to accept authority without putting it to his own test (the image of the apples in the barrel). What Bayle does essentially is to take the first principle of the Method—to accept only what is 'evidently' so according to one's own lights—and to apply it not to ideas but to sources of information, in other words to apply it empirically.

As to what is 'evidently' so, the problem is for the historiographer simply one of sceptical good sense. The value of a source does not lie in the 'authority' attributed to its writer. It lies in the evidence he has been able to adduce and in the clear absence of prejudice. Bayle was for instance extremely sceptical of the newest form of information, the gazette, an early form of the newspaper and highly subject to bias. In past records, if an enemy praised a leader, this is stronger evidence than if his followers praised him. Coinage, public records and inscriptions are fairly trustworthy, though Bayle is too astute to believe that the last two are never falsified. Above all, where reliable information is not available, the historian must profess his ignorance and simply leave a gap. Since, for example, we have Roman accounts of the Punic wars but no Carthaginian accounts we must admit to not having entirely reliable knowledge of these wars.

In brief, Bayle is the first French historiographer to insist on the criteria of reliability and objectivity already much explored in the physical sciences by his time, and which we expect today. Bayle's own critique of the Catholic Maimbourg's History of Calvinism is a model of impartiality, whereas Maimbourg was more concerned with Catholic apologetics than with history.[7] Little wonder that Bayle was indignant when the Catholic authorities had his own studies burned by the public hangman.[8] Bayle does not take his place in the first rank of historians because he envisaged his task as the correcting of earlier errors rather than the producing of an original thesis. None the less, he did a great deal towards refining the tools of historiography and, in so doing, shows us how the outlook of the Scientific Revolution, of Bacon, Pascal, but most directly Descartes, was being assimilated by the 'human sciences'.

The reader will recall that Bayle first studied Descartes in

Geneva. Let us now return to following his fortunes from 1672, when he went back to France. He was still, of course, a 'lapsed Catholic', and he lived obscurely as a household tutor, in Coppet in 1672, in Rouen in 1674 and in Paris in 1675. Then he won the professorship of philosophy at the Protestant Academy of Sedan, with a brilliant Cartesian-style dissertation on 'Time'. Taking up his chair late in 1675, he accepted his brief, which was to teach the traditional syllabus by the traditional methods. But, 'grand ami des nouveaux philosophes' to use his own words, he took what opportunities he could to introduce his students to Cartesianism.[9] In the summer of 1681 the first *dragonnades* took place in Poitou and the Protestant Academy of Sedan was suppressed in July. Bayle did like many other Protestants in those dark years—he fled to the 'Refuge' in Rotterdam. He obtained the chair of history and philosophy in that town's *Ecole illustre*. Almost at once began the period of his epoch-making works. He published his *Lettre sur la comète* in March 1682, his *Critique de . . . Maimbourg* in July, and then his study on the comet appeared in September 1683 under its modern title, *Pensées diverses sur la comète*. This work we shall now pause to discuss.[10]

The occasion of the work was the spectacular comet of 1680. On 29 November its tail extended through over fifty degrees of arc, a magnificent phenomenon such as had not been seen since 1618. Yet careful examination of the available evidence suggests that public reaction was not very strong, though Bayle claimed that it was. Prat finds that, whereas the comet of 1654 did cause widespread panic, this visitor of 1680 inspired more curiosity than fear, at least among the educated, and amusement on their part at the idea of warnings of 'God's animadversions' by such fiery messages.[11] The 'New Philosophy' had made great inroads on public gullibility since Galileo, Kepler and others had advanced their attempts at scientific explanation of the comets of 1618.[12] By 1680 many astronomers believed that comets moved in a predictable orbit, and in fact Halley correctly identified the smaller comet of 1682 and accurately predicted its orbit of more than seventy years.

Perhaps the best indication of the public's reaction comes from Bayle's own *Pensées diverses*; in the sections devoted to the related theme of astrology—which is described as 'la chose du monde la plus ridicule'—it is clear that Bayle feels he is fencing with shadows. Nearly all his observations on astrological superstitions in France relate to the sixteenth century, a few relate to the period of Louis XIV's minority, and of his own day Bayle has this to say:

> Peu à peu notre Nation s'est guérie de cette faiblesse, soit que nous aimions le change, soit que l'attachement qu'on a eu pour la Philosophie dans ce siècle ici, nous ait fortifié la raison . . . Aussi faut-il avouer qu'il n'y a qu'une bonne et solide Philosophie qui, comme un autre Hercule, puisse exterminer les monstres des erreurs populaires . . . [13]

It is clear that in this changing climate of opinion, with the tide of superstition receding, Bayle could scarcely have written a work of two hundred and sixty-three sections exclusively for the purpose of correcting popular error.

Thus, there must have been a more fundamental motive, and Walter Rex has maintained, in an admirably scholarly study, that the *Pensées diverses* was really a Protestant's attack on Catholicism and was recognised as such at the time, and that Bayle at certain points was merely wearing 'a Cartesian mask'.[14] Without denigrating this argument, which is a significant one, one may find that on studying exactly the same evidence one arrives at a rather different view, closer to Elizabeth Labrousse's carefully weighed judgement that Bayle is always less concerned to attack any particular church than to help make 'better Christians', that is, essentially, more peace-loving men.[15]

Bayle opens the *Pensées diverses* with an attack on the 'argument from Antiquity', the view that an argument must be true if it has a long enough history. We have seen that this was the strongest argument of the Counter-Reformation (as in Bossuet), and Rex rightly maintains that to argue against it was a commonplace of Calvinist controversy, here seen in 'one of [its] last significant reappearances'.[16] Yet in arguing against Antiquity and majority opinion, Bayle not only uses Descartes' expressions—like 'la pluralité des voix'—but Descartes' reasoning that Antiquity is improperly invoked for its 'authority' instead of for the reasons on which its testimony is based.[17] He uses simple modern physics to show that comets cannot have any of the Aristotelians' 'virtue' to influence our world.[18] He then shows how 'bon sens' indicates that they do not even presage events on earth. For example: the history of man is one long series of calamities for one nation or another, so that a comet's appearance is bound to coincide with some disaster. Again: it did not require the comets of 1618 to inform any intelligent man that there were empirical reasons that made war in Europe inevitable. And there are many other such reasonings.[19] All of them come into the category of what Descartes called 'les simples raisonnements que peut faire un homme de bon sens touchant les choses qui se présentent', and in them the *philosophes* of the eighteenth century were bound to see the thoughts of a man who shared their idea of what constitutes 'une bonne et solide Philosophie'.

It is true that in attacking superstition, Bayle most frequently attacks popular Catholic practices: the wearing of amulets (from Rome), the veneration of saints and relics (both abhorred by the Calvinists as worship of creatures and not the Creator). But Bayle's real objective seems to be to show that it is the superstitious mind that is most convinced of its own rightness and is therefore most ready to resort to force. The persecution of Protestants is a current and important example, of course.[20] But it is not the only possible example. Bayle, we may consider, was attacking not merely the Catholics, but a general mentality of 'unreason', such as Protestants—including some of Bayle's friends—were quite capable of showing. 'Unreason' as a source of inhumanity was to be the perennial enemy of the *philosophes*. The baron d'Holbach, for example, asks: Who is most ready to hunt for scapegoats, most intolerant of humanity?—and answers himself: He who is most fearful and superstitious in his own religious beliefs.[21]

The resorting to force is, as Bayle sees it, against 'natural light', and his argument shifts from scientific 'reason' to ethical 'reasonableness'. As we follow it, we can trace an essential link between the preoccupations of the Scientific Revolution and those of the Early Enlightenment: Bayle propounds a *theory of ethics*, and he propounds it from a quasi-scientific not a theological standpoint. He moves towards the 'humanisation', the 'desacralisation' of ethics.[22] It is not true, as once maintained in this context, that Bayle's contention that an atheist may be more ethically sound than a Christian was one of the most startling of his 'paradoxes' (he was fond of uttering 'paradoxes', meaning 'controversial opinions'). Many Christians already accepted this view, and it was not till more than ten years later that the Protestant militant Jurieu claimed the *Pensées diverses* to be 'full of dangerous and impious propositions' on this score—'with the greatest bad faith in the world', Bayle claimed, for Jurieu, once his friend, had quite different reasons for persuading the Flemish Consistory of Rotterdam to remove him from his professorship.

At the same time, one is led to think of early *libertins* like La Mothe le Vayer with his *De la vertu des päiens* (1641), for Bayle's 'desacralisation' of ethics was more fundamental than was realised till the eighteenth century. His argument is on these lines: religion does not imply good morals; the proof is that in the field of sexual licence where only religious prohibitions and no State sanctions apply, Catholics and many Protestants give free reign to what Bayle calls their 'bad impulses' (exception made in section 143 for the few who are truly led by the Spirit of God). Many things influence morals other than religion—the fear of punishment, State sanctions, fear of losing one's good name, and above all the simple fact that many, *by their own nature* ('tempérament'), prefer good to evil.[23] True, Bayle often refers to the Fall and the consequent need for grace.[24] It is God who gives us 'une disposition de cœur' which makes us find more joy in virtue than in vice. Yet, when one puts Bayle's idea of 'disposition de cœur'—even in its context—next to his idea of the atheist's 'tempérament' which may naturally incline him to the good, one finds it very hard to distinguish between them. Bayle really seems to be concerning himself with whether a 'desacralised' ethos may not account as well as does religion for love for one's fellow men, and to be pointing towards the 'humanistic' (in the modern sense) ethics of the *philosophes*. This concern was to become even clearer within two years.

Between March 1684 and February 1687 Bayle was engaged in the astonishing one-man task of composing a very substantial monthly literary review, the *Nouvelles de la République des Lettres*, as well as filling his chair.[25] In the midst of this period came the Revocation, accompanied by a surfeit of praises for Louis XIV's policy and of justificatory tracts from the Catholics of France. Shameful they were, but quite in the spirit of the times; even the Protestants harassed the handful of 'sectarians' who spoke of 'civil tolerance', and this remained true even into the 1690s. In November 1685 Bayle's brother Jacob, imprisoned as a pastor in France, died in his cell. Five months later, Bayle published in Amsterdam his quite brief *Ce que c'est que la France toute catholique sous le règne de Louis le Grand*.[26] It is in three letters, the second and third purportedly written by two exiled Huguenots. The second is the expression of Bayle's grief and anger, in memorable invective. The third, Bayle's passion having been purged as it were, speaks in more measured tones, but does not disclaim the previous letter. Reason speaks against the Revocation: it was a political mistake, for loyalist minorities were important to Louis XIV; it was against human decency and other nations now call Catholicism 'la religion des malhonnêtes gens' and the French dangerous neighbours. But most important is the ethical question of religious tolerance. Bayle does not adduce individual rights nor the freedom of the citizen—essentially English ideas—but the *sacredness of conscience, even in error* (including, for instance, that of Socinian heretics). Where previously we saw him 'desacralising' the concept of goodness, here we see him 'sacralising' a humanistic ethos: to force the conscience of the individual is to usurp a right that only God has, it is 'lèse-majesté divine'. Though no one can say ultimately what Bayle's religion was, it is certain that he was not a deist. Yet he leads us far in the direction of a view common in eighteenth-century deism: that a benign God allows man to work out his own salvation according to a purely humanistic ethos of private conscience.

Bayle was soon to bring the idea of sacredness of conscience together with his earlier concept of 'natural light' in an important synthesis, in the *Commentaire philosophique sur ces paroles de l'Evangile selon S. Luc, ch. 14 vers 23: 'Et le Maître dit au Serviteur, va par les chemins et par les haies, ET CONTRAINS-LES D'ENTRER, afin que ma Maison soit remplie'*.[27] We saw how Catholics like Bossuet used the doctrine of *compelle intrare* ('make them come in'), basing it on Augustine's commentary on Luke, to justify conversion by force. Bayle has now mastered his personal grief and has moved to a stance involving universal principle—the question of what is the source and guide of ethics.

Part 1 of the *Commentaire* opens with a highly significant chapter-heading 'Que la lumière naturelle, ou les principes généraux de nos connaissances, sont la règle matrice et originale de toute interprétation de l'Ecriture, en matière de mœurs principalement'.[28] The crux of the argument is the distinction between *literal* and *figurative* interpretations of Scripture, and Bayle argues that any literal interpretation of the words of Jesus which contains an obligation to commit crimes is false, *according to natural light*. Natural light has nothing to say on puzzling dogmas such as that of the Trinity, which are best accepted fideistically, but there are articles of faith ('rationalised' by the theologians, Bayle says mockingly) on which it has everything to say, and in particular ethics: '... sans exception, il faut soumettre toutes les lois morales à cette idée naturelle d'équité, qui, aussi bien que la lumière Métaphysique, *illumine tout homme venant au monde*'.[29] Of the nine refutations of the doctrine of *compelle intrare* the two most forceful are that this doctrine is contrary to the spirit of the Scriptures (ch. 3) and that it is contrary to natural light (ch. 2). Bayle shows by his vocabulary that he is consciously turning Descartes' 'bon sens' towards ethics: 'C'est donc une chose manifestement opposée au bon sens et à la lumière naturelle, aux principes généraux de la Raison, en un mot à la règle primitive et originale du discernement du vrai et du faux, du bon et du mauvais, que d'employer la violence à inspirer une Religion à ceux qui ne la professent pas'.[30] But really Bayle's argument is: My *intuition*, my whole *lived experience* of religion, tell me that Jesus could not have meant what Augustine thought. In other words, Bayle is not using Descartes' 'bon sens'; he is closer to Hobbes' view that 'natural Reason' is 'the undoubted Word of God'; but he is closest of all to Pascal's 'existential intuition', *le cœur*. It is a deeper tragedy for the inheritors of Bayle than we can know that he sensed but never clearly said that *knowledge of the good* is not arrived at by dialectical reason (method) but by a suprarational intuition. He stayed within the limits of Cartesianism when he could perhaps have transcended them in a manner more acceptable to the *philosophes* than Pascal's.

Part 2 of the *Commentaire* refutes possible objections to part 1. Part 3 gives forty quotations from Augustine and refutes them. Bayle's attitude here is important; he does not mince words, and it is clear that there is a strong element, not merely of anti-authoritarianism, but of 'desacralisation' in his attack on the most venerable Father of the Church.

We now approach the *Dictionnaire historique et critique* (complete version 1696), massive in scale and erudition, a monument of rational historical method and teeming with provocative ideas. At first, Bayle intended only to correct the errors of earlier historians, which is why we find Plato and Pascal but look in vain for Aristotle and Descartes. Bayle is indeed not merely selective but idiosyncratic in his choice of topics. We shall leave aside now the theme of tolerance, concerning which Bayle merely reinforces his earlier statements.[31] Nor shall we revert to the subject of the 'good atheist', which recurs frequently.[32] We shall not return either to the important article 'Pyrrhon', previously discussed. Nor is there scope in this study to report on the recent fascinating developments in the study of the political implications of the notorious 'David'.[33] We must content ourselves with pointing out that this article dramatically criticises both the *text* and the *ethos* of the Old Testament, attacking thus both its historical and its moral authority.[34]

There is an observation that must must be made on the structure of the *Dictionnaire*. It consists of short Articles, intended for reference, and long Remarks, intended to air Bayle's views. Both Articles and Remarks are accompanied in the margin by source- and cross-references. This kind of layout was notoriously used in the *Encyclopédie* edited by Diderot et al. to disguise the more controversial views contributed, and the *Encyclopédistes* were long held to have imitated Bayle in this. No modern scholar will now accept this view. There is no hiding-away of Bayle's thought (except that some of his private obsessions—such as his anger with Jurieu—can be traced only through consulting the source-references) and the Rotterdam Consistory had no difficulty in pinning down what it disapproved of. Nor does the general reader have any difficulty in following where Bayle wants to lead.

We shall follow Bayle on two fundamental and closely

related subjects: the problem of evil and the need for a fideistic religion. His views are widespread, but one can locate all the essentials in the articles 'Manichéens', 'Pauliciens', 'Rufin' and the 'Eclaircissements' asked for by the Rotterdam Consistory for the second edition.

The problem of how God in His goodness allows the existence of evil in His creation had exercised the partisans of rational theology from the Fathers of the Church through the whole era of scholasticism. It is perhaps true that the seventeenth century preoccupied itself rather with the problem of Free Will and Predestination, and it was almost incidental to this that so often the accent was on the miserable and evil condition of man without Grace and on the idea that pain was part of this condition. Bayle takes the emphasis away from the problem of Free Will to put it firmly back on the problem of evil.[35] In one place or another, he examines all the traditional explanations for evil by 'rational theology' and finds them all wanting. Bayle's debate centres on the Epicurean affirmation that God either can but will not prevent evil or that He does will but cannot. One alternative challenges God's infinite goodness, the other His omnipotence.

The Manichean heresy claimed that God is infinitely good but not omnipotent. The sect was held to have derived in the third century from Manes, a Persian who developed his view from Zoroaster, and Bayle maintains that it held the 'croyance aux deux principes'. The eternal good principle, which is God, created the world, but could not prevent the equally powerful and eternal evil principle from invading His creation. It is to little account that, in his 'Eclaircissements', Bayle listed six refutations of this heresy, and claimed that it was not to be feared because it was too horrifying to entertain. He gives all the good arguments to the Manicheans and concludes that neither logic nor natural light can oppose them:

Qui n'admirera et qui ne déplorera la destinée de notre raison? Voilà les Manichéens qui, avec une Hypothèse tout-à-fait absurde et contradictoire, expliquent les expériences cent fois mieux que ne font les Orthodoxes, avec la supposition si juste, si nécessaire, si uniquement véritable d'un premier principe infiniment bon et tout-puissant.[36]

If, Bayle says on the same page, one rejects the Manichean view, the only possible alternative is to say that it is a fact that

God put evil into man, 'donc cela ne répugne point à la bonté de Dieu'.

The Christian faced with this conclusion stands in dismay, for it is offensive to natural light. He then has only one recourse, to arm himself with the shield of faith, 'le bouclier de la foi'.[37] This leads us straight into the fideistic position: 'Mais, direz-vous, les voies de Dieu ne sont pas nos voies, Tenez-vous-en donc là: c'est un Texte de l'Ecriture'.[38] To engage in dispute through natural light must lead to Pyrrhonism or deism or atheism[39] and rather than face any of those prospects we must, asserts Bayle not once but many times, abdicate from natural light at this point. We must resist 'les tentations de la Raison incrédule et orgueilleuse'.[40] We must place the problem of evil among the Mysteries of faith, and recognize that: 'leur caractère essentiel est d'être un objet de Foi, et non pas un objet de Science', for, using either dialectical reason or natural light to combat objections, we can only come off worst: 'Ce qu'il faut conclure de cela est, que les Mystères de l'Evangile étant d'un ordre surnaturel ne peuvent point et ne doivent point être assujettis aux règles de la Lumière naturelle. Ils ne sont pas faits pour être à l'épreuve des Disputes Philosophiques . . .'[41]

Thus Bayle sounds the death-knell of 'rational theology'. In the face of the problem of evil, there remain two possible alternatives. One is pure fideism, but this entails the abandoning not only of 'rational theology' but also of 'natural light'. What a surprise to find Bayle, the champion of 'natural light' now asking us to abandon it in favour of blind fideism. But there is the crux: the other alternative is atheism. Of course, Bayle does not state this second alternative as a viable one. But all good students of Bayle are made suspicious by a kind of irony in the whole promotion of fideism, an element of black comedy; Elizabeth Labrousse calls it 'bonhomie enjouée' and for all her masterly work on Bayle is forced to leave open the question—Is he inviting us to fideism or to atheism? Whatever Bayle's deep intention, two things are clear about his treatment of the problem of evil and his apparent retreat into fideism: one, that they point unmistakably *in the direction of* atheism; two, that they question deeply the ability of rational philosophy to deal with metaphysical questions.

Though Bayle was acceptable to many eighteenth-century thinkers on these two counts, he did not go unchallenged. It was largely in reply to him that Leibniz produced his *Theodicy* in 1710. A theodicy is a treatise on the attributes of God with particular reference to His justice in relation to the existence of evil in the creation. As such, theodicy had existed as long as rational theology, but Leibniz was the first to call it by this name. Bayle denies the possibility of a rational explanation for evil's existence—so that one could call the relevant parts of the *Dictionnaire* an 'anti-theodicy'.[42] Bayle and Leibniz set off between them a new controversy on evil which exercised all the great minds of the eighteenth century, perhaps especially Voltaire,[43] but of which the issue was nothing less than the future limitations of philosphy. It was not resolved until the last years of the eighteenth century by Kant in Germany and later in England by John Stuart Mill.

The *Dictionnaire* was a seminal work for the *philosophes*, particularly from the start of the Regency. They used it as well as the other works we have discussed as they saw fit, and not by any means always with reference to Bayle's intentions; but it is not within the scope of this book to follow the fortune of Bayle's ideas in this later period.[44] We must read him both as a seventeenth-century Protestant and as an unmistakable pioneer of the Enlightenment.

CHAPTER SEVEN

FONTENELLE

Throughout the lifetime of Bayle there was an exchange of written courtesies and information between him and Fontenelle, for both men knew that at least one thing they had in common was their war on the superstitious and gullible mind. However, Fontenelle's situation was very different from that of Bayle. Whereas Bayle lived largely in exile, Fontenelle from his earliest years had the opportunity to move into the centre of French cultural life. He also appears to have been untroubled by financial difficulties and, though he worked very hard, he did not work 'for a living'.

Bernard le Bovier de Fontenelle lived from 1657 to 1757 and was born into a Catholic family of some means.[1] His home was in Rouen, where his father was a barrister in the *parlement* of Normandy and his mother sister to Pierre Corneille, who was still to write at least four of his great tragedies.

Born into a social situation not unlike that of Descartes, Fontenelle too studied under the Jesuits, in their college in Rouen. He received a thorough classical education and was and remained much more enthusiastic for the humanities than Descartes had been. Fontenelle, in spite of his anti-clericalism which we shall examine in due course, remained on friendly terms with the Jesuits, and his friend and first biographer, Trublet, was a cleric. Fontenelle studied law, but after his very first case turned to writing and began to create the image of a 'bel esprit' that was later to draw a sneer from La Bruyère, with poems, plays and other minor publications in the recently founded *Mercure galant*. From a fairly early date he had as a friend Du Hamel, the fellow-Norman whom he would eventually succeed as permanent secretary of the Académie des sciences. Among the scientists of repute that he knew in these early years were Rohault and Régis, two outstanding champions of Cartesianism.

Before 1686 he had made a considerable reputation as a society author and 'moraliste' with the *Dialogues des morts* (1683) and had shown his colours as an opponent of superstition with a one-act comedy *La comète* (1681), inspired by the same celestial visitation as Bayle's *Pensées diverses sur la comète*. The year 1686, however, was to establish Fontenelle's true place, which is in the history of ideas, with two books—the *Entretiens sur la pluralité des mondes* and the *Histoire des oracles*—an important essay, *Doutes sur le système physique des causes occasionnelles*—and one short letter destined for an embarrassing notoriety, the so-called *Lettre sur l'île de Bornéo*.[2] These were to be followed only two years later by the important though brief *Digression sur les Anciens et les Modernes* (1688). These are the works on which we shall concentrate much of our attention.

In 1697 Fontenelle became permanent secretary ('secrétaire perpétuel') of the Académie Royale des sciences, in time to write the history of its reorganisation in 1699 by the Secretary of State, Pontchartrain, the same who had recently found Fénelon's economic theory of Christian agrarianism a thorn in his side. The 'new-look' Academy was to be an authoritative voice in European science and Fontenelle was to write its history annually in a large volume, up to his retirement in 1740.[3] He had become a member of the Académie française in 1691 and was to be a member of many other intellectual bodies of the kind for which the pattern had recently emerged: the Royal Society in London, the Arcadian Academy of Rome, the Academies of Berlin and Nancy. With all this and his regular task as *secrétaire perpétuel* of publishing annually a complete account of the papers given before the Académie des sciences and of pronouncing the eulogies (*Eloges*) of its members deceased, Fontenelle became the extremely well-informed, technically competent, authoritative voice for the progress of the 'New Philosophy'.[4] His authority was reinforced by his mastery in the field of *belles-lettres*, long since acclaimed in the early *Dialogues des morts*. The combination made him a great populariser, not only authoritative but eminently readable.

Let us consider Fontenelle's character in general and then observe how it shows in one particular work, the *Entretiens*. Fontenelle was known as a great populariser of the new thought, particularly in the work named, but underneath his readily accessible thinking there are traces of a kind of aristocratic élitism: 'Contentons-nous d'être une petite troupe choisie qui les croyons, et ne divulguons pas nos mystères dans le Peuple', he says when asked about belief in inhabitants of other planets.[5] He also had a distaste for becoming upset. In a short essay of 1690, *Du bonheur*, he gives his personal formula for contentment: 'Le plus grand secret pour le bonheur c'est d'être bien avec soi'. Thus, his work is usually far from the tone of aggressive polemic, and Carré is justified in subtitling his study of Fontenelle's thought 'Le sourire de la raison'. Fontenelle might seem open to the accusation of evading commitment; he rarely appears to go out on a limb like Bayle, or to be fully involved from the moral point of view. Yet his lucid judgement could rarely be bought off; and unlike Bayle, Fontenelle, by his judicious appearance of moderation and good humour, the careful veiling of his aggression, was able to work towards the changing of the French outlook from the inside—and remaining on the inside it was not inappropriate that he should consider personal survival a prime necessity and good reputation the most powerful weapon in his armoury. His public image, carefully nurtured, allowed him to express from time to time ideas that he could never have propagated had he not profited from great intellectual and social prestige.

One can say that Fontenelle presented an object-lesson to the *philosophes* who were to follow him in how to conduct intellectual guerilla warfare and yet survive in a hostile environment. His constant effort was towards unobtrusively cultivating a flourishing climate of healthy scepticism—he could be healthily sceptical even of his beloved sciences on occasion. Calame does not exaggerate in claiming that the seeds of all the 'philosophie dite des lumières' are present in the *Entretiens*.[6] It must be said, however, that the *philosophes* did not always follow his example of disarming humour, preferring their own brand of rather more vitriolic laughter. Today too, in an era where aggressiveness is considered to pay dividends, the tone of Fontenelle can be mistaken for cowardice:

> Je n'ai pourtant jamais ouï parler de la Lune habitée, dit-elle, que comme d'une folie et d'une vision. C'en est peut-être une aussi, répondis-je. Je ne prends parti dans ces choses-là que comme on en prend dans les Guerres civiles, où l'incertitude de ce qui peut arriver, fait qu'on entretient toujours des intelligences dans le parti opposé, et qu'on a des ménagements avec ses Ennemis même. Pour moi, quoique je croie la Lune habitée, je ne laisse pas de vivre civilement avec ceux qui ne le croient pas, et je me tiens toujours en état de me pouvoir ranger à leur opinion avec honneur, si elle avait le dessus . . . [7]

If he returned today, Fontenelle could admit that the moon is not inhabited with good grace, while congratulating himself on his firm prognosis that science would carry men to set foot on the moon.[8] The *Entretiens sur la pluralité des mondes* (1686), on which we have just drawn twice, give us indeed a fair insight into how Fontenelle conducts his guerilla warfare.

The theory that the world is a planet and that other planets might well be inhabited had been proposed by many of those who favoured the Copernican (heliocentric) system. The thought of Giordano Bruno contained implicity the possibility of other inhabited worlds—the theory called 'pluralism'. Galileo's observations on the moon were published in French during the seventeenth century. Petrus Borel published his *Discours prouvant la pluralité des mondes* in Geneva in 1657. This was also the year of Cyrano de Bergerac's lunar travel fiction, *L'autre monde*. In 1658 Gassendi, in his *Syntagma philosophicum*, chapter 6, debated in Latin the question: 'Whether the sky and the stars are habitable'. Wilkins, Bishop of Chester, had written two books favouring pluralism, both of them published in French translation in Rouen in 1656.[9] Bayle wrote on the habitability of the moon in the *Nouvelles de la République des Lettres* of May 1686. By this date, pluralism was a major debating point among the knowledgeable. By now the Church, so strong against Galileo in 1633, must have felt that its battle against Copernicanism was lost. But pluralism was a newer and burning theological issue: if the moon were inhabited, was it by men who were not descendants of Adam, who had not inherited original sin and who had no need of Christ as Saviour? Such speculation the Church of course had no desire to countenance. The theologians were not yet by any means accustomed to temporising with the New Philosophy and its subversive implications.

Into this hot controversy Fontenelle stepped with a series of eminently readable and enjoyable conversation-pieces. The *Mercure galant* announced the forthcoming publication in January 1686:' . . . un livre nouveau, qui quoiqu'il soit de Philosophie, est tourné si galamment que la matière n'a rien de sauvage'; 'de la Philosophie déguisée'; and promised that the ladies could follow its argument with ease.[10] The *Entretiens* were published with Royal Privilege but anonymously. Not from prudence, because the 'gentilhomme-auteur', as a true *honnête homme*, remained anonymous for the second and third editions, even though Bayle had named him in his *République des Lettres* in May 1686. The book was during its author's lifetime to go through some thirty-three editions, of which Shackleton lists thirty-one.[11] This enormous success lay in the ease and clarity with which the Philosopher explains the Copernican heliocentric system combined with the Cartesian cosmology, the provocative nature of his speculations, his inventive teaching method, and by no means least in the real charm of his pupil, perhaps based on the Marquise de la Mésangère, a widow of twenty-seven or so and third child of Madame de la Sablière. She is a perfect pupil, who listens with moderate interest to the Philosopher's opening gambit on the affinity between blondes and sunshine, brunettes and night, and is soon plying him with eager questions and with an appealing naïveté referring to 'us Copernicans', having never heard the name of Copernicus till ten minutes earlier. From then on she has scant patience with the gallantries of her tutor, which none the less probably had quite an appeal for Fontenelle's readers. This *marquise* must have done more to justify education for women than the writings we touched on in discussing Fénelon's *Education des filles*. She is intelligent though unknowlegeable, quick-minded, ready to cope with new concepts, a fine mind waiting to be filled (and Fontenelle expresses his admiration for this kind of mind in the fictitious letter that opens his account of the discussions).[12]

The reader of 1686 found himself compellingly persuaded to abandon Aristotle and Ptolemy in favour of Descartes and Copernicus, and plunged into a fully-developed purely mechanistic universe.[13] He was also invited to believe that we could well not be the only inhabitants of our solar system, and that there could be multitudes of similar systems, equally likely to be inhabited by an endless variety of living forms throughout the universe. Fontenelle's description of the cosmos was at that date as good as could have been produced (though of course the next year, 1687, was to see the whole of Descartes' celestial mechanics thrown into doubt by Newton's *Principia mathematica*). If points of detail showed that the twenty-nine-year-old author was not quite as well up on the newest findings in astronomical measurement as he should have been, his long years of hard work for the Académie des sciences were to make this good. Of course, the cruces of the work were: the Cartesian idea that man is not the centre of the universe; and the theological question of Adam's progeny and the rôle of Christ among the planets. The first Fontenelle propagates as taken for granted. The second he approached from the outset by expounding the problem from the theologians' point of view and then affirming that he visualises the inhabitants of the moon as not men but some other product of the vast diversity of nature: 'J'y mets des Habitants qui ne sont point du tout des Hommes'.[14] The *Journal des savants* was not in the least taken in by this, pointing out that the author soon forgets it, to the point of talking about his Selenites as having all the characteristics of men.[15] Fontenelle had calculated perfectly what he could get away with. His reasonings are so lucid, so well-informed and above all so gracefully and humorously offered that hostile critics were bound to put themselves into the stance of bad-tempered and irrational carpers. In fact, the *Entretiens* brought their author no serious trouble until twenty years later, when the gross hardening of the régime had encouraged the theologians into an energetic bout of 'witch-hunting'. His personal contacts, probably particularly with d'Argenson, chief of police, got him out of difficulty in the event. The *Entretiens* were none the less placed on the Catholic Church's *Index* as undesirable reading within a year of publication, perhaps not so much for their pluralistic theory as for their purely mechanistic description of the cosmos.

Having taken a sample of Fontenelle's polemical method, let us proceed to examine what may be considered the three most important aspects of his work as a whole: his scientific view of the universe; his view of the concept of progress; and his views on God and religion.

In considering the first of these three one finds oneself totally involved in the question of Fontenelle's attitudes to Descartes and Newton, and in dealing with this question alone we shall at least touch on all the salient aspects of his scientific world-picture. Fontenelle having presented Cartesian cosmology so faithfully in the *Entretiens* in 1686 and having returned to its defence in one of his very last works, the *Théorie des tourbillons cartésiens* (1752),[16] a last-ditch stand against Newton, it is no surprise that for long years he was held to be the champion of Descartes and the arch-enemy in France of Newton. In recent years, scholars have become aware that this view is a very misleading simplification and have done much to correct it. A close examination of Fontenelle's views shows, in summary, that he defended Descartes on only one specific issue—his cosmology—and on three general convictions: that the universe is not specifically made for man; that the laws of nature are mechanistic laws; and finally that systematic doubt—or scepticism—is a good thing.

The initial debt to Descartes is clear from the beginning of the *Entretiens*. Fontenelle expounds Descartes' cosmology of 'tourbillons' (vortices) to his lady-friend in the fourth conversation, drawing on the master's *Principes de la philosophie*.[17] His description of light is based on the *Dioptrique*.[18] His denial of anthropocentrism—'Notre folie à nous autres, est de croire aussi que toute la nature, sans exception, est destinée à nos usages'—is again drawn from the *Principes de la philosophie*, if not from Galileo.[19] Where he is not drawing directly on Descartes Fontenelle is probably making good use of his friends Rohault and Régis.[20] The mechanistic view set out in the first conversation is straight Descartes and proclaims the fact.

Fontenelle held faithfully to the mechanistic cosmology of the vortices. Yet when we look further, we find that there is little else of Descartes that he would accept. Not Descartes' metaphysics. The ontological proof of God does not interest him. He expounds, rather, Giordano Bruno's view that God, though omnipresent, is knowable only through the laws of nature. He rejects the concept of 'clear and distinct ideas' known 'évidemment être telles' by the mind alone, and especially the 'idea of perfection' which yields Descartes' first proof of God. Take away ideas coming from my senses, he claims, and you will never prove God to me. All universal ideas are formed from particulars.[21] Not Descartes' faith in the community of 'bon sens'. Fontenelle constantly affirms that men are all alike because of their passions, not their reason. Not Descartes' 'animal-machine'. For Fontenelle, as for Fénelon, even instinctive behaviour—what he describes is in fact what we would call 'reflex behaviour'—is a proof of thought; such reflexes he defines as 'une sorte de raison qui veille à me conserver'. Animal and man are both machine-like but neither is a machine. Both have intelligent behaviour, and intelligent behaviour is a function of will. What are they then? 'Mystère!' says Fontenelle; the question remains open.[22] The only point conceded to Descartes is that the absence of language in animals is hard to explain. Finally, not Descartes' need for a God who sustains the universe from instant to instant. Not occasionalism. The theory of occasionalism is in embryo in Descartes, but it is normally attributed to Malebranche, in discussing whom we studied it. Fontenelle indeed wrote his *Doutes sur le système physique des causes occasionnelles* (1686) in answer to Malebranche's *Traité de la nature et de la grâce* of 1680; but in it he attributes the theory of 'causes occasionnelles' directly to Descartes.[23] The theory is outlined by Fontenelle in *Doutes sur . . . [les] causes occasionnelles*, chapter 2, and is followed by this historical analysis: 'Tel fut l'accroissement des causes occasionnelles dans la physique: elles l'occupèrent tout entière sous M. Descartes. Le père Malebranche est venu, aussi grand philosophe et théologien que M. Descartes était grand philosophe, et il a transporté les causes occasionnelles dans la théologie'.[24]

In the last words lies the key to Fontenelle's rejection of Descartes on this issue. He did not want physics mixed up with theology, or with metaphysics in any guise. He wanted the universe to be explicable as a machine to which God initially gave a certain quantity of motion and which was thereafter self-sustaining and self-regulating: 'La nature d'une machine est, qu'après avoir reçu du mouvement de dehors, elle exécute ensuite, étant abandonnée à elle-même, le dessein pour lequel on l'a faite.'[25] To get rid of God's intervention in physical events was to drive metaphysics out of physics, and, incidentally, to rob Malebranche of his rationalist explanation of miracle. Instead, Fontenelle offers a purely mechanistic theory of cause and effect. The title of chapter 3 of the *Doutes* is: 'Qu'il semble que les corps ne sont point causes occasionnelles, mais causes véritables du mouvement les uns à l'égard des autres'. Similarly, against Descartes' mind–body dualism Fontenelle asserts the unity of mind and matter and thus opens the way for the materialism of much of the Enlightenment; materialism being the theory that the universe is entirely material and that mind is a phenomenon of matter, independently of any spiritual First Cause. God was on the way to being driven out of mental events too.

If Fontenelle rejects Descartes on so many issues, why was he ever seen as Descartes' champion against Newton? Because he could not countenance Newton's theory of gravitation ('attraction')—action at a distance—and consistently opposed Newton on that issue. The theory of gravitation required one body to attract another over an intervening void. Fontenelle, like some of his peers in France, saw this as a quasi-mystical idea, totally alien to mechanism, and reminiscent both of Aristotelian obscurantism and mediaeval occultism. Fontenelle had attacked the turn of mind of which he was to suspect Newton a year before the *Principia* appeared—in the *Entretiens sur la pluralité des mondes*. Imagine, he says to his lady-friend, that you are at the Opéra and you see the actor playing Phaëton fly (a typical sort of happening in baroque entertainment). You know that he is on a cord. Descartes and some other Moderns say that Phaëton flies because he is pulled by a cord over a pulley with a weight heavier than himself at the other end. But imagine, he says, a Pythagoras, a Plato, an Aristotle in the audience. They will say: 'C'est une certaine Vertu secrète qui enlève Phaëton'; or: 'Phaëton est composé de certains nombres qui le font monter'; or: 'Phaëton a une certaine amitié pour le haut du Théâtre'.[26]

Shackleton quotes the mathematician Antoine Parent also objecting in 1709 to being dragged by Newton back into the old obscurities of peripatetic (Aristotelian and scholastic) philosophy, heaven forbid![27] Fontenelle was still speaking in similar vein in 1757 in his *Théorie des tourbillons cartésiens*: 'Si l'on dit que l'attraction mutuelle est une propriété essentielle aux corps, quoique nous ne l'apercevions pas, on en pourra dire autant des sympathies, des horreurs, de tout ce qui a fait l'opprobre de l'ancienne Philosophie scolastique'.[28]

But even in his magnificent praise of Newton in his *Eloge*, with its lucid and apparently sympathetic exposition of the theory of gravitation—pointing out how it could explain weight, tides, and the very complex behaviour of the moon—he was unable to resist contradicting Newton's denial of dealing in 'scholastic occultism'.[29] It is well known that, in the *Eloge de Newton*, Fontenelle sings the praises of both Descartes and Newton, Descartes as an *a priori*-stic mind that worked brilliantly from pure theory to the phenomena, Newton as a speculative mind that worked from the phenomena to brilliant theory; both men at the absolute limit of human ability. The fact was that Fontenelle did not think science was ready for vast syntheses and, in principle, ought to have found the purely rationalistic mechanical universe of Descartes as difficult to countenance as the purely mathematical universe of Newton. According to Fontenelle, the Académie des sciences was right to have 'nul système général' for fear of forcing its observations to fit into a false synthesis, one of the 'systèmes précipités'; and he affirmed that ' . . . il faut que la physique systématique attende à élever des édifices que la physique expérimentale soit en état de lui fournir les matériaux nécessaires'.[30]

As Marsak neatly puts it: 'Fontenelle wanted to be reasonably sure that whatever law was announced was in fact an expression of nature and not simply an extension of human logic'.[31] In other words Fontenelle had a greater affinity with Galileo and Francis Bacon than with either Descartes or Newton.[32]

Now to our second general question, which is: To what extent did Fontenelle hold to a concept of progress? This question presents itself with some inevitability, since Fontenelle plunged into the *Querelle des Anciens et des Modernes* in 1688, with considerable brio, and had a good deal to say in favour of the Moderns. Therefore he must have seen some sort of progress from the Ancient to the Modern world. But it remains worth while to look at the issue a little more closely, to see what *kind* of progress he believed historically real, or possible in the future.

The first blow for the Moderns in the *Querelle* was really struck in the field of philosophy, by Descartes in the *Discours de la méthode*. Descartes shattered the principle of 'authoritative antiquity' by producing a new style of reasoning which, undoubtedly to the astonishment of many a reader, simply ignored it. However, most students of literature are naturally more acquainted with that aspect of the quarrel which centred in the 'rules for good writing' grounded more of less in Aristotle and Horace. At the time of Descartes' *Discours*, Corneille had already found, with *Le Cid* (1636), that respecting the rules placed something of a constraint on his inspiration. By 1663, Molière dared pronounce, actually on stage, in favour of the Moderns' equality with the Ancients as regards 'bon sens', which he claimed was the basis of Aristotle's approach to the theory of drama; and he also asserted the empirical principle that a successful drama without obedience to old rules proves itself better than an unsuccessful drama written within the rules. This was in *La critique de l'Ecole des femmes*, his one-act conversation-piece.[33] Naturally, this kind of polemic was what most captured the attention of the educated public. At the same time, many of the participants in the Quarrel seem to have been more at home in discussing modernism in art than in seeing the implications of the New Philosophy.[34] Yet the rights of the New Philosophy were the most fundamental issue; what was at stake was essentially the basic principles of the new science—including the new criticism of the Bible.

Fontenelle was well aware of this in his *Digression sur les Anciens et les Modernes* of 1688, and more so as time passed. But he was too much of a populariser to ignore the literary debate. Techniques in both the arts and the sciences can be perfected. Thus, Homer was somewhat barbaric—he must have talked the language of the Gods, laughs Fontenelle, for no Greek ever talked like his verse, which is full of a mixture of jargons and dialects.[35] But literature reached its perfection in the Augustan age of Rome, and is never likely to do any better than did Virgil and his contemporaries.[36] The same is not true of the sciences. The sciences depend on 'bon sens', equal in all generations, and experience; but experience is cumulative. Thus, Fontenelle finds himself propounding the formula, well-tried by Mersenne, Pascal, Malebranche and others, that the Ancients were at the youth of the world and that (humanity—like a single individual—growing older and wiser) the Moderns are the better-informed Elders. Fontenelle was convinced of this. He recognised that if science is cumulative, the historian of ideas has the difficulty of explaining the static or retrogressive character of science in the Dark Ages. He adopts the historian's view that there are always great minds, but that some centuries are more propitious to their flourishing than others. There can be world wars, barbarian invasions, governments hostile to progress, fashionable prejudices.[37]

What is most remarkable is the clarity with which Fontenelle saw the great leap forward made by science in the hundred years before 1688. Indeed, what he describes is the Scientific Revolution, and he is not far from calling it by that name; and in envisaging it, he gives the greatest rôle to Descartes, not to his science and metaphysics (the two subsumed under 'philosophie') but to the new manner of reasoning, as a result of which 'il règne non seulement dans nos bons ouvrages de physique et de métaphysique, mais dans ceux de religion, de morale, de critique, une précision et une justesse qui jusqu' à présent n'avaient été guère connues'.[38] Convinced as he was that his century had left the past far behind in science, he later made clear that he considered mankind to be still only at the start of a vast exploration: 'Il est permis de compter que les sciences ne font que de naître . . .'[39]

But did the Scientific Revolution mean for Fontenelle progress in an absolute sense, that is, for the good of man as a species? None of the scholars who have studied Fontenelle has failed to be impressed by the violently pessimistic way he berates the eternal 'sottise des hommes'.[40] Since he believed that man is fundamentally ruled by passion, there might seem to be little hope of moral progress. Yet Fontenelle does see man's conduct improving, not indeed through any softening of his heart, but through culture and the progress of ideas. If Descartes believed that reason could make man virtuous, Fontenelle is at least prepared to believe that 'bon sens' can teach man that good conduct is a rational and profitable choice. Paganism, as Bouchard points out, Fontenelle depicts in his early years as 'une sottise où il n'y avait pas ombre de bon sens ni de raison'.[41] Later, in *De l'origine des fables* (1734), Fontenelle shows the development of culture and civilisation as a phenomenon closely tied in with the growth of a more sophisticated world-picture, and as something which comes from philosophers.[42] He does not put too much emphasis on the practical benefits of the new science. He gives a good account of them, naturally, for he is always something of the salesman; but he also knew from the bad period of the Académie des sciences between about 1675 and 1699 that the material fruits of science can bring unwelcome attention and directives from a greedy government. The new charter of 1699 had largely set the Academy free of such interference, and Fontenelle had no desire to show science as a mere tool for the economist or the soldier. Thus, he is always more ready to assert that the scientific habit of mind can set man free from ignorance, superstition and prejudice and that, though it can never master passion, it can rid man of many of the causes of an uneasy relationship with his fellow men, and societies of many sources of hostility towards other societies.[43]

Fontenelle's own contribution to the spreading of light, apart from his popularising of science, is to be found largely in his constant attack on superstition and the taste for the 'merveilleux' he found characteristic of his own generation: 'Assez de gens ont toujours dans la tête un faux Merveilleux enveloppé d'une obscurité qu'ils respectent. Ils n'admirent la Nature, que parce qu'ils la croient une espèce de Magie où l'on n'entend rien; et il est sûr qu'une chose est déshonorée auprès d'eux, dès qu'elle peut être conçue'.[44] As soon as one comes on to this aspect of his thought, one is led, in Fontenelle's case, to the subject of religion, so we shall leave this discussion of 'progress' with one final reference, to a story that Fontenelle made famous.

This is the story of the 'gold tooth'.[45] In 1593 there was a rumour that a Silesian child of seven had grown a gold tooth. Horstius, professor of medicine at the University of Helmstadt, wrote a book on this tooth, claiming that it was partly miraculous, sent by God to this child to console the Christians under Turkish persecution. Controversy raged among the erudite. Finally, a goldsmith examined the tooth, and found it to be a normal tooth skilfully plated with gold leaf. But, concludes Fontenelle, they wrote their books first, and consulted the goldsmith later. 'Je ne suis pas si convaincu de notre ignorance', he adds as an afterthought, 'par les choses qui sont, et dont la raison nous est inconnue, que par celles qui ne sont point, et dont nous trouvons la raison.' In the light of his attack on Malebranche's theory of angels as the 'causes occasionnelles' of certain miracles, it is not unjust to believe that Fontenelle may here be attacking not only the 'rational proof' of miracles but belief in the very reality of miracles.

This leads us naturally to our last topic of discussion, Fontenelle, religion and God. Fontenelle never ostensibly removed himself from the Catholic Church. Occasionally he pays homage briefly to Christianity, as in his short essay *Sur l'histoire*: 'Nous sommes éclairés des lumières de la vraie religion, et, à ce que je crois, de quelques rayons de la vraie philosophie, et par conséquent nos erreurs sont incomparablement moindres que celles des anciens peuples; cependant elles se sont établies, et elles se conservent tout comme les leurs'.[46] One can say that the above quotation detracts from as much as it gives to a religion that Fontenelle saw as largely hostile to his 'vraie philosophie' (the critical method), and largely imbued with the 'erreurs' of 'le merveilleux', to which he was just as antagonistic as Bayle.

Some things are clear about Fontenelle's views on religion. One is his anti-clericalism. If the *Histoire des Ajaoiens* is correctly attributed to Fontenelle he is clearly anti-clerical.[47] There is a passage in the *Entretiens* where, by withholding the fact that he is talking about a beehive, Fontenelle tempts us to believe that what he later tells us are the drones are in fact the Catholic clergy.[48] But if such evidence is shaky, there remain the letter on Borneo and the *Histoire des oracles*. The *Extrait d'une Lettre écrite de Batavia dans les Indes Orientales, le 27 Novembre 1684, contenu dans une Lettre de M. de Fontenelle reçue à Rotterdam par M. Basnage* was published by Bayle in the *Nouvelles de la République des Lettres* in January 1686.[49] Bayle apparently noticed nothing odd about this letter; but others did. The names Mréo, Mliseo and Eénegu were seen to be anagrams of Rome, Solime (Jerusalem) and Geneva. The letter was a satire on Catholic–Protestant controversy, especially over communication under one species and transubstantion, with provocative allusions to the Catholic clergy as 'eunuchs', to the quarrel over 'legitimate faith proved by antiquity', and to the Revocation of the Edict of Nantes (the last proves the dating of the letter to be fictitious, but one has to see the meaning of the allegory to realise this). Fontenelle was profoundly embarrassed. It has been suggested that his later, very uncharacteristic, poem in praise of the Revocation, *Le triomphe de la religion*, was a public 'penance' forced on him under threat of worse things.[50]

The *Histoire des oracles* (also 1686) is an attack on the belief that pagan oracles ceased to be uttered (by demons) at the birth of Christ, who instantly quelled them. This belief, stated as fact by Bossuet in his *Histoire universelle*, was an ancient accretion to Catholicism, not a dogma but very nearly an article of faith, and very dear to the Catholic heart. Fontenelle attacks it with every weapon of the critical method, historical and logical. But chapters X to XVIII of the 'Première dissertation' argue in particular that the 'oracles' were a device invented by the priests to mould the minds of men, and pure trickery. The priests in question are of course the priests of paganism, but the general tenor of this long section is that all clergy are a deceitful, power-hungry breed and that human gullibility is the chief source of that power. In general, Fontenelle is constantly bemoaning the ease with which men accept 'le merveilleux', and frequently hints that the Christian faith has grown largely as a consequence of this human weakness.[51]

To say that Fontenelle dislikes Christianity as a faith burdened with a priesthood and a multitude of fabulous accretions is not to say that he does not believe in God, though he can rarely get near to speaking of Christ without finding himself in the hated realm of 'le merveilleux'. Thus he is not very amenable to Revelation and is far from being a fideist. At the same time, he rejects Descartes' first proof of God's existence from the idea of perfection, on the grounds that we have already seen, namely that our concept of 'perfection' comes from experience and is not 'put into us' by God. Fontenelle's personal proof of God's existence is by the critical and speculative method of the scientist. We may deduce that, when animals appeared, the world was very much as it is now, since the animals needed a world that could sustain them with vegetation and water. Hence, animals were not created out of a fortuitous coming together of atoms out of chaos, as one theory of the universe held. Thus they must have been created at a given moment in time, when the world already existed, by an outside agent, God.[52] Consequently, all we can really say about this God is that he is immensely clever and far-sighted to have created such complex creatures which would henceforth be self-sustaining and self-propagating.

Fontenelle was tremendously impressed by the animal world, especially what he learned of it through anatomy. His God creator of the animal kingdom does not fail to move him in his discreet way. But this God is not much concerned in a drama of redemption. Fontenelle believed that man is largely a slave to his passions, but he does not have the dreadful sense of 'la corruption de la nature' that we have spoken of in La Bruyère, La Rochefoucauld and Racine. God need not even be concerned to teach us morals; the civilising process of 'philosophie' will do that. Neither need this God intervene in nature, having made it as a good machine.

Thus, there is really nothing to stop us from concluding that Fontenelle was a deist fully-fledged before his numerous successors in the Enlightenment. Let us end with his words as read in English by the Fellows of the Royal Society:

> We must not look upon the sublime reflections which Natural Philosophy leads us to make, concerning the Author of the Universe, as mere curiosities. For this stupendous Work, which appears always more wonderful the more we know it, gives us such exalted notions of its Maker, that they fill our minds with admiration and respect. But above all, Astronomy and Anatomy are the two sciences which more palpably lay before us two great attributes of our Creator; one His immensity by the distance, magnitude and number of celestial bodies; the other His infinite knowledge by the mechanism of animals. True Natural Philosophy is a kind of Theology.[53]

'Admiration and respect.' ('Respect' could conceivably have been translated as 'awe'). But of worship and love, not a word.

NOTES

Notes to Chapter One

1. Méthivier: *La France de Louis XIV*, documents 1–3.
2. *Ibid.,* document 1, my italics.
3. See passage from Louis' *Mémoires* quoted by Lough: *Introduction to Seventeenth Century France*, p. 135.
4. This Catholic revival is studied in detail by Daniel-Rops: *The Church in the Seventeenth Century*.
5. A detailed account of scholasticism is clearly not within the scope of this book, but we may recommend Copleston: *A History of Medieval Philosophy*, Leff: *Medieval Thought: St. Augustine to Ockham*, and Gilson: *History of Christian Philosophy in the Middle Ages* and *Reason and Revelation in the Middle Ages*.
6. See *The Ontological Argument, from St. Anselm to Contemporary Philosophy*, ed. Plantinga.
7. See G. E. R. Lloyd: *Aristotle: The Growth and Structure of his Thought*, Cambridge University Press, 1968, chapters 7, 8.
8. *Discours*, ed. Gadoffre, pp. 66 and 17–18.
9. *Histoire de l'Académie Royale des Sciences, année 1699*. That he was overoptimistic with regard to the civil authorities at that time in respect even of his own case will be seen in Chapter 7.
10. Viz. Koestler: *The Sleepwalkers*, Russell on Descartes in his *History of Western Philosophy*, Butterfield: *The Origins of Modern Science*, and others too numerous to list.
11. See for example D. C. Potts and D. G. Charlton: *French Thought since 1600*, London, Methuen, 1974, pp. 13–22.
12. Especially Spink's excellent: *French Free-Thought from Gassendi to Voltaire*. See also Antoine Adam: *Les libertins au 17e siècle, textes choisis*, his *Théophile de Viau et la libre pensée française en 1620,* Pintard: *Le libertinage érudit dans la première moitié du 17e siècle*, and Weber's informative edition of Cyrano de Bergerac: *L'autre monde*.
13. See Brunschvicg: *Descartes et Pascal, lecteurs de Montaigne*.
14. *Apologie de Raimond Sebond, Essais*, ed. Thibaudet, p. 604.
15. See Pierre Humbert: *Un amateur: Peiresc*; and Spink, *op. cit.*, p. 13 gives names of Peiresc's contacts.
16. See Charbonnel: *La pensée italienne au 16e siècle et le courant libertin*.

17. Naudé's *Apologie pour tous les grands personnages qui ont été faussement soupçonnés de magie* (1625) (there is an edition printed in offset by Gregg International, Farnborough, 1972), Le Vayer's *De la vertue des païens* (1641), Gassendi's Latin essay on 'Whether the sky and the stars are habitable' *(Syntagma philosophicum*, chap. 6, post., 1658) all clearly influenced the 'Pre-Enlightenment' in the 1680s and 1690s.
18. In so far as Cyrano's thought can be systematised, this has been done by Alcover: *La pensée philosophique et scientifique de Cyrano de Bergerac*, and Harth: *Cyrano de Bergerac and the Polemics of Modernity.*
19. *L'Autre monde*, ed. Weber, p. 39.
20. *Ibid.*, p. 50.
21. *Ibid.*, pp. 53–66.
22. It is a commonly held view that Cyrano formed his thought essentially in the years 1641–8 on the basis of the Epicureanism of Gassendi, who during that time was professor of 'mathematics' (in fact, astronomy) at the Collège Royal.
23. *Oeuvres*, ed. Ribemont-Dessaignes, p. 308.
24. Cited by Adam: *Les libertins*, etc. See also Lachèvre: *Disciples et successeurs de Théophile de Viau.*
25. This is one of the main contentions of A. G. R. Smith: *Science and Society in the Sixteenth and Seventeenth Centuries.*
26. *Discours de la méthode*, ed. Gadoffre, p. 6. Another famous Jesuit college was the Collège de Clermont.
27. Except for the Collège Royal, established independently of the faculties of the rest of the University of Paris by François I.
28. See Lenoble: *Mersenne, ou la naissance du Mécanisme.*
29. See Strowski: *Pascal et son temps*, vol. 2, appendix 1: 'Les réunions savantes au milieu du dix-septième siècle'; Ornstein: *The Rôle of Scientific Societies in the Seventeenth Century* which deals with other countries as well as France; Daumas: 'La vie scientifique au 17e siècle'; H. Brown: *Scientific Organisations in Seventeenth-century France, 1620–80.*
30. But it is not possible to take seriously Hall's description of Louis XIV as 'the greatest of all scientific patrons' (*From Galileo to Newton*, p. 25).
31. Wiener: 'Leibniz's project of a public exhibition of scientific inventions'.
32. Thorndike: *History of Magic and Experimental Science*, vols. 7, 8, is the most exhaustive account of this credulity. Her chapter on Descartes, however, strains credibility. K. Thomas: *Religion and the Decline of Magic*, though it relates to England, is excellent.
33. *La pensée religieuse française de Charron à Pascal*, pp. 351–2.
34. *The Devils of Loudun*, p. 156.
35. Méthivier: *La France de Louis XIV*, p. 18.
36. For a full account, see Huxley, *op. cit.* and Michelet, *op. cit.* Michelet also goes into the cases of Gauffridi (1610), and Madeleine Bavent at Louviers (1643).
37. See Funck-Brentano: *Le drame des poisons*; Sévigné: *Lettres*, section X, 'La Voisin'.
38. A movement in Kepler's thought from animism to mechanism is excellently studied in Koestler: *The Sleepwalkers.*

Notes   179

39. *Discours*, ed. Gadoffre, p. 10.
40. This animistic view can be called 'holism', in that matter and mind are one. For Descartes with his 'dualism'—the view that matter and mind are entirely distinct—the rejection of any belief based on some concept of 'world-soul' was even easier.
41. For a good account of the fortunes of Copernicus, see Boas: *Scientific Renaissance 1450–1630*; Taton, ed.: *Histoire générale des sciences*, vol. 2, is also helpful here and for all this section.
42. See Drake: *Discoveries and Opinions of Galileo*.
43. See Ridgely: 'Dalibray, Le Pailleur, and the "New Astronomy" in French seventeenth-century poetry'.
44. See Guerlac: 'Copernicus and Aristotle's cosmos'.
45. See *Discours de la méthode*, ed. Gadoffre, pp. 39–40.
46. See Koyré: *From the Closed World to the Infinite Universe*.
47. Other significant figures can be found in Shackleton, ed.: *Fontenelle: Entretiens; Digression*, p. 17.
48. Copernicus is said to have tried it, but basing his calculations of the radius of Earth's orbit at twenty times less than the true figure. See Knight: *Copernicus*, pp. 164 ff.
49. Johann Fabricius of Emden, son of a friend of Kepler, first publicly announced the existence of sunspots in the summer of 1611. Galileo had already shown them. In Rome in 1613 a *History and Demonstrations Concerning the Solar Spots*, written but not signed by C. Scheiner, a Jesuit from Ingolstadt, was circulated by Scheiner's friends.

    Around 1750, Buffon did an experiment by measuring the time taken to cool by two large iron spheres and assigned to earth a minimum age of 74,832 years. In 1862, Lord Kelvin undertook similar experiments and arrived at a minimum figure of twenty million years and a maximum of four hundred million. Today's estimate, based on the 'uranium clock', is between three and a half and five thousand million years.
50. *Discours de la méthode*, ed. Gadoffre, pp. 41–3.
51. See Dobell: *Antony van Leeuwenhoek and his 'Little Animals'*, and *Reason: The Road to Modern Science*, pp. 239–44.
52. See Hazard: *La crise de la conscience européene*, ch. 'Ferveurs'.
53. See Taton, ed., *op. cit.*, Ornstein, *op. cit.*, and in the Bibliography, section 3, articles by Caullery, Daumas, Lenoble.
54. Hall: *From Galileo to Newton*, p. 22.
55. Wendt: *Before the Deluge*, pp. 37–9. The skeleton was correctly identified by Cuvier in 1825.
56. '1st Book of Aphorisms', xxxi, *Novum Organum*. My italics.

Notes to Chapter Two

1. For a discussion of the date, see the *Oeuvres*, ed. Alquié, 2, pp. 1101–3.
2. A good English text, except that it does not give the *Discourse* in its entirety, is *Descartes: Philosophical Writings*; a selection translated and edited by Anscome and Geach. A very useful French text is *Descartes:*

Oeuvres philosophiques, ed. Alquié (3 tomes, Garnier). This collection contains much correspondence; the Pléiade text of *Oeuvres et lettres de Descartes* in one volume is handy, but not so well annotated as Alquié and does not contain the three technical works to which the *Discours* served as introduction. The classic text for detailed research is: Adam et Tannery: *Oeuvres de Descartes* (13 tomes) (called AT).

3. See also Baillet: *Vie de Monsieur Descartes*; Haldane: *Descartes, His Life and Times*; Charles Adam: *Vie et œuvres de Descartes*, together with his longer account of Descartes' life in volume 12 of AT; Fischer: *Descartes and his School*, book I; and, for shorter accounts, Kenny: *Descartes: A Study of his Philosophy*, chapter 1; Bréhier: *The History of Philosophy: The Seventeenth Century*, pp. 46–52; Bronowski and Mazlish: *The Western Intellectual Tradition*, chapter 12; Keeling: *Descartes*, chapter 1; and Russell: *History of Western Philosophy*, pp. 542 ff. Rodis-Lewis, in *Descartes: initiation à sa philosophie*, expounds the development of Descartes' philosophy on a biographical pattern. The most recent biography, which adds little that is new, is Vrooman: *René Descartes*, 1970.

4. Hereafter in this chapter, page references in the text refer to *Discours de la méthode*, ed. Gadoffre.

5. Descartes read little, for this reason, set out at length in *Regulae* (*Règles pour la direction de l'esprit*, règle III).

6. *Discours*, p. 12. The other account, in the *Olympica*, is fragmentary, and must be supplemented from Baillet.

7. Bréhier: *Seventeenth Century*, p. 47; Maritain: *Dream of Descartes*, pp. 12–13. Haldane places Descartes' search for the Rosicrucians slightly later, in 1620, and concludes, in accord with Baillet: 'Descartes' efforts to lay hold of this ever-vanishing society were in vain'. (*Descartes*, pp. 72–3.) The first uncontested document of the Rosicrucians was the *Fama Fraternitatis, dess Löblichen Ordens des Rosenkreuzes*, published in Germany in 1614. For a period of a few years from this date, many intellectuals were to hope for great things from the Rosy Cross, which promised total knowledge of the universe, seen and unseen. The first two Rosicrucian documents are given in trans. in Frances Yates: *The Rosicrucian Enlightenment*, London, Paladin, 1975, appendix.

8. See Baillet: *Vie de M Descartes;* Alquié: *Descartes: Oeuvres*, under 'Olympiques'; Maritain: *Dream of Descartes*; and, for an interesting meditation on the event, Krailsheimer: *Studies in Self-interest*.

9. Alquié: *ed. cit.*, 1, p. 52.

10. E.g., ' . . . mon inclination, qui m'a toujours fait haïr le métier de faire des livres . . . ' (*Discours*, p. 58).

11. Cf. Rodis-Lewis: *Descartes: initiation etc.*, p. 40.

12. Alquié: *ed. cit.*, 2, p. 91, letter to Mersenne of 11 October 1638.

13. This is no doubt why he calls philosophy the best occupation 'des hommes purement hommes' (p. 5), meaning that it should not concern itself with the supernatural.

14. Scott: *Scientific Work of Descartes*, pp. 168–9. See these pages for a discussion of the events of 1633, and, following them, a detailed exposition of the theory of 'vortices'. See also Section (iii) of the present chapter.

15. These essays are not given with Gadoffre's text. *La dioptrique* is given in

full and *Les météores* in summary in Alquié's edition, 1. For the three works in full one must go to AT.
16. Denissoff considers rather perversely that there *is* irony here: *Descartes, premier théoricien etc.*, p. 51.
17. E.g. in *Méditations*, IV, in ed. Alquié, vol. 2, p. 455.
18. Consider, for instance, how it emerges in *The Sceptical Chymist*, of 1661, which was to make of Robert Boyle the 'Father of Modern Chemistry'; and on Boyle see Reason: *The Road to Modern Science*, pp. 76 ff.
19. *Petit Robert*: '*Induction, 1*: Opération mentale qui consiste à remonter des faits à la loi, de cas donnés (*Propositions inductrices*) le plus souvent singuliers ou spéciaux, à une proposition plus générale.' Contrast: '*Déduction II*. (*Abstrait*): Procédé de pensée par lequel on conclut de propositions prises pour prémisses, à une proposition qui en résulte, en vertu de règles logiques.'
   Descartes used both induction and deduction. The proofs of God are made basically by deduction; most of the medical theories are arrived at by induction, but the cosmology is almost entirely deductive.
20. *Règles*, III (ed. Alquié, 1, p. 87)
21. Cf. *Règles*, XIII.
22. Alquié, 1, p. 90 and p. 100.
23. Cf. *Règles*, III, VII, XII (Alquié, I), and *Méditations*, IV (Alquié, 2, p. 467).
24. One contention, that Descartes introduced parts III and IV into the *Discours* as sheer 'opportunism', seems unacceptable. Denissoff invites us, in studying the *Discours*, 'à négliger les textes que Descartes a introduits dans ce traité par opportunisme, tout spécialement ceux relatifs à la métaphysique et à l'éthique . . . ' (*Descartes, premier théoricien etc.*, p. 109). Astute Descartes certainly was, but he was also a gentleman ('*un honnête homme*') and his ethics are exactly what one would expect from such in the climate of ideas; furthermore, it would be perverse to neglect the metaphysical proofs of God, which are the *only* thing that guarantees for Descartes the existence of the physical universe he wants to study.
   T. Keefe's recent article: 'Descartes's "Morale Provisoire": a reconsideration' adequately counters the view represented by Denissoff and others.
   Descartes wrote: 'Il est vrai que j'ai été trop obscur en ce que j'ai écrit de l'existence de Dieu dans ce traité de la Méthode, et *bien que ce soit la pièce la plus importante*, j'avoue que c'est la moins élaborée de tout l'ouvrage . . . ' (To Père Vatier, 22 February 1638, Pléiade, p. 768, my italics). Also: 'Pour mes raisons de l'existence de Dieu, j'espère qu'elles seront à la fin autant ou plus estimées qu'aucune autre partie du livre . . . ' (To Mersenne, 1 March 1638, Pléiade, p. 775). He was writing to two priests, but Mersenne was also an intimate friend.
25. Descartes tries to justify and explain this attitude of perseverance' in a letter to an unknown person, March 1638, Pléiade, pp. 777 ff.
26. *Oeuvres etc.*, Pléiade, pp. 582 and 627.
27. Alquié, 2, p. 462. cf. *Principes*, 42 (Pléiade, p. 451) and *Passions de l'âme*, art. 49 (Pléiade, p. 581).
28 It is quite obvious that, while Descartes is ready to discuss God, he does not discuss Christ.

29. Alquié, 2, p. 412.
30. Cf. *ibid*: 'Mais je me suis persuadé qu'il n'y avait rien du tout dans le monde, qu'il n'y avait aucun ciel, aucune terre, aucuns esprits, ni aucuns corps; ne me suis-je donc pas aussi persuadé que je n'étais point? Non certes, j'étais sans doute, si je me suis persuadé, ou seulement si j'ai pensé quelque chose. Mais il y a un je ne sais quel trompeur, qui emploie toute son industrie à me tromper toujours. Il n'y a donc point de doute que je suis, s'il me trompe; et qu'il me trompe tant qu'il voudra, il ne saurait jamais faire que je ne sois rien, tant que je penserai être quelque chose' (Alquié, 2, p. 415).
31. Criticised also by Hobbes in the *Troisièmes objections aux Méditations (Objection seconde sur la seconde Méditation)*, Alquié, 2, p. 602: 'Mais d'où vient la connaissance de celle-ci: *je pense*? Certes, ce n'est point d'autre chose, que de ce que nous ne pouvons concevoir aucun acte sans son sujet, comme la pensée sans une chose qui pense, la science sans une chose qui sache, et la promenade sans une chose qui se promène.' To which Descartes peremptorily replies: '*Il est certain* que la pensée ne peut pas être sans une chose qui pense, et en général aucun accident ne peut être sans une substance de laquelle il soit l'acte.' (Alquié, 2, p. 605, my italics.)
32. To Paul Demeny, 15 May 1871 (*Oeuvres complètes*, Gallimard, Paris, 1972, p. 250).
34. Rimbaud adopted a quasi-mediaeval occult belief in the *anima mundi*, of which the poet is a mere receptacle: 'Le poëte définirait la quantité d'inconnu s'éveillant en son temps dans l'âme universelle . . . ' (*loc. cit*). If one does not like to think of him in this way, one can compare him to the mystic who, in Huxley's *Doors of Perception*, is open to 'Mind-at-Large.'
35. Mallarmé to Cazalis, 14 May 1867 (*Correspondance*, I, éd. Mondor avec Richard, Gallimard, Paris, 1959, pp. 240–2).
36. See Descartes' letter to an unknown person, Leyden, November 1640 (Pléiade, p. 874) and letter to Mersenne of December 1640 (Pléiade, p. 879) in which he locates the relevant part of Augustine as *De civitate dei*, book II, chap. 26.
37. ' . . . ce moi, qui pense, est une *substance immatérielle* . . . ', letter to an unknown person, Leyden, November 1640 (Pléiade, p. 874).
38. For another exposition of all the foregoing reasoning, see *Recherche de la vérité* (Alquié, 2).
39. Alquié, II, pp. 420—1. On conceiving and feeling as acts of the thinking mind, see also *Règles*, XII (Alquié, 1, p. 140): 'Il faut se représenter enfin, cinquièmement, que cette force par laquelle à proprement parler nous connaissons les choses, est une force purement spirituelle, et n'est pas moins distincte du corps pris dans son ensemble que le sang n'est de l'os, ou la main de l'œil . . . En toutes ces occasions, cette force cognitive est tantôt passive, tantôt active . . . ' That is to say, the activity of the mind is sometimes triggered from within, sometimes from without (by sensation—but Descartes elsewhere makes it clear that for him sensation is an act of consciousness and therefore of the mind, not of the body).

40. He re-examines these proofs at greater length in the *Méditations*, and in Meditation V adds the 'ontological' proof similar to the ontological argument invented by Anselm about 1070 in chapters 2 to 4 of *Proslogion*. In *The Ontological Argument, from St. Anselm to Contemporary Philosophers*, ed. Plantinga, we are given the ontological proofs of Anselm, Aquinas and Descartes; Descartes' proof is correctly quoted from Meditation V, though the note incorrectly states that it is taken from Meditation III.
41. Cf. *Méditations*, III (Alquié, 2, p. 441).
42. '. . . l'étendue en longueur, largeur et profondeur, constitue la nature de la substance corporelle; et la pensée consitue la nature de la substance qui pense' (*Principes*, partie I, No. 53, Pléiade, p. 456).
43. See *Méditations*, V (Alquié, 2, p. 479); *Méditations*, VI (Alquié, 2, p. 481 and p. 484, especially: '. . . en sorte qui je ne pouvais sentir aucun objet, quelque volonté que j'en eusse, s'il ne se trouvait présent à l'organe d'un de mes sens . . . '); in the same, pp. 481–90; *Response à l'objection dernière (XVIe)* in the *Troisièmes objections* (those of Hobbes; Alquié, 2, p. 631); *Principes de la philosophie, première partie*, No. 69 (Pléiade, p. 467) and *deuxième partie*, Nos. 1–4 (Pléiade, pp. 473–4).
44. On the pineal gland, also called by Descartes *conarium*, see *Passions de l'âme*, articles 31–5 (Pléiade, pp. 571–4). The 'Cartesian dualism' of mind-matter has never been satisfactorily resolved.
45. See Scott: *Scientific Work of Descartes*, p. 22, and Gilson: *La pensée médiévale dans la formation du système cartésien: 'Descartes, Harvey et la scolastique'*.
46. 'Mechanistic' because it requires only activities also found in inanimate nature (heat, rarefaction) and not the muscular activity of Harvey, which seemed to require the intervention of mind.
47. Cf. *Méditations*, VI (Alquié, 2, p. 497).
48. This may be a slightly unfair anachronism. Harvey did not know of the capillaries, and they were seen under the microscope by Malpighi (born 1628) and Leeuwenhoek (born 1632) after the time of the *Discours*. However the possibility of their existence was guessed at in Descartes' day. Descartes' satisfaction with the evidence of the naked eye is curious, considering that he was an expert in optics and dioptrics–including the practice of lens-grinding.

   For a succinct account of the development of research, especially Harvey's, into the workings of the heart see Wightman: *The Emergence of Scientific Medicine*, chap. 6: 'Physiology in a New Key'; also Reason: *The Road to Modern Science*, pp. 235–40; and, for relevant extracts from Harvey's writings, *A History of Medicine, Selected Readings*, edited by King, pp. 98–111.
49. Vesalius (1514–64), the Flemish anatomist and author of *De humanis corporis fabrica* (1543), who taught at the University of Padua, had gone one better than Descartes in dissecting human bodies and discovering many errors in the great authority of the Middle Ages, Galen (A.D. 130–200), who had based his theories of the human body on dissection of apes and dogs. Descartes wrote to Mersenne that he had done many dissections over eleven years (20 February 1639, Pléiade. p. 827).

50. Cf. *Passions de l'âme*, articles 10, 11, 37 (Pléiade, pp. 560–1, 575).
51. Cf. letter to an unknown person, March 1638 (Pléiade, pp. 781–3 *et seq.*)
52. See Leonora Rosenfield: *From Beast-Machine to Man-machine;* Balz: 'Cartesian doctrine and the animal soul; an incident in the formulation of the modern philosophical tradition', and Shugg: 'The Cartesian beast machine in English literature (1663–1750)'.
53. The evidence of various parts of the Correspondence may justify the view that Descartes believed animals to have no soul of any kind.
54. One such 'artifice' usually ascribed to a Frenchman shortly after Descartes' day is the steam-engine: Dionysius Papin (1647–1712) is credited with the theory, though he had difficulty in making his steam engines work.
55. See in contrast Pascal's *Prière pour le bon usage des maladies*. However, Descartes did not always limit the 'souverain bien' to physical health, but more particularly to moral health. See letter to Christina of Sweden, 20 November 1647 (Pléade, pp. 1042–3).
56. The most relevant place, *Principes,* troisième partie, is given neither in Alquié nor in the Pléiade. We therefore quote in English from Anscombe and Geach:

    'II. Secondly, we must beware of thinking too proudly of ourselves. We should be doing this . . . , and that in a special degree, if we imagined everything had been created by God for our sake . . .

    III. In ethics indeed it is an act of piety to say that God made everything for our sake, that we may be the more impelled to thank him, and the more on fire with love of him; and in a sense this is true; for we can make *some* use of all things—at least we can employ our mind in contemplating them, and in admiring God for his wonderful works. But it is by no means probable that all things were made for our sake in the sense that they have no other use. In physical theory this supposition would be wholly ridiculous and absurd . . . ' (*op. cit.*, pp. 222–3).
57. See Adams: 'Social responsibilities of science in *Utopia, New Atlantis* and after'. Zilsel: 'The genesis of the concept of scientific progress' regards the idea as fully-fledged in Francis Bacon, but remarks: 'Manifestly, the idea of science we usually regard as "Baconian" is rooted in the requirements of early capitalist economy and technology; its rudiments appear first in treatises of fifteenth-century craftsmen.' See also Zilsel: 'The sociological roots of science' in *Origins of the Scientific Revolution,* ed. Kearney; Prior: 'Bacons's man of science'; Bury: *The Idea of Progress,* chap. 'Cartesianism.'
58. See for example Voltaire: 'Sur l'insertion de la petite vérole', in *Lettres philosophiques* (1734).
59. The best available work on Descartes' science, in particular his mathematics and cosmology, is Scott: *Scientific Work of Descartes*. On his physics and physiology, see also Bréhier: *Seventeenth Century*, pp. 83–97.
60. The main sources of Descartes' physics are *Le monde*, the essay *Les météores*, the *Principes*, and much of the *Correspondance*.
61. Parhelia are the appearance of several mock-suns or bright spots in a

solar halo, caused by ice-crystals in the atmosphere. Observed by Scheiner at Frascati on 20 March 1629.
62. Even Einstein found it necessary to demonstrate that the existence of the 'luminiferous ether' could be neither proven nor disproven.
63. On how Roemer calculated (fairly accurately) the speed of light, see J. A. Coleman: *Relativity for the Layman*, London, Pelican, 1959 (first publ. William-Frederick Press, New York, 1954), pp. 15–17.
64. Main sources: the *Discours*, *L'Homme*, *Les passions de l'âme*, *Principes*, quatrième partie (called *De la terre*, but largely concerned with the body; in full only in AT), *Correspondance*, esp. to Elizabeth of Bohemia. Cf. Bréhier, *op. cit.*, pp. 94–7.
65. See Scott, *op. cit.*, p. 197 on *La dioptrique*. Consult the relevant parts of *La dioptrique*: 'De l'œil'; IV, 'Des sens en général'; V 'Des images qui se forment sur le fond de l'œil'; VI, 'De la vision' (Alquié, 1, pp. 678–717. The 'discours' which follow are devoted to the improving of sight, the making of spectacles and the grinding of lenses. These are not given in Alquié and must be seen in AT).
66. *Art. cit.*, p. 161.
67. Bréhier; *Seventeenth Century*, p. 104.
68. See *Règles*, XII and *Passions*, article 41.
69. See for example Descartes to Mersenne, 27 May 1641? (Pléiade, pp. 895–7) and to Père Mesland, Leyden, 2 May 1644? (Pléiade, pp. 934ff.).
70. See Lenoble, *art. cit.*, pp. 168–9.
71. See Descartes to Elizabeth, 21 May 1647 (Pléiade, p. 921): 'Premièrement, je considère qu'il y a en nous certaines notions primitives, qui sont comme des originaux, sur le patron desquels nous formons toutes nos autres connaissances.' And he lists: being, number, time; and, for the body in particular, extension, shape and motion, and, for the soul in particular, awareness of thought.
72. *Seventeenth Century*, p. 94.
73. Alquié, 2, gives *Cinquièmes objections* (selected), Descartes' *Réponses* and letter to Clerselier. It does not give Gassendi's *Instances*. The most convenient way of studying Gassendi's side of the controversy is in Brush, trans.: *Selected Works of Gassendi*, containing the essential of his 'Doubts', Descartes' 'Replies' and Gassendi's 'Rebuttals'.
74. Brush, *ed. cit.*, pp. 241ff.
75. *Ibid.*, pp. 261ff. The objections of others to the ontological proof may be found in Plantinga, ed.: *The Ontological Argument*.
76. Brush, *ed. cit.*, p. 180.
77. *Ibid.*, p. 199.
78. In his views on sight and awareness of heat, however, Gassendi seems almost unwittingly to have returned to a 'qualitative' explanation.
79. Brush, *ed. cit.*, p. 176. We have seen of course that this doubt was, in Descartes, 'une feinte'.
80. *Ibid.*, p. 235.
81. *Ibid.*, p. 256.
82. See Rochot, in *Pierre Gassendi, etc.*, p. 90 (in Bibliography under *Gassendi*).

83. Alquié: *Le cartésianisme de Malebranche*, pp. 17–18.
84. *Recherche de la vérité*, *Oeuvres*, 1, pp. 15–18.
85. On the foregoing, which consists of simple illustrations not actually set out by Malebranche, see: *Traité de la nature et de la grâce*, premier discours, première partie, *Oeuvres*, 5, pp. 11–37. In the *Recherche de la vérité*, Malebranche speaks throughout as though the general concept of 'causes occasionnelles' is already well established in his reader's mind (as in the discussion of the 'occasional causes' of human error, needed in order to make man desire freedom from error, in livre I, ch. 4, *Oeuvres*, 1) but the most illuminating passage is livre VI, seconde partie, ch. 3, *Oeuvres*, 2.
86. *Traité de la nature etc.*, second discours, première partie, *Oeuvres*, 5.
87. *Vie de Monsieur Descartes*, p. 197.
88. Pléiade, p. 788.
89. Pléiade, p. 851.
90. Pléiade, p. 983, note 1. See also Spink: *op. cit.*, pp. 192–5, on the Jesuit and Oratorian attitudes to Descartes. Gouhier: *La pensée religieuse de Descartes*, pp. 128–1, is useful on Descartes and the Jesuits.
91. Antoine Arnauld *(fils)*—'le grand Arnauld'—was of course the author of the *Quatrièmes objections* to Descartes' *Méditations*. Leonora Rosenfield remarks however: 'But Descartes' answer appears to have convinced him, or else the objections were designed simply to bring out more amply the great philosopher's thought on the subject' (*From Beast-machine to Man-machine*, pp. 281–2). Spink adduces much evidence to show the official hostility of the Oratorian colleges to Descartes, and concludes that such official efforts to suppress his thought bear witness to its popularity among the college teachers (*op. cit.*, p. 194).
92. Spink considers that the struggle for the old still went on in the *Journal des savants* and reached its peak as late as 1690, after which date Cartesianism appears to have emerged triumphant (*op. cit.*, pp. 195–6).
93. See Mouy, *Le développement de la physique cartésienne*, section 'La persécution', pp. 169–72.
94. Descartes to Elisabeth, 10 May 1647 (Pléiade, p. 1029).
95. For names, see Spink, *op. cit.*, p. 190.
96. See the following, listed in our Bibliography: *Fischer*, on Rohault, Sylvain Régis, La Forge, Cordemoy, Clauberg, Bekker, Geulincx, Malebranche; *Mouy*, on Henricus Regius (Henri le Roy), Cordemoy, La Forge, Rohault, Gadrois, Sylvain Régis, Joseph Sauveur, Fontenelle, Huyghens, Malebranche; *Bréhier*, on Rohault, Geulincx, Clauberg, Digby, La Forge, Cordemoy, Sylvain Régis, Spinoza; *Scott* (in his appendix), on Chanut, Clerselier, De Beaune (Debaune), Heydanus (Abraham Van Der Heyden), Henricus Regius, Henri Reneri (Renier); *Spink*, on Rohault, La Forge, Cordemoy, Sylvain Régis, Malebranche; *Keeling*, on Régis, La Forge, Cordemoy, Geulincx, Malebranche, Regius, Clauberg, Arnauld.

On one particular question, the Cartesian 'animal-machine', we may follow Descartes' partisans and enemies in *Rosenfield*.

97. See the following articles, listed in our Bibliography: Ware: 'The influence of Descartes on John Locke'; Saveson: 'Descartes' influence on John Smith, Cambridge Platonist'; also: 'Differing reactions to Descartes among the Cambridge Platonists'; Laird: 'L'influence de Descartes sur la philosophie anglaise du XVIIe siècle'; Shugg: 'The Cartesian beast-machine in English literature (1663–1750)'.
98. On the backwardness of the French universities in the seventeenth century, see Ornstein: *The Rôle of Scientific Societies in the Seventeenth Century*, pp. 220ff. Spink tells us that, at the Collège Royal—one of the most advanced teaching establishments—in the 1720s, 'the abbé de Molieres was teaching Cartesian physics and rebutting the attacks of the Newtonians' (*op. cit.*, p. 191).
99. See Shugg: *art. cit.*
100. There is a very informative little critical edition of this text by H. Busson and F. Gohin, Droz, Paris, 1938. Rosenfield, *op. cit.*, also discusses it.
101. Offroy de la Mettrie (1709–51) was to be the extreme advocate of the theory of 'l'homme-machine' in the development of the 'materialism' of the Enlightenment. See Rosenfield, *op. cit.*
102. Nicole: *Essai de morale*.
103. A good example of the cross-fertilisation between Cartesianism and the Early Enlightenment may be seen in the *Tractatus theologico-politicus* of Spinoza (1670), abhorred by the authorities as a denial of Providence, of Final Causes and of Free Will: 'The method of interpreting Scripture does not widely differ from the method of interpreting nature—in fact it is almost the same' (trans. R. H. M. Elwes (1891), quoted by Burke: *Renaissance Sense of the Past*, p. 65).
104. *Descartes*, p. 66.
105. Professor Langer offers a brilliant, well-documented criticism of those modern thinkers 'whose immediate objective is to 'mathematicize' their findings as fast as they are found and even faster, evidently feeling that the dress of mathematics bestows scientific dignity no matter how or where it is worn'; in *Mind: An Essay on Human Feeling*, vol. I, John Hopkins Press, Baltimore and London, paperback ed. 1970, pp. 38ff.

Notes to Chapter Three

1. In this chapter, bracketed numbers following quotations refer to fragments in the *Pensées* as numbered by Brunschvicg. I have used the *Pensées*, Garnier-Flammarion, 1976 (not the 1973 edition, which used Lafuma's numbering), but there are numerous other well-established texts which use the Brunschvicg numbering, e.g. *Oeuvres de Pascal*, Paris, Hachette, 1921–5, vols. 12–14.

    For the rest of Pascal's work I refer to the *Oeuvres complètes* in the one-volume crit. ed. by Lafuma, Ed. du Seuil, 1963, henceforth called *O.C.*

2. The *Histoire générale des sciences*, vol. 2, published under the direction of René Taton, for example, mentions Pascal's work on the cycloid and gives an adequate account of his work in hydrostatics. It does not appear

to mention the calculating machine. The section is written by Lenoble. Mason's *History of the Sciences* does not index Pascal.
3. Maire, 1912, and Humbert, 1947. Koyré contributes a worth-while chapter on 'Pascal savant' in the Cahiers de Royaumont: *Blaise Pascal, l'homme et l'œuvre*. Most other writers pay lip-service to his scientific genius, but usually only to show how remarkable they find it that he should later have become holy!
4. Broome: *Pascal*, 1965. There is one writer in French (not a Frenchman) who has produced a short and worthwhile study of *La pensée philosophique créatrice de Pascal*. He is D. Nedelkovitch. However, his interesting examination is somewhat vitiated by his concluding section, which attempts to prove his thesis from the *Discours sur les passions de l'amour*, without mentioning that this essay has never been definitively ascribed to Pascal.
5. In a famous passage of *Micromégas*.
6. *Monsieur Pascall's Thoughts, etc.*, trans. by Joseph Walker.
7. The best biography remains that of Strowski in three volumes, *Pascal et son temps*. The English-language biographies of Ernest Mortimer and Morris Bishop are both acceptable, though neither is profound in thought or scholarship. Broome's *Pascal* is more fruitful, but biography is subordinated to critique. There is a useful chronology in O.C. and in Béguin: *Pascal par lui-même*, 1953, which also contains interesting biographical interpretations.
8. See Koyré: 'Pascal savant', *loc. cit.*, p. 262.
9. O.C., pp. 35 ff. Leibniz's views (p. 37) are interesting, and flattering for Pascal.
10. A model built by Pascal survives in the Conservatoire des arts et métiers in Paris. Many books on Pascal contain a photograph of this, as do many reference books on French literary history.
11. Since the French monetary system was not at that time decimalised, twelfths and twentieths also occur, but the principle is exactly the same.
12. In the calculating machines he built in 1694 and 1706 Leibniz overcame this problem in multiplication and division with a device called a 'stepped reckoner'.
13. O.C., pp. 195 ff. Strowski, II, p. 71, describes this syringe as the first pneumatic machine.
14. Torricelli said: We live submerged in an ocean of air, and it is certain that the air has weight. Pascal does not distinguish in fluids ('liqueurs') between gases and liquids. He therefore continues to speak of the 'weight or pressure' of the atmosphere where we speak only of its 'pressure'.
    That Pascal actually overcame the technical difficulties of performing the experiment of the 'vacuum within a vacuum' is attested by none other than his main adversary in the controversy, Noël. For a full account, see Strowski, II, pp. 142–5. Pascal takes Florin Périer to witness in his letter of 15 November 1647 to Périer.
15. Noël's letter and Pascal's reply are in O.C., pp. 199–204.
16. He returns to the problem of definition and to the same example in *De l'esprit géométrique*, O.C., p. 350.

17. Second letter of Noël and letter from Pascal to Le Pailleur, *O.C.*, pp. 204 and 208 respectively.
18. *O.C.*, pp. 221–2.
19. *O.C.*, pp. 221–5.
20. Torricelli had guessed at the principle of the barometer. After Pascal's experiments, many people made their own. Von Guericke built a forty-foot water barometer on the side of his house for all to see. On the popularity of home-made barometers, see Daumas: *Instruments scientifiquees aux 17e et 18e siècles*, pp. 80–1. See the same, p. 83 on Papin's publication of 1674 on pumps for extracting air.
21. *O.C.*, p. 230.
22. *O.C.*, pp. 231–2 '... la nature n'ayant pour objet que de maintenir les animaux dans un ordre de perfection bornée, elle leur inspire cette science nécessaire, toujours égale [l'instinct] ... Il n'en est pas de même de l'homme, qui n'est produit que pour l'infinité'. Etc. In this passage one finds also the argument which was to become familiar in the latter part of the century, in the Quarrel of Ancients with Moderns, that the Ancients were really the youth of mankind and that the Moderns are his maturity.
23. *O.C.*, p. 230.
24. *Ibid.*
25. *Ibid.*
26. *O.C.*, pp. 285 ff.
27. *Adresse à l'Académie Parisienne* (1654), *O.C.*, pp. 101–3.
28. *O.C.*, pp. 50–103.
29. *Pensées ed. cit.* reproduces the text, pp. 43–4.
30. See Béguin: *Pascal par lui-même*, pp. 21–2; and Lafuma, *O.C.*, p. 493.
31. *O.C.*, p. 50, for Lafuma's remarks on the arithmetical triangle and pp. 104–85 for the cycloid and related problems. The most important conclusions for the Calculus are in *Potestatum numericarum summa*, *O.C.*, pp. 90 ff. On the place of Pascal's work on the cycloid in the development of the Integral Calculus, see Humbert: *Cet effrayant génie, etc.*, pp. 215–19.

    In 1658, Pascal offered a prize for an international competition of geometers on the cycloid. Among competitors was the English algebrist John Wallis, and Christopher Wren sent a contribution which, though not within the terms of the contest, was described by Pascal as the finest thing he had seen on the cycloid. Wren found the length of the cyloid's arc to be four times the diameter of the generating circle. None of the competitors was up to Pascal's own standard, and ultimately he withheld the prize. See Humbert, *op. cit.*, pp. 205–13.
32. On an enormous scale in Sainte-Beuve's *Port-Royal*. Most readers will find enough factual details to satisfy them in Daniel-Rops: *The Church in the Seventeenth Century*, Cognet: *Le jansénisme*, Strowski: *Pascal et son temps*, III and Orcibal: *Saint Cyran et le jansénisme*.
33. Stewart: *Provinciales*, crit. ed., is informative on the situation as it had developed.
34. Pascal was no theologian, though he had written an *Abrégé de la vie de Jésus-Christ* (c. 1655–6), and his fragmentary *Ecrits sur la grâce* (probably

begun after the series of *Provinciales* had started) show him better-informed than do the *Provinciales* themselves.
35. The Jesuits and Thomists had made an alliance of expediency based on a similarity of terminology which when analysed by Pascal proved to be factitious.
36. See Stewart, *ed. cit.*, p. 329, note to p. 233 line 3; and Daniel-Rops, *op. cit.*, p. 341.
37. On the psychology of Pascal, see Strowski: *Pascal etc.*, III, p. 55.
38. Lafuma has given us two kinds of presentation. One is a direct transcription from Pascal, guided by the *Copie, Bibliothèque nationale ms. 9203*, which Lafuma is satisfied is the one Etienne Périer refers to in the preface to the Port-Royal edition (which did not use all the materials): 'La première chose que l'on fît fut de les faire copier tels qu'ils étaient et dans la même confusion qu'on les avait trouvés . . . ' (Let us note that the confusion was not complete, in that many of the papers had been tied in bundles—'papiers classés'.) This presentation is used by Lafuma in his edition for Editions du Luxembourg and in O.C., Editions du Seuil. The alternative presentation is his own classification of the materials of ms. 9203 according to what he thinks were Pascal's intentions, and this we find in his edition for Delmas and re-used in the Garnier-Flammarion edition of 1973 whereas Brunschvicg is used in their 1976 edition.

There is a concordance between the Port-Royal edition of 1670 (printed by Guillaume Desprez), Lafuma (Luxembourg) and Brunschvicg; this is by Thérèse Goyet, and is in Mesnard et al.: *Les 'Pensées' de Pascal ont trois cents ans*. In the same book Jean Mesnard gives a lot of information on the saga of Pascal editions.

Couton and Jehasse have recently edited a facsimile of the Edition of Port-Royal (1670). For details of this, of other texts mentioned above and some not mentioned, see our Bibliography.
39. Keeling: *Descartes*, pp. 73–4.
40. *De l'esprit géometrique etc.*, section 1, *O.C.*, p. 350.
41. Cruickshank: 'Knowledge and belief in Pascal's *Apology*', p. 97. It was because Bertrand Russell disingenuously chose to interpret 'cœur' as 'irrational emotionalism' that his silence on Pascal was broken only to make a grossly inaccurate comparison between him and J.-J. Rousseau (*History of Western Philosophy*, p. 666, note 1).
42. Readers of Suzanne Langer's *Mind: An Essay on Human Feeling* will know exactly what is meant here. Unfortunately, there are not many philosophers as well equipped as Professor Langer to draw intelligently on the multitude of disciplines in which she is at home.
43. On the false rationalisation of attitudes to which we are unwittingly predisposed, Pascal wrote no lines more subtle and modern than *Pensée* 276: 'M de Roannez disait: 'Les raisons me viennent après, mais d'abord la chose m'agrée ou me choque sans en savoir la raison, et cependant cela me choque par cette raison que je ne découvre qu'ensuite.' Mais je crois, non pas que cela choquait par ces raisons qu'on trouve après, mais qu'on ne trouve ces raisons que parce que cela choque.'

44. 'Philosophie' here clearly has largely the sense of 'natural philosophy', that is, science. But Pascal, as we shall se, also rejects philosophy in its other major form up to that date, rational theology.
45. The three sects referred to are the dogmatists, the Epicureans and the Stoics, in that order.
46. *O.C.*, pp. 292–7. The *Entretien* was not published until 1728.
47. See Cruickshank, *art. cit.*, p. 93. *Pensée* 72, on *Disproportion de l'homme*, is on similar lines.
48. Pascal seems consistent in his distinctive use of *savoir* and *connaître*, the first for useless 'geometric' knowledge, the second for the recognition of one's true state. See the use of *connaître* in 397, above.
49. See *'Les pensées de M Pascal sur les miracles,* publiées par Monseigneur Colbert (1727)' in the facsimile of the Port-Royal edition edited by Couton and Jehasse, pp. 525–30 (see Bibliography); and 'Notes pour un *Ecrit sur le miracle opéré sur Mlle Périer*' in the 1976 Garnier-Flammarion *Pensées*, pp. 291–306.
50. Huxley, 'Holy Face', *Collected Essays*, pp. 351–2. The essay 'Pascal' follows on directly. On the sickness of Pascal's body, see pp. 359–60.
51. Huxley, 'Pascal', *op. cit.*, p. 360.
52. Grégoire: *Fontenelle: une 'philosophie' désabusée.*
53. This is precisely the message of Caligula in the play of that name: he tries to show the people that, since death is inevitable, it is pointless to fear it, but that one should fear living without values. Caligula, of course, tries to teach this lesson in the wrong way.

Notes to Chapter Four

1. Preface to *Histoire des variations des églises protestantes, Oeuvres complètes de Bossuet* (henceforth in this chapter called *O.C.*), vol. 14, p. 11.
2. *O.C.*, vol. 23.
3. cf. Goyet: *L'humanisme de Bossuet*, pp. 554–63.
4. *Louis XIV et les protestants*, appendice 3.
5. Not in *O.C.* Bibliography under *Bossuet (a) Texts*.
6. Adam: *Grandeur and Illusion*, pp. 108–10; and Martimort: *Le Gallicanisme de Bossuet*, p. 707.
7. He may well have hoped to be archbishop of Paris, and many critics consider that jealousy against the elevation of his erstwhile disciple Fénelon to the archbishopric of Cambrai was a factor in his anti-Quietism. After 1678 Pope Innocent XI was eager to make Bossuet a cardinal and was deterred only by the resistance of Louis XIV, who had reasons of internal and almost family politics for wanting Bossuet not to be preferred—though he himself gave his moderate Gallican bishop many responsible tasks. See Martimort: *op. cit.*, pp. 341–57.
8. On the foregoing, see Martimort: *op. cit.*, and Giraud: *Bossuet*, ch. 7.
9. *Histoire des variations*, *O.C.*, vol. 15, p. 179.
10. 'II. Les variations dans la foi, preuve certaine de fausseté. III. Caractère des hérésies, d'être variables'. (*Histoire des variations*, préface, *O.C.*, vol. 14). See also: *Politique tirée de l'Ecriture sainte*, book VII, article 3, propositions i–ii.

11. See the writings of John Gilbert, Joseph Johnston and William Wake (Archbishop of Canterbury) between 1686 and 1688.
12. See Gaxotte: *La France de Louis XIV*, pp. 239–53, and especially Orcibal: *Louis XIV et les protestants*.
13. See Truchet: *La prédication de Bossuet*, vol. 2, p. 47.
14. *3e sermon pour le Dimanche des Rameaux, sur les devoirs des rois*, O.C., vol. 9, pp. 618–35.
15. Rébelliau: *Bossuet, historien du protestantisme* (1891), pp. 300–7; Truchet: *op. cit.*, vol. 2, pp. 40–52; Pépin: 'Bossuet et la Révocation'. The last, by a priest in the *Revue catholique de Normandie* (1892), has a clear bias against the 'stubbornness' of the Protestants, but is well documented.
16. O.C., vol. 12.
17. Giraud: *Bossuet*, p. 124.
18. Bossuet: *Correspondance*, vol. 3, letter 374.
19. *Ibid.*, letters 352, 368, 384.
20. For the full text of this *mandement*, see Pépin: *art. cit.*, pp.309–13.
21. O.C., vol. 17.
22. Source given by Orcibal: *op. cit.*, p. 159.
23. O.C., vols. 23–24, or Le Brun's critical edition.
24. See Rébelliau: *Bossuet*, pp. 97 ff. and Schmittlein: *L'Aspect politique du différend Bossuet-Fénelon*, p. 5.
25. *Leviathan*, ch. 44, my italics.
26. cf. Thomas: *Religion and the Decline of Magic*, p. 108.
27. *Renaissance Sense of the Past*, p. 104.
28. Bossuet regarded history as 'La maîtresse de la vie humaine et de la politique' and also wrote for the Dauphin an *Abrégé de l'histoire de France* (from the fifth century to Charles IX) which was not published till 1767. He claimed 'une grande exactitude' for this work included in O.C., vol. 25).
29. See Hardy: *Le 'De civitate Dei', source principale du 'Discours sur l'histoire universelle'*; and, for some qualifications, Goyet: *L'Humanisme de Bossuet*, vol. 2, pp. 330–34; in Goyet, all vol. 2, ch. 1 is also on Bossuet's historiography.
30. Bracketed numbers in this section are page-references to the 1966 Garnier-Flammarion paperback edition of the *Histoire universelle*.
31. Fénelon, who had undoubtedly read Bossuet's *Histoire* at the time, discourses in *De l'éducation des filles* (1684–7) on Augustine's historical method as showing 'par la suite de l'histoire, la religion aussi ancienne que le monde' (*Oeuvres*, vol. 3, p. 504).
32. Cf. Gusdorf: *L'avènement des sciences humaines etc.*, pp. 247 ff. for a sophisticated discussion of Bossuet's 'space-time'.
33. Saint-Evremond: *Réflexions sur les divers génies du peuple romain dans les divers temps de la République* (*Oeuvres en prose*, vol. 2) was published in *Oeuvres mêlées* in 1684, parts of it having been published previously. A first draft may have existed in 1665. Its programme, writes Saint-Evremond is 'de suivre le génie de quelques temps mémorables, et l'esprit différent dont on a vu Rome diversement animée' (ch. 1).

Notes to Chapter Five

1. See *Plans de gouvernement* (1711): '8: Libertés gallicanes sur le spirituel', *Oeuvres de Fénelon* (henceforth in this chapter called *O.F.*), vol. 5. There seems little justification for seeing him as sometimes 'un ultramontain exagéré' as does Leroy: *Fénelon*, p. 1.
2. See letters to le père Le Tellier in 1711–12: *O.F.*, vol. 5, letters 243, 263, 272. The partisanship of the Jesuits for either Bossuet of Fénelon in the Quietist controversy is dealt with by Hillenaar: *Fénelon et les jésuites*.
3. Both texts in *O.F.*, vol. 1.
4. *O.F.*, vol. 5, letter 10, and *Correspondance de Fénelon*, ed. Orcibal, vol. 2, pp. 34–5.
5. December 1685 to July 1686 and May–July 1687.
6. Letters to his superior, Seignelay, minister for naval and coastal affairs: *O.F.*, vol. 5, letters 7, 8, 9 and a larger collection in *Correspondance*, ed. cit., vol. 2.
7. cf. Rothkrug: *Opposition to Louis XIV*, which is much more convincing than Schmittlein's: *Aspect politique du différend Bossuet–Fénelon*. Rothkrug, however, overstates the ideological importance of the quarrel as between 'the forces of tradition and reform', calling it their 'first large-scale encounter' (*op. cit.*, p. 287).
8. See Schmittlein, Rothkrug, Joppin, Carcassonne, Janet, Daniel-Rops in our Bibliography.
9. *Introduction à la vie dévote*, paperback by Editions du Seuil, 1962. Extracts from Saints Teresa and John of the Cross in *Mysticism: A Study and an Anthology* by F. C. Happold, London, Pelican Books.
10. *O.F.*, vol. 3. Translations of this and other documents in Barnard: *Fénelon on Education*.
11. See Fagniez: *La femme et la société française dans la première moitié du 17e siècle*, esp. p. 48; Reynier: *La femme au 17e siècle, etc.*, esp. pp. 240–9; for modifications to both, Dubois: 'The Education of women in seventeenth-century France'.
12. *O.F.*, vol. 3, p. 480.
13. *Ibid.*, p. 481.
14. *Ibid.*, pp. 481–2. On the characteristic female weaknesses of jealousy and vanity, chaps. 9 and 10 speak at length.
15. *Ibid.*, p. 483.
16. *Télémaque*, vol. 2, pp. 186–8. Given in trans. by Barnard: *Fénelon on Education*.
17. *O.F.*, vol. 3, pp. 514, 516.
18. *O.F.*, vol. 3.
19. Unless one counts the *Essai philosophique sur le gouvernement civil*, written by Ramsay 'on the principles of the late Fénelon' (*O.F.*, vol. 5. pp. 41–122).
20. See *Ecrits politiques*, *O.F.*, vol. 5, and Urbain: *Fénelon: écrits et lettres politiques*.
21. *Plans de gouvernement*, *O.F.*, vol. 5, p. 193.
22. Rothkrug: *Opposition to Louis XIV*, chaps. 1–6.

194   *Ideas in seventeenth-century France*

23. Apart from the Quietist affair, *Télémaque*, circulated at court in 1698, contributed to Fénelon's disgrace. Louis XIV allowed himself to be convinced that the criticisms contained in the novel were directed against himself, though Fénelon always denied this with apparent sincerity.
24. *O.F.*, vol. 5; Leroy, pp. 84–104.
25. *Mémoires sur les mesures à prendre après la mort du Duc de Bourgogne*, *O.F.*, vol. 5.
26. *O.F.*, vol 5; Urbain, *ed. cit*. Published as *Examen de conscience pour un roi* in 1734. Published in London in 1747 in the original and in trans. as *Proper Heads of Self-examination for a King*.
27. The timidities of Madame de Maintenon and Beauvillier are berated in the *Lettre*, but this may well have been to avoid rendering them suspect.
28. *Lettre au duc de Chevreuse*, 4 August 1710, *O.F.*, vol 5, p. 619.
29. The foregoing paragraph refers to the *Plans de gouvernement*, *O.F.*, vol. 5, pp. 190–202.
30. Rothkrug: *loc. cit*.
31. See Chérel, *Fénelon au 18e siècle*, 'Tableaux bibliographiques'. Ozell translated the book into English in 1715.
32. The reigns of Louis XIII and Louis XIV had in fact seen twelve 'sumptuary edicts' attempting to regulate private expenditure on luxury goods.
33. Clearly a criticism of the existing crop and land taxes which discouraged peasants from doing so much as mend a barn or buy a plough.

Notes to Chapter Six

1. A succinct account of Bayle's fortunes with the critics and historians is given in Dibon's introduction to *Pierre Bayle, le philosophe de Rotterdam*. For the reader without access to the massive *Oeuvres diverses* (henceforth referred to in this chapter as *O.D.*) and *Dictionnaire*, there are useful selections edited by Beller and Lee (in English), by Labrousse, Raymond, Niderst, and Solé—though the selections in the last are not very characteristic.
2. Delvolvé's attempt to make a synthesis of Bayle's thought is not very successful. The eclectic approach of Labrousse does greater justice to the reality of Bayle.
3. His teachers were Louis Tronchin, who regarded Cartesianism as 'the True Philosophy', and Jean-Robert Chouet who taught essentially the experimental method, which he regarded as Cartesian rather than Baconian.
4. *Dictionnaire historique et critique,* henceforth called *Dictionnaire*, pp. 2306 B–2307 A. Except where otherwise stated my references are to the Rotterdam edition of 1720, and, since the pagination is continuous throughout the four vols., I do not give the vol. number. A and B refer to the left- and right-hand columns on a given page.
5. *Dictionnaire*, 'Pyrrhon', Remarque B, p. 2306A.
6. *Projet d'un dictionnaire*, ix, in *Dictionnaire*, p. 2984. Bayle goes on to argue, against Descartes, that the 'object of mathematics' (that to which the mathematician applies his thought) 'ne peut être qu'une idée de notre

âme'. Like Gassendi, Bayle had little grasp of mathematics, and in fact his Pyrrhonism is in some senses more Gassendist than Cartesian.
7. Bayle: *O.D.*, vol. 2, pp. 1–59, 161–335.
8. Bayle's indignation over the 'Inquisition against the Republic of Letters' is clear in his *Avis de M. Bayle au lecteur* heading the *Recueil . . . concernant la philosophie de M Descartes*, published Rotterdam, 1684 (*O.D.*, vol. 4, p. 186).
9. His lectures are recorded as *Systema totius philosophiae* with parallel French text, O.D., vol. 4. Teachers like Bayle were very important in the triumph of Cartesianism late in the century.
10. *Pensées diverses sur la comète*, éd. crit. Prat, will be the source of our references. Text, with additions thereto, also in *O.D.*, vol. 3, pp. 1–500.
11. Prat's study of this question (*ed. cit.*, vol. 1, Intro.) is the most scholarly to date.
12. See texts gathered in *The Controversy on the Comets of 1618; Galileo, Grassi, Guidicci, Kepler*, trans. by Stillman Drake and C. D. O'Malley, Philadelphia, Univ. of Pennsylvania Press, 1960, publ. in Britain by Oxford University Press.
13. Ed. Prat, vol.1, p. 80. Astrology is dealt with in sections 17–22. On the use of the word 'Philosophie' in this quotation, Prat observes that this is one of the first times the word is clearly used in the eighteenth-century sense. One may indeed contrast its use here with the way it is used in section 8: '*Pourquoi on ne parle point de l'autorité des Philosophes*', where the accepted philosophy based on Aristotle is meant.
14. Rex: *Essays on Bayle and Religious Controversy*, part I, esp. pp. 35, 72–4.
15. Labrousse: *Pierre Bayle et l'instrument critique*, p. 30.
16. Rex: *op. cit.*, p. 74.
17. Prat: *ed. cit.*, section 8.
18. *Ibid.*, sections 9–15.
19. *Ibid.*, sections 23, 24, 35–42, 49, 206–14, 242, and others.
20. As Rex does not fail to notice: *op. cit.*, note 67 lists the textual evidence, the best being in sections 88, 148, 244–5.
21. *La contagion sacrée, ou histoire naturelle de la superstition*. The edition I use is given as London, 1768. See vol. 1, pp. 151–2.
22. This is a view of earlier commentators which I cannot follow Rex in rejecting.
23. 'Tempérament' is discussed in section 144.
24. Section 157: 'Raison très-forte pour prouver la nécessité de la grâce'.
25. *O.D.*, vol. 1.
26. March 1686. Ed. crit. Labrousse; also *O.D.*, vol. 2.
27. Published Amsterdam, parts 1 and 2 in October 1686, part 3 in June 1687, and a long supplement (undated) *O.D.*, vol. 2.
28. *O.D.*, vol. 2, p. 367.
29. *Ibid.*, p. 371B. Italics in the text.
30. *Ibid.*, p. 371B. Cf. the opening lines of Descartes' *Discours de la méthode*.
31. E.g. 'Marcionites', pp. 1909ff. (esp. remarques D, F), and 'Pauliciens', p. 2203, remarque A.
32. E.g. 'Eclaircissements', pp. 2987ff., 'Eclaircissement I', with its fifteen subheadings.

33. See Rex: *op. cit.* and his earlier article 'Pierre Bayle: the theology and politics of the article on David' (*Bibliothèque d'Humanisme et de Renaissance*, XXIV and XXV, 1 in 1962, 2 in 1963); Labrousse: *Pierre Bayle*, vol, 2, pp. 346ff.; Dodge, *op. cit.*, ch. 7: 'Theocracy and the menace of Bayle'.

34. On textual irrationalities, see 'David', remarques D and H. Richard Simon's *Histoire critique du Vieux Testament* was published in French in 1678, in Latin in 1681. It lost Simon his place in the Oratory. His *Histoire critique du Nouveau Testament* appeared in English translation in 1689.

    Bayle wrote an admiring but discreet review of Simon's *Vieux Testament*, wondering why it had been banned in France, in his *Nouvelles de la République des Lettres*, December 1684, art. 9 (*O.D.*, 1, pp. 190–3). In the March 1685 number he wrote a shorter review of yet another edition together with a review of a work by Pierre Ambrun attacking Simon ('Catalogue de livres nouveaux', *O.D.*, 1, pp. 255–6).

    On the *ethos* of the Old Testament, Bayle points out that its authors make no moral comment at all on David's treacheries and injustices, nor on his violence and cruelty in war. We may easily see the tenor of Bayle's argument by reading the parts 'expurgated' by him at the demand of the Rotterdam Consistory of 1687. These parts are given in the 1820 Desoer edition as 'Variants' (vol. 5, pp. 408–18).

35. Labrousse, in *Pierre Bayle*, vol. 2, treats both Fideism (chap. 10) and The problem of evil (chap. 12) in a more detailed way than we can. In particular, she makes clear the recent developments in the argument on evil in Malebranche, with whose work Bayle was well acquainted, and she also firmly grounds Bayle's preoccupation with evil in his own psychology and experience, showing him to be an extremely pessimistic man.

36. 'Pauliciens', remarque E, p. 2205.
37. *Ibid.*, remarque M, p. 2214.
38. *Ibid.*, remarque E, p. 2205.
39. 'Eclaircissements', II, p. 2992.
40. *Ibid.*, III (on 'Pyrrhon'), subheading 8, p. 3006.
41. *Ibid.*, II, p. 2991 for both quotations.
42. See also André Robinet: 'L'aphilosophie de Bayle devant les philosophies de Malebranche et de Leibnitz', in *Bayle, le philosophe de Rotterdam*, éd. Dibon.
43. The reader may be familiar with Voltaire's constant mockery of metaphysics, and particularly of Leibniz's theodicy as interpreted by Pope and others, in *Candide*. In respect of the special interest Voltaire took in Bayle's presentation of Manicheism and in the whole problem of 'le mal moral et le mal physique', it is curious that the Manicheism professed by Martin in *Candide* is defective in that, of the 'deux principes', he speaks only of the principle of evil.
44. The subject has been excellently treated by Rétat: *Le dictionnaire de Bayle et la lutte philosophique, etc.* See also C. Louise Thijssen-Schouten: 'La diffusion européenne des idées de Bayle' in Dibon, *ed. cit.*, and Mason: *Pierre Bayle and Voltaire*.

Notes to Chapter Seven

1. Of the books on Fontenelle, which are slowly continuing to increase in number, Carré's remains the classic. The undergraduate reader would do well, however, to approach Fontenelle through Marsak's slim but lucidly argued *Fontenelle: The Idea of Science in the French Enlightenment*, the splendid editiorial material by Roelens in his *Fontenelle: textes choisis*, and Calame's excellent critical edition of the *Entretiens*.
2. The *Histoire des oracles* dates from 1686, whereas the date 1687 given by some literary histories is that of a later and inaccurate edition. See Maigron's critical edition, p. j.
3. Fontenelle gives an account of the new charter from Louis XIV in *Histoire du renouvellement de l'Académie Royale des Sciences (Oeuvres*, Vol. 6, pp. 15 ff.; also in *Eloges des Académiciens*, etc., 1740, vol. 1, pp. 1–21). Among interesting details are the following: bigger accommodation in the Louvre; membership of seventy; meetings twice weekly for most of year, with attendance virtually compulsory; emphasis on international correspondence and information, and the accepting of foreign members as Associates; and Article 48: The King will continue to finance research and experiment.
4. Fontenelle's maturing abilities in the sciences are shown by his *Des éléments de la géométrie de l'infini (Oeuvres*, 10) and the corrections made over the years to errors of detail (especially dimensions and distances) in the successive editions of the *Entretiens*. On the latter, see the critical editions of Calame and Shackleton.
5. *Entretiens*, ed. Calame, p. 158.
6. *Ibid.*, p. xxxii.
7. *Ibid.*, p. 47.
8. *Ibid.*, p. 68.
9. Wilkins: *Discovery of a New World* (1638) and *Discourse tending to prove that 'tis probable our Earth is one of the Planets* (1640). Shackleton attaches prime importance to Wilkins as a source for Fontenelle; I favour however the view of Calame: '. . . Ici l'information de Fontenelle est donc indépendante de Wilkins, et nous pensons qu'elle l'est partout' (Calame, *ed. cit.*, p. xxvi).
10. Calame, *ed. cit.*, pp. vii–viii.
11. Shackleton: *Entretiens and Digression*, *crit. ed.*, pp. 41–5.
12. Calame, *ed.cit.*, p. 11.
13. Roelens summarises this aspect of the work in *Fontenelle: textes choisis*, section: 'L'explication mécanique de l'univers: une tendance matérialiste', pp. 89–91. See particularly *Entretiens*, ed. Calame, pp. 17–19.
14. Calame, *ed. cit.*, *Préface*, p. 9.
15. See Calame, *ed. cit.*, p.xxxvii.
16. *Oeuvres*, 9.
17. *Entretiens*, ed. Calame, pp. 114 ff.
18. *Ibid.*, p. 50.
19. *Ibid.*, pp. 23–4.

20. Rohault: *Traité de physique*, 1671; Régis: *Cours entier de philosophie*, 1681.
21. *Fragments d'un traité de la raison humaine*, Oeuvres, 9, pp. 199–200, 209–14, esp. the last. Here we have a Fontenelle closer to Gassendi than to Descartes.
22. *Sur l'instinct*, Oeuvres, 9.
23. *Doutes, etc.*, Oeuvres, 9.
24. *Doutes, etc.*, Oeuvres, 9, p. 41.
25. *Ibid.*, p. 56.
26. *Entretiens*, ed. Calame, pp. 18–19.
27. *Entretiens, and Digression*, ed. Shackleton, pp. 27–8.
28. *Théorie, etc.*, Oeuvres, 9, p. 192.
29. Oeuvres, 6, p. 186; also in *Eloges des Académiciens, etc.*, 1740, vol. 2, pp. 329–30.
30. *Préface sur l'utilité des mathématiques et de la physique et sur les travaux de l'Académie des sciences*, Oeuvres, 5; also in Roelens: *Textes choisis*.
31. Marsak: *Fontenelle, etc.*, p. 23.
32. In spite of his inclination towards Descartes' *a priori* mechanistic cosmology, Fontenelle, believing that science was by no means ready to explain systematically 'les premières causes de la nature', would surely have sided with Galileo on this principle. 'Sure tidings', Fontenelle says, are brought best by scientists using telescopes (*Entretiens*, ed. Calame, pp. 59–60).

    Incidentally, Fontenelle wrote a rather derisive little poem *Sur un portrait de Descartes*, Oeuvres, 4, p. 262. Yet he consistently adopts Descartes' systematic doubt, his derision of 'le faux merveilleux', and his rejection of argument from authority.
33. Molière was disingenuous in trying to have the best of both worlds. While asserting that successful drama can laugh at the rules, he also insisted that *L'école des femmes* was a 'regular' play, that is, one that broke no rules.
34. This is true of Charles Perrault in the *Parallèle des Anciens et des Modernes en ce qui regarde les Arts et les Sciences* (1688), in spite of its title. Perrault deals with the sciences certainly, and suggests that: 'nous sommes plus sages dans les choses que nous inventons de nous-mêmes que n'ont été les Grecs, et [qu'] à l'égard de celles que nous avons prises d'eux, nous les avons rendu meilleures qu'elles n'étaient . . . ' (p. 105). Yet he does not convince us that he has a firm grasp on what is happening in the science of his era.
35. Fontenelle: Oeuvres, 4, p. 127.
36. *Ibid.* 123. None the less, antiquity itself lends a patina to art, and, by generations long in the future, Fontenelle believed, Corneille, Racine and Molière would be held in awe. Perhaps the Americans would one day be the Moderns, and face a derisive world (p. 129). Virgil was a Modern in his day.
37. *Ibid.*, p. 125.
38. *Ibid.*, p. 121.
39. *Préface sur l'utilité des mathématiques et de la physique*, Oeuvres, 5, p. 12; also in Roelens: *Textes choisis*, p. 277.

40. *Entretiens*, ed. Calame, p. 58: '. . . je ne sache rien au monde qui ne soit le monument de quelque sottise des hommes'.
41. Bouchard: *L'histoire des oracles de Fontenelle*, p. 70.
42. *De l'origine des fables*, ed. Carré, pp. 19–20.
43. See Marsak's study of this aspect in *Bernard de Fontenelle, etc.*, section VI: 'The meaning of science'.
44. *Entretiens*, ed. Calame, pp. 21–2.
45. *Histoire des oracles*, ed. Maigron, pp. 32–3.
46. *Oeuvres*, 9, pp. 249–50.
47. See Roelens: *Textes choisis*, esp. p. 75: 'Point de culte religieux, point de sacerdoce non plus.'
48. *Entretiens*, ed. Calame, p. 98.
49. Bayle: *Oeuvres diverses*, I, p. 477. Also given in Roelens: *Textes choisis*.
50. This poem, often alluded to, is not in *Oeuvres*, and I have not seen it.
51. See, for example, *De l'origine des fables*, ed. Carré, pp. 26, 34.
52. *De l'existence de Dieu*, *Oeuvres*, 3, pp. 137–43.
53. *Of the usefulness of mathematical learning* in *Miscellania curiosa* (see Bibliography under *'Fontenelle (a)'*. Translated from *Préface sur l'utilité des mathématiques et de la physique*, 1699. See in *Oeuvres*, 5, p. 10, or Roelens: *Textes choisis*, p. 275.

BIBLIOGRAPHY

The Bibliography is divided into three sections:
Section I is subdivided under the names of the six main thinkers treated, in alphabetical order, with, for each name, a list of (*a*) texts and (*b*) related reading.
Section II is a list of books not clearly related to any single thinker, and is alphabetical under the name of the author.
Section III is a list of articles, alphabetical under the name of the author.

Section I

(i) BAYLE

(a) Texts

BAYLE, *Ce que c'est que la France toute catholique,* texte établi, présente et annoté par Elisabeth Labrousse, Paris, Vrin, 1973.
——, *Dictionnaire historique et critique*, 3e éd., revue, corrigée, et augmentée par l'auteur, Rotterdam, Michel Bohm, 1720, 4 vols. with continuous pagination; and Paris, Desoer, 1820, 16 vols.
——, *Oeuvres diverses* (excepté son *Dictionnaire*), Hildesheim, Georg Olms, 1964–8, 4 vols; facsimile ed. of the Hague ed. of 1727–31, each volume introduced by Elisabeth Labrousse.
——, *Pensées diverses sur la comète*, éd. crit. par A. Prat, Paris, Droz, 1939, 2 vols.
——, *Réponse aux questions d'un provincial*, Rotterdam 1704–7, 5 vols.
BELLER, ed., *Selections from Bayle's Dictionary*, ed. by E. A. Beller and M. du P. Lee, Princeton N.J., Princeton U.P., 1952.
LABROUSSE, ed., *Pierre Bayle et l'instrument critique,* présentation, choix de textes, biblio. par Elisabeth Labrousse, Paris, Seghers, 1965. (The presentation of the texts is extensive and valuable.)
NIDERST, ed., *Pierre Bayle: Oeuvres diverses*, ed. Alain Niderst, Paris, Editions sociales, 1971.
RAYMOND, ed., *Pierre Bayle: choix de textes*, avec intro. par Marcel Raymond, Paris, Egloff, 1948.
SOLE, ed., *Bayle polémiste: extraits du Dictionnaire historique et critique*, avec intro. et notes par Jacques Solé, Paris, Robert Laffont, 1972.

(b) Related reading on Bayle

BARBER, W. H., 'Pierre Bayle: Faith and Reason', in *The French Mind, studies in honour of Gustave Rudler*, ed. Moore, Sutherland and Starkie, Oxford, Clarendon, 1952.
BRUSH, C. B., *Montaigne and Bayle: variations on the theme of Skepticism*, The Hague, Nijhoff, 1966.
COURTINES, L.-P., *Bayle's relations with England and the English*, New York, Columbia U.P., 1938. Contains biblio. of English translations of Bayle on pp. 234–5.
DELVOLVE, JEAN, *Essai sur Pierre Bayle: religion, critique et philosophie positive*, Geneva, Slatkine Reprints, 1970 (reprinted from Paris ed. of 1906).
DIBON, ed., *Pierre Bayle, le philosophe de Rotterdam, études et documents*, publiés sous la direction de Paul Dibon, Paris, Vrin (Elsevier Publishing Co.), 1959.
LABROUSSE, ELISABETH, *Pierre Bayle*, La Haye, Nijhoff, 1963–4, 2 vols.
MASON, HAYDN TREVOR, *Pierre Bayle and Voltaire*, London, Oxford U.P., 1963.
RETAT, PIERRE, *Le Dictionnaire de Bayle et la lutte philosophique au 18e siècle*, Paris, Imprimerie Audin, 1971.
REX, WALTER EDWIN, *Essays on Pierre Bayle and religious controversy*, The Hague, Nijhoff, 1965.
ROBINSON, HOWARD, *Bayle the Sceptic*, New York, Columbia U.P., 1931.
SERRURIER, CORNELIA, *Pierre Bayle en Hollande*, Apeldoorn, Dixon et Cie, 1913.

(ii) BOSSUET
(a) Texts

BOSSUET, *Oeuvres complètes*, éditées par F. Lachat en 31 tomes, Paris, Librairie de Louis Vivès, 1863.
——, *Correspondance*, nouvelle éd. par Ch. Urbain et E. Levesque en 15 tomes, Paris, Hachette, 1910, reprinted by Kraus Reprint Ltd., 1965. Vol. 3 (1681–8) covers the period of the Revocation.
——, *Discours sur l'histoire universelle*, chronologie et préface de Jacques Truchet, Paris, Garnier-Flammarion, 1966.
——, *Politique tirée des propres paroles de l'Ecriture Sainte*, éd. crit. avec intro. et notes par Jacques Le Brun, Genève, Droz. 1967.
——, *Traité de la concupiscence*, texte établi et présenté par Ch. Urbain et E. Levesque, Paris, Fernand Roches, 1930.
——, *Oraisons funèbres. Sermons. Maximes et réflexions sur la comédie*, London, Paris, Dent, 1913.

(b) Related reading on Bossuet

CALVET, J., *Bossuet, l'homme et l'œuvre*, Paris, Boivin, 1941.
GIRAUD, VICTOR, *Bossuet*, Paris, Flammarion, 1930.

GOYET, THERESE, *L'humanisme de Bossuet*, 2 vols. with cont. pagination, Paris, Klincksieck, 1965.
HARDY, GEORGES, *Le 'De civitate dei', source principale du 'Descours sur l'histoire universelle'*, Paris, Bibliothèque de l Ecole des Hautes-Etudes, 1913.
LE BRUN, JACQUES, *Bossuet,* Paris, Desclée de Brouwer, 1970.
——, *La spiritualité de Bossuet*, Paris, Klincksieck, 1973.
MARTIMORT, AIME-GEORGES, *Le Gallicanisme de Bossuet*, Paris, Editions du Cerf, 1953.
REBELLIAU, ALFRED, *Bossuet*, 6e éd, revue, Paris, Hachette, 1927.
——, *Bossuet, historien du protestantisme*, Paris, Hachette, 1891.
TRUCHET, JACQUES, *La prédication de Bossuet*, 2 vols., Paris, Editions du Cerf, 1960.

(iii) DESCARTES

(a) Texts

DESCARTES, *Oeuvres de Descartes, éd.* par Charles Adam et Paul Tannery, Paris, 1896–1910, 13 vols.; new ed. in progress.
——, *Oeuvres philosophiques de Descartes*, textes établis, présentés et annotés par Ferdinand Alquié, Paris, Garnier Frères, 1963, 3 tomes.
——, *Descartes: oeuvres et lettres*, textes présentés par André Bridoux, Paris, Bibliothèque de la Pléiade, nrf., 1937.
——, *Descartes: Discours de la méthode*, avec intro. et remarques de Gilbert Gadoffre, Manchester U.P., 2nd ed., 1961.
——, *Descartes: Discours de la méthode*, texte et commentaire par Etienne Gilson, Paris, Vrin, 1947.
ANSCOMBE, trans., *Descartes: Philosophical Writings*, selection translated and edited by Elizabeth Anscombe and Peter Thomas Geach, intro. by Alexandre Koyré, London, Nelson's Univ. Paperbacks, Open University, 1970; first publ. 1954 in Nelson Philosophical Texts.
BAIR, trans., *Essential Works of Descartes*, trans. by Lowell Bair for the Library of Basic Ideas, intro. by D. J. Bronstein, New York, Bantam Books Inc., 1961.
SUTCLIFFE, trans., *Discourse on the method/Meditations*, trans. and intro. by F. E. Sutcliffe, Harmondsworth, Middlesex, Penguin, 1968.
HALDANE trans., *Philosophical Works of Descartes*, trans. by Elizabeth S. Haldane and G. T. R. Ross, 2 vols., Cambridge, Cambridge U.P., 1967.
WILSON, ed., *The Essential Descartes*, (selected writings based on trans. by Haldane and Ross (q.v.) except correspondence with Elizabeth of Bohemia trans. by Emmett Wilson) edited with an intro. by Margaret D. Wilson, N.Y., Toronto, London, Mentor, 1969.

(b) Related reading on Descartes

ADAM, CHARLES ERNEST, *Vie et œuvres de Descartes*, Paris, 1910, abridged and corrected as *Descartes, sa vie et son œuvre*, Paris, Boivin, 1937.

ALQUIE, FERDINAND, *Descartes*, Paris, Hatier, nouvelle éd. 1956.
BAILLET, ADRIEN, *Vie de Monsieur Descartes*, Paris, La Table Ronde, 1946, appears to be slightly abridged. Baillet first publ. in 1691.
DENISSOFF, ELIE, *Descartes, premier théoricien de la physique mathématique: trois essais sur le 'Discours de la méthode'*, Louvain, Publications Universitaires de Louvain, 1970, Paris, Ed. Béatrice-Nauwelaerts.
DONEY ed., *Descartes, A collection of critical essays*, edited by Willis Doney, London and Basingstoke, Macmillan, U.S.A. 1967, U.K. 1968.
FISCHER, KUNO, *Descartes and his School*, trans. from the third and revised German ed. by J. P. Gordy, ed. by Noah Porter, London, T. Fisher Unwin, 1887.
GILSON, ETIENNE, *Etudes sur le rôle de la penseé médiévale dans la formation du système cartésien*, Paris, Vrin, 1930.
GOUHIER, HENRI, *La penseé religieuse de Descartes*, Paris, Vrin, 1924.
HALDANE, ELIZABETH S., *Descartes: his life and times*, London, John Murray, 1905.
KEELING, S. V., *Descartes*, London, Oxford, N.Y., Oxford U.P., 1968, an Oxford Paperback first publ. by Ernest Benn, 1934.
KENNY, ANTHONY, *Descartes: a study of his philosophy*, New York, Random House, 1968.
MARITAIN, JACQUES, *The Dream of Descartes*, (trans. by Mabelle L. Andison from *Le songe de Descartes*), London, Editions Poetry London, Nicholson & Watson, 1946.
MOUY, PAUL, *Le développement de la physique cartésienne*, 1646–1712, Paris Vrin, 1934.
RODIS-LEWIS, GENEVIEVE, *Descartes—initiation à sa philosophie*, Paris, Vrin, 1964.
——, *La morale de Descartes*, Paris, Presses Universitaires de France, 1970.
SCOTT, J. F., *The Scientific Works of René Descartes*, London, Taylor & Francis, 1952.
SMITH, NORMAN K., *Studies in the Cartesian philosophy*, London, Macmillan, 1902.
——, *New Studies in the Philosophy of Descartes*, London, Macmillan, 1952.
VROOMAN, J. R., *René Descartes, a Biography*, New York, Putnam's Sons, 1970.

(iv) FENELON

(a) Texts

BARNARD, trans., *Fénelon on Education*, trans. of *De l'éducation des filles* and other documents illustrating Fénelon's educational theories and practice, with an intro. and notes by H. C. Barnard, Cambridge, Cambridge U.P., 1966.
FENELON, *Aventures de Télémaque*, nouvelle éd. par Albert Cahen, 2 tomes, Paris, Hachette, 1920.
——, *Explications des Maximes des Saints sur la vie intérieure*, éd. crit. d'Albert Chérel, Paris, Bloud, 1911.

——, *Examen de conscience*, trans. as *Proper heads of self-examination for a king*, London, 1747, and publ. as *Directions pour la conscience d'un roi*, La Haye, 1747.

——, *Oeuvres de Fénelon*, en 5 tomes, avec avertissement daté 1821, Paris, Lefèvre et Pourrat, sans date.

——, *Lettre à Louis XIV*, avec une préface de Henri Guillemin, Neuchâtel, Ides et Calendes, undated but before 1966.

LEROY, ed., *Fénelon, collection de textes*, éd. par Maxime Leroy, Paris, Alcan, 1928.

ORCIBAL, ed., *Correspondance de Fénelon*, texte établi par Jean Orcibal avec intro., notes et commentaires, 3 tomes, Paris, Klincksieck, 1972.

OZELL, trans., *Adventures of Telemachus*, London, 1715.

——, *Reflections on Learning*, London, 1718.

URBAIN, ed., *Fénelon: écrits et lettres politiques*, éd. par Charles Urbain, Paris, Bossard, 1920.

(b) Related reading on Fénelon

CARCASSONNE, ELY, *Fénelon, l'homme et l'œuvre*, Paris, Boivin, 1946.

CHEREL, ALBERT, *Fénelon au 18e siècle en France, 1715–1820*, Paris, Hachette, 1917, with a useful supplement: 'Tableaux bibliographiques'.

DOUEN, E. O., *L'intolérance de Fénelon*, Paris, Sandoz et Fischbacher, 1872.

GORCE, AGNES DE LA., *Le vrai visage de Fénelon*, Paris, Hachette, 1958.

HILLENAAR, HENK, *Fénelon et les jésuites*, La Haye, Nijhoff, 1967, extensive bibliography.

JANET, PAUL, *Fénelon*, 3e éd., Paris, Hachette, 1912.

JOPPIN, GABRIEL, *Fénelon et la mystique du pur amour*, Paris, Beauchesne et fils, 1938.

LEROY, MAXIME, *Fénelon*, Paris, Alcan, 1928.

SCHMITTLEIN, RAYMOND, *L'aspect politique du différend Bossuet–Fénelon*, Bade, Editions Art et Science Bade, 1954.

VARILLON, le R. P. FRANCOIS, *Fénelon et le pur amour*, Paris, Ed. du Seuil, 1957.

ZERMATI, DAVID -J., *La place de Fénelon dans l'histoire des doctrines économiques* (thèse de droit), Alger, Imprimerie Solal, 1934.

(v) FONTENELLE

(a) Texts

FONTENELLE, *Oeuvres*, nouvelle éd., augmentée, avec figures, 12 vols., Amsterdam, chez François Changuion, 1764.

——, *De l'origine des fables, 1724*, éd. crit. par J.-R. Carré, Paris, Alcan, 1932.

BAYLE, ed., 'Extrait d'une Lettre écrite de Batavia dans les Indes Orientales le 27 Novembre 1684, contenu dans une lettre de M. de Fontenelle, reçue à Rotterdam par M. Basnage', *Nouvelles de la République des Lettres*, janvier 1686, article X (Bayle, *Oeuvres diverses* (q.v.), vol. I, pp 476–7). Also included in Roelens (q.v.).

FONTENELLE, *Entretiens sur la pluralité des mondes*, éd. crit. par Alexandre Calame, Paris, Didier, 1966.
——, *Entretiens sur la pluralité des mondes; Digression sur les Anciens et les Modernes*, ed. by Robert Shackleton, Oxford, Clarendon, 1955.
——, 'A translation of part of Monsieur Fontenelle's Preface to the Memoirs of the Royal Academy at Paris, in the year 1699, treating of the usefulness of mathematical learning', *Miscellanea Curiosa*, vol. 1, 3rd ed., London, James and John Knapton, 1726.
FONTENELLE, *Histoire des Oracles*, éd. crit. par Louis Maigron, Paris, Edouard Cornély et Cie., 1908.
——, *Eloge des Académiciens, avec l'histoire de l'Académie Royale des Sciences en 1699, par M. de Fontenelle, Secrétaire perpétuel*, The Hague, Isaac vander Kloot, 1740, 2 vols., facsimile by Impression Anastaltique, Culture et Civilisation, Brussels, 1969.
ROELENS, ed., *Fontenelle, textes choisis*, intro. et notes par Maurice Roelens, Paris, Editions Sociales, 1966.

(b) Related reading on Fontenelle

BOUCHARD, MARCEL, *L'histoire des oracles, de Fontenelle*, étude, Paris, S.F.E.L.T., 1947.
CARRE, J.-R., *La philosophie de Fontenelle (ou le Sourire de la Raison)*, Paris, Alcan, 1932.
GREGOIRE, FRANCOIS, *Fontenelle: une 'philosophie' désabusée*, Paris, Vrin, 1947.
LABORDE-MILAA, AUGUSTE, *Fontenelle*, Paris, Hachette, 1905.
MAIGRON, LOUIS, *Fontenelle: l'homme, l'œuvre, l'influence*, Paris, Plon, 1906.
MARSAK, LEONARD, M., *Bernard de Fontenelle: the idea of science in the French Enlightenment*, (transactions of American Philosophical Society; new ser., vol. 49, pt. 7, 1959), Philadelphia, American Philosophical Society, 1959.
NIDERST, ALAIN, *Fontenelle à la recherche de lui-même*, Paris, Nizet, 1972.

(vi) PASCAL

(a) Texts

PASCAL, *Oeuvres*, 14 vols., éd. par Léon Brunschvicg et Pierre Boutroux, 'Grands Ecrivains de la France', Paris, Hachette, 1921.
COHEN, trans., *Pascal, The Pensées*, trans. with an intro. by J. M. Cohen from ed. Chevalier (q.v.), Harmondsworth, Middlesex, Penguin, 1961.
PASCAL, *Oeuvres complètes*, texte établi et annoté par Jacques Chevalier, (nrf, 'Bibliothèque de la Pléiade'), Paris, Gallimard, 1962.
——, *Pensées de M. Pascal sur la religion, et sur quelques autres sujets*, L'Edition de Port-Royal (1670) et ses compléments (1678–1776), présentée par Georges Couton et Jean Jehasse, Centre Interuniversitaire d'éditions et de rééditions, Editions de l'Université de Saint-Etienne, 1971.
GOUNELLE, ed., *L'entretien de Pascal avec M. de Sacy*, étude et comm. par André Gounelle, Paris, P.U.F., 1966.

KENNET, trans., *Thoughts on Religion, and other subjects*, trans. B. Kennet, London, 1704.

PASCAL, *Pensées*, éd. par Louis Lafuma, Paris, Editions du Luxembourg, 1951, 3 vols.: I Textes, II Notes, III Documents.

——, *Oeuvres complètes*, présentation et notes de Louis Lafuma, Paris, Editions du Seuil, 1966. The *Pensées* in this volume (called O.C. in the present book) are as in Editions du Luxembourg.

——, *Pensées*, avant-propos et notes de Louis Lafuma, Paris, Delmas, 1952.

——, *Pensées*, texte établi par Léon Brunschvicg, Paris, Garnier-Flammarion, 1976. The numbering of the *Pensées* in this ed., used in the present book, is as in numerous eds. using the order established by Brunschvicg.

——, *Les Provinciales*, texte établi et annoté par José Lupin, préface de Henri Gouhier, Paris, 'Livre de poche', Editions Gallimard et Librairie Générale Française, 1966.

——, *Oeuvres complètes*, 2 vols., éd. par Jean Mesnard, Paris, Desclée de Brouwer, vol. I 1964, II 1970.

——, *Les Provinciales, de Blaise Pascal*, ed. by H. F. Stewart, Manchester, Manchester U.P., 1920, reprinted 1951.

(b) Related reading on Pascal

BEGUIN, ALBERT, *Pascal par lui-même*, Paris, Editions du Seuil, 1953.

BERA ed., *Blaise Pascal, l'homme et l'œuvre*, 'Cahiers de Royaumont, Phil., No. 1', multiple authorship, presented by M.-A. Béra, Paris, Editions de minuit, 1956.

BISHOP, MORRIS, *Pascal: the life of genius*, London, G. Bell & Sons, 1937.

BROOME, J. H., *Pascal*, London, Arnold, 1965.

CRUICKSHANK, JOHN, 'Knowledge and belief in Pascal's *Apology*', in *Studies in French Literature presented to H. W. Lawton*, Manchester, Manchester U.P., N.Y., Barnes & Noble Inc., 1968.

GIRAUD, V., *Pascal, l'homme, l'œuvre, l'influence*, Paris, Fontemoing, 1900.

GOUHIER, HENRI, *Blaise Pascal, commentaires*, Paris, Vrin, 1966.

HUMBERT, PIERRE, *Cet effrayant génie . . . L'Oeuvre scientifique de Blaise Pascal*, Paris, Albin Michel, 1947.

HUXLEY, ALDOUS, 'Holy Face' and 'Pascal', in *Collected Essays*, London, Chatto & Windus, 1960.

JOVY, ERNEST, *Etudes pascaliennes, vol. I: Pascal et St-Ange; Jacques Forton, sieur de Saint-Ange, ses écrits et ses infortunes*, Paris, Vrin, 1927.

KOYRE, ALEXANDRE, 'Pascal Savant', in *Blaise Pascal, l'homme et l'œuvre*, see above under Béra.

MAIRE, ALBERT, *L'œuvre scientifique de Blaise Pascal, bibliographie critique et analyse de tous les travaux qui s'y rapportent*, Paris, Librairie Scientifique A. Hermann, 1912.

MAURIAC, FRANCOIS, *Blaise Pascal et sa sœur Jacqueline*, Paris, Hachette, 1931.

MESNARD, JEAN, *Pascal, l'homme et l'œuvre*, Paris, Boivin, 1951, and

Pascal, Paris, Hatier, 4e éd., 1962. These two books are identical except that the second has a table of contents and a more up-to-date bibliography.
MESNARD et al., *Les 'Pensées' de Pascal ont trois cents ans*, multiple authorship, Clermont-Ferrand, Bussac, 1971.
MORTIMER, ERNEST, *Blaise Pascal, the life and work of a realist*, London, Methuen, 1959.
NEDELKOVITCH, D., *La pensée philosophique créatrice de Pascal*, Paris, Alcan, 1925.
STEINMANN, JEAN, *Pascal*, nouvelle éd. revue et augmentée, Paris, Desclée de Brouwer, 1962 (1st ed. 1954).
STEWARD, H. F., *Pascal's Apology for Religion extracted from the 'Pensées'*, Cambridge, Cambridge U.P., 1948.
STROWSKI, FORTUNAT, *Pascal et son temps*, 3 vols., Paris, Plon, 3e éd. 1907.
VIALLANEIX et al., *Pascal présent, 1662–1962*, multiple authorship, Clermont-Ferrand, Bussac, 1962.
VOLTAIRE, 'Sur les Pensées de M. Pascal' in *Lettres philosophiques*, ed. by F. A. Taylor, Oxford, Blackwell, revised ed. 1946.

Section II

General books consulted

ADAM, ANTOINE, *Grandeur and Illusion: French Literature and Society, 1600–1715*, trans. by Herbert Tint, London, Weidenfeld & Nicolson, 1972.
——, *L'âge classique*, vol. 1, 1624–1660, vol. 2, 1660–1720, Paris, Arthaud, 1968. (Vol. 3 is edited by Pomeau.)
ADAM, ANTOINE, ed., *Les libertins au 17e siècle*, textes choisis et présentés par Antoine Adam, Paris, Buchet/Chastel, 1964.
——, *Le mouvement philosophique dans la première moitié du 18e siècle*, Paris, S.E.D.E.S., 1967.
——, *Théophile de Viau et la libre pensée française en 1620*, Paris, Droz, 1936.
ALCOVER, MADELEINE, *La pensée philosophique et scientifique de Cyrano de Bergerac*, Genève, Droz, 1970.
ALQUIE, FERDINAND, *Le Cartésianisme de Malebranche*, Paris, Vrin, 1974.
BACON, FRANCIS, *The Advancement of Learning/New Atlantis*, ed. Arthur Johnston, Oxford, Clarendon, 1974.
——, *Novum organum* (including *First Book of Aphorisms*), in *Lord Bacon's Works*, vol. 4, ed. by Spedding, Ellis and Heath, London, Longman et al., 1858.
BAUDIN, E., *Pascal et Descartes*, Neuchâtel, Ed. de la Baconnière, 1946.
BERGERAC, CYRANO DE, *L'autre monde (Les états et empires de la lune, Les états et empires du soleil)*, présenté par H. Weber, Paris, Editions Sociales, 1959.

——, *Oeuvres libertines*, 2 vols., ed. F. Lachèvre, Paris, Garnier, reprint 1932.
——, *Oeuvres*, préface de G. Ribemont-Dessaignes, Paris, Club français du livre, 1957, contains *L'autre monde, Lettres diverses, Mazarinade*.
BLOCH, OLIVIER R., *La philosophie de Gassendi*, La Haye, Nijhoff, 1971.
BOAS, MARIE, *The Scientific Renaissance, 1450–1630*, London and Glasgow, Fontana, Collins, 1970; first publ. by Collins in 1962.
BOUCHARD, M., *L'Histoire des Oracles de Fontenelle*, Paris, S.F.E.L.T., 1947.
BOULENGER, JACQUES, *Le Grand Siècle*, Paris, Hachette, undated.
BREHIER, EMILE, *The Seventeenth Century*, trans., by Wade Baskin, Chicago and London, Univ. of Chicago Press, 1966; originally publishe as *Histoire de la philosophie. I. Le dix-septième siècle*, Paris P.U.F., 1938.
BRINTON, ed., *The Portable Age of Reason Reader*, ed. Crane Brinton, New York, Viking Press, 1956.
BRONOWSKI, J. and MAZLISH, BRUCE, *The Western Intellectual Tradition*, first published by Hutchinson, 1960; then Pelican, 1963; reprinted with revisions 1970.
BROWN, HARCOURT, *Scientific organisations in seventeenth century France, 1620–1680*, Baltimore, Williams & Wilkins, 1934.
BRUNSCHVICG, LEON, *Descartes et Pascal, lecteurs de Montaigne*, New York, Brentano's, 1944.
BRUSH, CRAIG C., *Montaigne and Bayle: Variations on the theme of skepticism*, The Hague, Nijhoff, 1966.
——, *Selected Works of Pierre Gassendi*, ed. and trans. Brush, N.Y., London, Johnson Reprint Co., 1972.
BURKE, PETER, *The Renaissance Sense of the Past*, London, Edward Arnold, 1969.
BURY, J. B., *The Idea of Progress*, London, Macmillan, 1932; New York, Dover Publications, 1955.
BUSSON. H., *La pensée religieuse française de Charron à Pascal*, Paris, Vrin, 1933.
BUTTERFIELD, HERBERT, *The Origins of Modern Science, 1300–1800*, new ed. revised and enlarged, London, Bell, 1968.
CALMETTE, JOSEPH, *L'ère classique*, Paris, Fayard, 1949.
CALVET, J., *La littérature religieuse de François de Sales à Fénelon*, Paris, J. de Gigord, 1938.
CATEL, MAURICE, ed., *Les écrivains de Port-Royal: intro. et choix de Maurice Catel*, Paris, Mercure de France, 1962.
CHARBONNEL, J.-ROGER, *La pensée italienne au 16e siècle et le courant libertin*, Paris. Champion, 1919 (new ed. with intro. and revised biblio. by Robert E. Taylor, New York, 1973).
CHEREL, ALBERT, *De Télémaque à Candide*, Paris, J. de Gigord, 1933.
CLARK, GEORGE NORMAN, *The Seventeenth Century*, 2nd ed., Oxford, O.U.P., 1947, issued as an Oxford Paperback 1960.
COHEN, BERNARD, *The Birth of a New Physics*, London etc. Heinemann, first publ. in Britain 1961.

Bibliography

CONLON, PIERRE M., *Prélude au Siècle des lumières, Répertoire chronologique de 1680 à 1715*, vols. 1–6, Geneva, Droz., 1970–5.
COPLESTON, F. C., *A History of Medieval Philosophy*, London, Methuen, 1972.
——, *A History of Philosophy*, London, Burns and Oates, 1958, vol. 4 'Descartes to Leibniz'.
CROMBIE, A. C., *Augustine to Galileo*, 2 vols.; vol. I, *Science in the Middle Ages, 5th–13th century*; vol. 2, *Science in the Later Middle Ages and Early Modern Times, 13th–17th century;* Harmondsworth, Middlesex, Penguin, 1969 (first publ. 1952).
CROSLAND, M. P., ed., *The Science of Matter: a historical survey; selected readings*, Harmondsworth, Middlesex, Penguin, 1971.
DANIEL-ROPS, H., *Le Grand Siècle des âmes*, Paris, Fayard, 1963; trans. by J. J. Buckingham as *The Church in the Seventeenth Century*, London, Dent, N.Y., Dutton, 1963.
DAUMAS, MAURICE, *Les instruments scientifiques aux 17e et 18e siècles*, Paris, P.U.F., 1953; trans. and ed. by Mary Holbrook as *Scientific Instruments of the Seventeenth and Eighteenth Centuries and their Makers*, London, Batsford, 1972.
DICKENS, A. G., *The Counter Reformation*, London, Thames & Hudson, 1968.
DOBELL, CLIFFORD, *Antony van Leeuwenhoek and his 'little animals';* ed. used London, etc., Staples Press, 1932 for 300th anniversary of Leeuwenhoek's death; see also New York, Dover Publications, 1960.
DODGE, GUY H., *Political Theory of the Huguenots of the Dispersion, etc.*, New York, Columbia U.P., 1947.
DRAKE, STILLMAN, ed., *Discoveries and opinions of Galileo*, trans. with intro. and notes by Stillman Drake, N.Y., Doubleday (Anchor Books), 1957.
FAGNIEZ, GUSTAVE, *La femme et la société française dans la première moitié du 17e siècle*, Paris, Gamber, 1929.
FUNCK-BRENTANO, FRANZ, *Le drame des poisons*, Paris, Hachette, ed. used 1935; trans. by G. Maidment as *Princes and Poisoners. Studies of the Court of Louis XIV*, London, Duckworth, 1901.
GAIFFE, FELIX, *L'Envers du Grand Siècle*, Paris, Albin Michel, 1924.
GADOFFRE, G. F. A., "Le 'Discours de la méthode' et la Querelle des anciens", in *Modern Miscellany, presented to Eugène Vinaver*, Manchester and N.Y., Manchester U.P. and Barnes & Noble, 1969, pp. 79–84.
GALILEO GALILEI, *Dialogue Concerning the Two Chief World Systems—Ptolemaic & Copernican*, trans. by Stillman Drake, foreword by Albert Einstein, Berkeley and Los Angeles, Univ. of California Press, 1953.
——, See under DRAKE, ed.
GASSENDI, P., *Pierre Gassendi, sa vie et son œuvre*, multiple authorship, Paris, Albin Michel, 1955.
——, *Selected Works*,. See under BRUSH, trans.
GAXOTTE, PIERRE, *La France de Louis XIV*, Paris, Hachette, 1946.
GILSON, ETIENNE, *History of Christian Philosophy in the Middle Ages*, London, Sheed & Ward, 1955.

———, *Reason and Revelation in the Middle Ages*, New York, London, Scribner's Sons, 1939.

———, *The Unity of Philosophical Experience*, London, Sheed & Ward, 1938, reprinted 1955; esp. Part 2: 'The Cartesian Experiment'.

GOUBERT, PIERRE, *Louis XIV et vingt millions de Français*, Paris, Fayard, 1966.

GUSDORF, GEORGES, *La révolution galiléenne*, Paris, Payot, 1969, 2 tomes; and *L'avènement des sciences humaines au siècle des lumières*, Payot, Paris, 1973; respectively vols. 3 and 6 of Gusdorf's *Les sciences humaines et la conscience occidentale*.

HAHN, ROGER, *The Anatomy of a Scientific Institution: the Paris Academy of Sciences, 1666–1803*, Berkeley, Los Angeles, London, Univ. of California Press, 1971.

HALL, A. RUPERT, *The Rise of Modern Science, 2: From Galileo to Newton, 1630–1720*, London, Glasgow, Fontana, Collins, 1970; first published by Collins 1963.

HARTH, ERICA, *Cyrano de Bergerac and the Polemics of Modernity*, N.Y., Columbia U.P., 1970.

HATTON, RAGNILD, *Europe in the Age of Louis XIV*, London, Thames & Hudson, 1969.

HAZARD, PAUL, *La crise de la conscience européene, 1680–1715*, 3 vols., Paris, Boivin, 1935; trans. in Pelican as *The European Mind, 1680–1715*.

HOBBES, THOMAS, *Leviathan*, intro. by A. D. Lindsay, London and Toronto, Dent, New York, Dutton (Everyman), 1914, reprinted 1924.

HOFMAN, JOSEPH E., *Leibniz in Paris, 1672–1676: His growth to mathematical maturity*, trans. from the German, Cambridge, Cambridge U.P., 1974.

HOWARTH, W. D., *Life and letters in France, vol. 1: The Seventeenth Century*, London, Nelson, 1965; Nelson's University Paperbacks, 1970.

HUMBERT, PIERRE, *Un amateur: Peiresc*, Paris, Desclée de Brouwer, 1933.

HUXLEY, ALDOUS, *The Devils of Loudun*, London, Chatto & Windus, 1952; Penguin, 1971.

KEARNEY, HUGH, *Science and Change, 1500–1700*, London, Weidenfeld & Nicolson, 1971.

———, ed., *Origins of the Scientific Revolution*, London, Longmans, 1964.

KING, LESTER S., ed., *A History of Medicine, selected readings*, Harmondsworth, Middlesex, Penguin, 1971.

KNIGHT, DAVID C., *Copernicus: Titan of Modern Astronomy*, London, N.Y., Franklin Watts, 1965.

KOESTLER, ARTHUR, *The Sleepwalkers, a History of Man's changing vision of the Universe*, Harmondsworth, Middlesex, Penguin, reissued 1968: first publ. Hutchinson, 1959.

KOYRE, ALEXANDRE, *From the Closed World to the Infinite Universe*, originally Baltimore, John Hopkins Press, 1957, now John Hopkins Paperbacks, 1968. Also obtainable as *Du monde clos à l'univers infini* in Idées/Gallimard.

———, *Mystiques, spirituels, alchimistes*, Paris, Armand Colin, 1955.

KRAILSHEIMER, A. J., *Studies in Self-Interest, from Descartes to La Bruyère*, Oxford, Clarendon, 1962.
KUHN, THOMAS S., *The Copernican Revolution*, Cambridge, Mass., Harvard U.P. (a Harvard Paperback), 1957.
LABBAS, LUCIEN, *L'Idée de science dans Malebranche et son originalité*, Paris Vrin, 1931.
LACHEVRE, FREDERIC, *Disciples et successeurs de Théophile de Viau. (La vie et les poésies libertines inédites de Des Barreaux, Saint-Pavin)*, Paris, Champion, 1911.
LA ROCHEFOUCAULD, *Réflexions ou sentences et maximes morales*, éd. par S. de Sacy, Paris, Gallimard et L.G.F., 1965.
LATREILLE, A. AND REMOND, R., *Histoire du catholicisme en France*, vol. 2, Paris, Editions Spes, 1962.
LAVISSE, ERNEST, *Histoire de France illustrée depuis les origines jusqu'à la révolution*, vols. 6–8, Paris, Hachette, 1911.
LEFF, GORDON, *Medieval Thought: St. Augustine to Ockham*, Harmondsworth, Middlesex, Penguin, 1958.
LENOBLE, ROBERT, *Esquisse d'une histoire de l'idée de nature*, Paris, Albin Michel, 1969.
——, *Mersenne, ou la naissance du Mécanisme*, Paris, Vrin, 1943.
LEVY-BRUHL, LUCIEN, *History of Modern Philosophy in France*, London, Kegan Paul, 1899.
LEYDEN, W. VON, *Seventeenth-Century Metaphysics*, London, Duckworth, 1968, paper 1971.
LOCKE, JOHN, *Locke's Essay concerning Human Understanding*, abridged, edited and introduced by Maurice Cranston, London, Collier, 1965.
LOUGH, JOHN, *An Introduction to Seventeenth Century France*, London and Harlow, Longmans, Green & Co., 1954; 8th impression, revised, 1969.
MAINDRON, E., *L'Académie des Sciences*, Paris, Alcan, 1888.
MALEBRANCHE, NICHOLAS, *La recherche de la vérité* (1674–5), vols. 1–3 in *Oeuvres completes*, éd. par G. Rodis-Lewis, Paris, Vrin, 1958–68, 20 vols.; *Traité de la nature et de la grâce* is in vol. 5, ed. G. Dreytus.
MASON, STEPHEN FINNEY, *A History of the Sciences. Main currents of scientific thought*, London, Routledge & Kegan Paul, 1953.
MERSENNE, MARIN, *L'usage de la raison*, Paris, Taupinart, 1623.
METHIVIER, HUBERT, *La France de Louis XIV: un grand règne?*, Paris, P.U.F., 1975.
MICHELET, JULES, *Satanism and Witchcraft*, trans. by A. R. Allinson from *La sorcière*, London, Tandem, 1965.
MONGREDIEN, GEORGES, *Cyrano de Bergerac*, Paris, Berger-Levrant, 1964.
MONTAIGNE, *Essais*, ed. Albert Thibaudet, Paris, Bibliothèque de la Pléiade, 1950.
MOORE, W. G., 'Montaigne's Notion of Experience', in *The French Mind. Studies in honour of Gustave Rudler*, Oxford, Clarendon, 1952.
MUELLER, FERNAND-LUCIEN, *Histoire de la psychologie de l'antiquité à nos jours*, Paris, Payot, 1960; chap. 15: 'Le dualisme cartésien', chap. 16: 'Les réactions à Descartes'.
NUSSBAUM, FREDERICK L., *The Triumph of Science and Reason, 1660–*

1685, New York, Harper & Row, 1953; paper 1962.

ORCIBAL, JEAN, *Louis XIV et les protestants*, Paris, Vrin, 1951.

——, *Port-Royal entre le miracle et l'obéissance*, Paris, Desclée de Brouwer, 1957.

——, *Saint-Cyran et le jansénisme*, Paris, Editions du Seuil, 1961.

——, *La spiritualité de Saint-Cyran, avec ses écrits de piété inédits*, Paris, Vrin, 1962.

ORNSTEIN, MARTHA, *The Rôle of Scientific Societies in the Seventeenth Century*, Chicago, Chicago U.P., 1928.

PENNINGTON, D. H., *Seventeenth Century Europe*, London, Longman, 1970; first paperback ed. with corrections and revisions, 1972.

PERRAULT, CHARLES, *Parallèle des Anciens et des Modernes en ce qui regarde les arts et les sciences*, Munich, Eidos Verlag, 1964.

PINTARD, RENE, *Le libertinage érudit dans la première moitié du 17e siècle*, Paris, Boivin, 1943.

PLANTINGA, ed., *The Ontological Argument, from St. Anselm to Contemporary Philosophy*, a selection of readings ed. by Alvin Plantinga, intro. by Richard Taylor, London, Melbourne, Macmillan, 1968, first publ. USA 1965.

REASON, H. A., *The Road to Modern Science,* London, Bell, 3rd revised ed. 1959.

REYNIER, G., *La femme au XVIIe siècle: ses ennemis et ses défenseurs,* Paris, Tallandier, 1929.

REYNOLD, GONZAGUE DE, *Synthèse du dix-septième siècle: la France classique et l'Europe baroque*, Paris, Editions du Conquistador, 1962.

ROSENFIELD, LEONORA COHEN, *From Beast-machine to Man-machine*, N.Y., Octagon Books, new and enlarged ed. 1968, first publ. 1940.

ROTHKRUG, LIONEL, *Opposition to Louis XIV: the political and social origins of the French Enlightenment*, New Jersey, Princeton U.P., 1965.

RUSSELL, BERTRAND, *History of Western Philosophy (and its connection with political and social circumstances from the earliest times to the present day)*, London, Unwin University Books, 1961; first publ. 1946.

SAINTE-BEUVE, *Port-Royal*, 7 vols., Paris, Hachette, vols. 1–6 1840–59, vol. 7 ('Table') 1871.

SAINT-EVREMOND, CHARLES DE, *Oeuvres en prose*, 4 vols., ed. R. Ternois, Paris, Didier, 1962–9.

SEVIGNE, Mme de, *Sévigné, choix de lettres*, ed. N. Scarlyn Wilson, London etc., Harrap, 1955.

SIMON, RENEE, *Henry de Boulainviller; historien, politique, philosophe, astrologue*, Paris, Boivin, 1942.

SIMON, RICHARD, *Histoire critique du Vieux Testament* (1678), Rotterdam, nouvelle éd., 1685.

——, *Critical History of the Text of the New Testament*, trans., London, R. Taylor, 1699.

SMITH, ALAN G. R., *Science and Society in the Sixteenth and Seventeenth Centuries*, London, Thames & Hudson, 1972.

SPINK, J. S., *French Free-Thought from Gassendi to Voltaire*, London, Athlone Press, 1960.

TATON, directeur, *Histoire générale des sciences; tome 2, La science moderne (de 1450 à 1800)*, Paris, P.U.F., 1958.
THOMAS, KEITH, *Religion and the Decline of Magic: studies in popular beliefs in sixteenth and seventeenth century England*, London, Weidenfeld and Nicolson, 1971.
THOMAS, P.-FELIX, *La philosophie de Gassendi*, N.Y., Burt Franklin, 1967.
THORNDIKE, LYNN, *A History of Magic and Experimental Science*; vols. 7, 8, *The Seventeenth Century*, N.Y., Columbia U.P., 1958.
WADE, IRA OWEN, *The Intellectual Origins of the French Enlightenment*, Princeton, Princeton U.P., 1971. Includes an extensive study of Bayle.
WENDT, HERBERT, *Before the Deluge*, London, Gollancz, 1968, trans. by R. and C. Winston from *Ehe die Sintflut kam*, Oldenburg and Hamburg, Gerhard Stalling Verlag, 1965.
WHITEMAN, W. P. D., *The Emergence of Scientific Medicine*, Edinburgh, Oliver & Boyd, 1971.
———, *Science and the Renaissance*, 2 vols., Edinburgh, London, publ. for Univ. of Aberdeen by Oliver & Boyd, 1962.
ZINNER, ERNST, *The Stars Above Us*, trans. by W. H. Johnston, London, Allen & Unwin, 1957; chap. 4 'Comets and Portents'.

Section III

Articles consulted

Hereunder *Journal of the History of Ideas* is abbreviated to *JHI*.

ADAMS, ROBERT P., 'The social responsibilities of science in *Utopia, New Atlantis* and after', *JHI*, vol. 10, no. 3, June 1949, pp. 374–97.
BALZ, ALBERT G. A., 'Cartesian doctrine and the animal soul: an incident in the formulation of the modern philosophical tradition', *Columbia University Studies in the History of Ideas*, III (N.Y., 1935), pp. 117–77.
CAULLERY, MAURICE, 'La biologie au 17e siècle', *XVIIe Siècle*, Jan. 1956, no. 30, pp. 25–45.
CRONIN, T. J., 'Eternal truths in the thought of Descartes and of his Adversary', *JHI*, vol. 21, no. 4, Oct.-Dec. 1960, pp. 553–9.
DAUMAS, MAURICE, 'La vie scientifique au 17e siècle', *XVIIe Siècle*, Jan. 1956, no. 30, pp. 110–13.
DUBOIS, ELFRIEDA, 'The education of women in seventeenth-century France', *French Studies*, vol. 32, no. 1, Jan. 1978, pp. 1–19.
GUERLAC, HENRY, 'Copernicus and Aristotle's cosmos', *JHI*, vol. 29, no. 1, Jan.-March 1968, pp. 109–13.
JASPERS, KARL, 'La pensée de Descartes et la philosophie', *Revue philosophique*, tome 123, mai-août 1937, section: 'La portée historique de Descartes', pp. 134–48.
KEEFE, T., 'Descartes's 'morale provisoire': a reconsideration', *French Studies*, vol. 26, no. 2, April 1972, pp. 129–42.
LAIRD, J., 'L'influence de Descartes sur la philosophie anglaise du XVIIe siècle', *Revue philosophique*, tome 123, mai-août 1937, pp. 226–55.

LENOBLE, ROBERT, 'La psychologie cartésienne', *Revue internationale de philosophie*, vol. 4, 1950, pp. 160–89.
———, 'La représentation du monde physique à l'époque classique', *XVIIe Siècle*, Jan. 1956, no. 30, pp. 5–24.
MARSAK, LEONARD M., 'Bernard de Fontenelle: in defence of science', *JHI*, vol. 20, no. 1., Jan. 1959, pp. 111–22.
MASON, STEPHEN FINNEY, 'The Scientific Revolution and the Protestant Reformation', *Annals of Science*, vol. 9, nos. 1, 2, March, June 1953.
PATRIDES, C. A., 'Renaissance thought on the celestial hierarchy', *JHI*, vol. 20, no. 2, April 1959, pp. 155–66.
PEPIN, LEON, 'Bossuet et la Révocation de l'Edit de Nantes', *Revue catholique de Normandie*, 1892; in 3 parts: pp. 311–28, 500–26, 628–40.
PRIOR, MOODY E., 'Bacon's man of science', *JHI*, vol. 15, no. 3, June 1954, pp. 348–70.
RIDGELEY, BEVERLY S., 'Dalibray, Le Pailleur, and the "New Astronomy" in French seventeenth-century poetry', *JHI*, vol. 17, no. 1, Jan. 1956, pp. 3–27.
ROSEN, EDWARD, 'Calvin's attitude towards Copernicus', *JHI*, vol. 21, no. 3, July-Sept. 1960, pp. 431–41.
SAVESON, J. E., 'Descartes' influence on John Smith, Cambridge Platonist', *JHI*, vol. 20, no. 2, April 1959, pp. 258–63.
———, 'Differing reactions to Descartes among the Cambridge Platonists', *JHI*, vol. 21, no. 4, Oct.-Dec. 1960, pp. 560–7.
SHARRATT, MICHAEL, 'Copernicanism at Douai', *Durham University Journal*, vol. 67, no. 1 (New Series vol. 36, no. 1) Dec. 1974, pp. 41–9.
SHUGG, WALLACE, 'The Cartesian beast-machine in English literature (1663–1750)', *JHI*, vol. 29, no. 2, April-June 1968, pp. 279–92.
WARE, CHARLOTTE S., 'The influence of Descartes on John Locke. A bibliographical study', *Revue internationale de philosophie*, vol. 4, 1950, pp. 210–30.
WEISINGER, HERBERT, 'Ideas of history during the Renaissance', *JHI*, vol. 6, no. 4, Oct. 1945, pp. 415–35.
WIENER, PHILIP J., 'Leibniz's project of a public exhibition of scientific inventions', *JHI*, vol. 1, no. 2, April 1940, pp. 232–40.
ZILSEL, EDGAR, 'The genesis of the concept of scientific progress', *JHI*, vol. 6, no. 3, June 1945, pp. 325–64.
XVIIe Siècle, no. 30, Jan. 1956, whole number devoted to 'Les sciences au 17e siècle' (see also Caullery, Daumas, Lenoble).
XVIIe Siècle, nos. 12–14, 1951–2, whole numbers devoted to 'Fénelon et le tricentenaire de sa naissance, 1651–1951'.
Revue philosophique, vol. 123, 1937, May-Aug., whole number devoted to Descartes.

INDEX

Abrégé de la philosophie de Gassendi, 68–9
Académie Royale des sciences, 20, 61, 76, 161, 162, 170, 173, 197 n. 3
Aix-en-Provence, 14, 68, 70
Alais, Grâce d', 4
Alpha Centauri, 27
Alquié, 73, 81, 180 n. 2
Anselm, St, 8, 183 n. 40
Apologie de la religion chrétienne, see *Pensées*.
Aquaviva, 95
Aquinas, St Thomas, 8, 9, 10, 46, 95, 127, 183 n. 40
d'Argenson, 166
Aristotelianism, see scholasticism; *and under* Descartes
Arnauld, Angélique, 96
Arnauld, Antoine *(fils)*, 76, 96–7
Arrêt burlesque, 76
atomists, see Gassendi
Augustine of Hippo, St, 16, 95, 127, 128, 157
Augustinus, 96
Autre monde, L', 15–17, 164
Averroes, 8, 14, 23
Avicenna, 8

Bacon, Francis, 21, 31, 62, 78, 170
Baillet, 16, 180 n. 3
Barre, Poulain de la, 138, 139
Bavent, Madeleine, 85, 178 n. 36
Bayle, Jacob, 155
Bayle, Pierre, 12, 13, 15, 116, 147–60, 161, 162, 164, 165

Bayle, Pierre—*contd*.
and atheism, 153–4, 157, 159
and authority, 148, 150, 152, 157, 163, 164
and biblical criticism, 157
and civil tolerance, see Bayle—and ethics
and Descartes, 72, 148–50, 151, 152–3, 156, 157
and ethics, 13, 153–7
and fideism against rational theology, 159
and historiography, 72, 150
and intuition, 156
and Pyrrhonism, 149
and religion, 147–8, 152, 153, 154
and right reason, 13, 72, 149, 150, 153, 156, 159
and superstition, 151–2, 153, 174
and problem of evil, 158–60
and the Revocation, 148, 151, 154–7
Beauvillier, duc de, 141, 142, 144
Beeckman, 35, 38
Bellarmine, St Robert, 9
Bergerac, Cyrano de, 15–18, 24, 29, 164
Bernier, 69, 71
Bérulle, 10, 40, 96
Bodin, 126
Boileau, 76
Borel, 164
Bossuet, J.-B., 2, 28, 91, 117–31, 147, 175
and authority, 117, 120, 122, 123–6, 128, 130, 152

216 Index

Bossuet, J.-B.—contd.
  and Descartes, 79, 117, 123
  and *'le merveilleux'*, 128
  and political theory, 123–6, 145
  and Providence, 112, 126–31
  and Protestantism, 2, 118, 119–22, 126
  and Quietism, 119, 135, 142, 191 n.7
  and the Revocation, 120–122
  as Gallican, 118, 119
  as historian, 28, 126–31, 192 n. 28
  as preceptor to the Dauphin, 118, 125
  as *'Prédicateur'*, 118, 122
Bossuet, l'abbé, 136
Boullé, 85
Boyle, 92
Brahe, 26
Bréhier, 67
Bridoux, 76
Bruno, 14, 24, 164, 167
Buffon, 179 n. 49
Burke, P., 126
Busson, 22

Calvin, 6, 95
Calvinism, *see* Protestantism
Cambrai, Archbishop of, *see* Fénelon
Cambridge Platonists, 78
Camisards, Revolt of the, 122, 133
Campanella, 15, 24
Camus, Albert, 116
Candide, 114
Caractère, Les, 13
Cardano, 14
Cartesians, 20, 73, 77–81, 96, 133, 138, 167, 186 n. 96, 194 n. 3
Cavendish, 78
Ce que c'est que la France toute catholique, 155
'Chambre ardente', La, 23
Champvallon, 119
Chandoux, 40
Charles IX, 2
Charlet, 75
Charron, 14

'Charte gallicane', see *'Declaration des quatre articles'*
Chateaubriand, 82
Chevreuse, duc de, 141, 142
Christina, Queen, 36
Church Party, the, 6, 120, 121
Cid, Le, 4, 51, 171
City of God, The, 127, 182 n. 36
Colbert, 20, 119, 141, 144
Collège Royal, 10, 68, 187 n. 98
Comète, La, 162
Commentaire philosophique sur . . . S. Luc . . . ET CONTRAINS - LES D'ENTRER, 155–7
Concord of Free Will with the Gifts of Grace, 95
Condom, Bishop of, *see* Bossuet.
'convulsionnaires, L'Affaire des', 22
Copernicus, 25–6, 42, 164, 165, 179 n. 48
Corneille, Pierre, 4, 51, 84–5, 161, 171
Cornet, 119
Creation, date of, 28, 127
Critique de l'Ecole des femmes, La, 171
Critique générale de l'Histoire du calvinisme de M. Maimbourg, 149, 150, 151
Cruickshank, 101–2
Cudworth, 78
Culverwell, 78
Cur Deus homo, 8
Cuvier, 179 n. 55

D'Alembert, 79
'Déclaration des quatre articles, La', 119
De la vertue des païens, 154
De l'éducation des filles, 137–40, 165
De l'esprit géométrique, 97
Democritus, 17, 70
De motu cordis, 58
De l'origine des fables, 173
De revolutionibus orbium coelestium, 25
Desargues, 84, 85
De vita et moribus Epicuri, 68

Index

Descartes, Francine, 35
Descartes, René, 5, 8, 10, 11, 12, 13–14, 19, 21, 24 25–6, 28, 29, 32–81, 106–7, 167–9
  and the animal-machine, 59–61, 73, 79–80, 186 n. 96
  and Aristotelianism, 10, 32, 36, 37, 45, 46, 64, 70, 165
  and Beeckman, 35, 38, 39
  and Bérulle, 35, 40, 50
  and the *cogito*, 53, 100–2
  and cosmology, 42, 63–4, 71, 89, 184 n. 59
  and dualism, 33, 55, 56–7, 73, 179 n. 40, 183 n. 44
  and fideism, 37, 38
  and Galileo, 35, 41–2, 68
  and Gassendi, 69–72
  and Harvey, 58
  and immortality, 61
  and innate ideas, 47–8, 53, 66–7
  and intuition, 47, 53–4, 69, 100–2
  and the Jesuits, 36, 50, 75–7
  and the '*mauvais génie*', 52–3
  and mathematics, 32, 49, 63, 103
  and Mechanism, 11, 58, 64, 170
  and metaphysics, 31, 52–7, 74
  and method, 33, 44–9, 61, 67–8
  and morality, 25, 41–2, 50–2, 62
  and physics, 32, 46–7, 56, 57, 63–4, 71, 74–5, 184 n. 60
  and physiology, 58–9, 63, 64–5
  and psychology, 65–6
  and rationalism, 39, 42, 44, 47–8, 68, 171
  and the Rosicrucians, 39
  and theology, 36, 38, 51–2, 66
  and universal doubt, 50, 52, 70, 101, 102, 149
  at La Flèche, 35, 36–8
  at Neuburg, 35, 38–40
D'Holbach, 153
Dialogue concerning the two great World-Systems, 25
Dialogues des morts, 162
Dictionnaire historique et critique, 149, 157–60
Diderot, 134, 147
Digby, 78
Digression sur les Anciens et les Modernes, 162, 171
Dinet, 75
Dioptrique, La, 34, 43, 67, 75, 167, 185 n. 65
Discours de la méthode, 10, 13, 34, 35, 36–68, 75, 171
Discours prouvant la pluralité des mondes, 164
Discours sur les passions de l'amour, 92
Discours sur l'histoire universelle, 28
Dom Juan, 20
Dominicans, 95
Doutes sur le système physique des causes occasionnelles, 162, 168
'dragonnades, Les', *see* Nantes, Revocation of Edict of
Du Hamel, 161
Duras, Mlle de, 120

Einstein, 185 n. 62
Elizabeth, Princess of Palatine (of Bohemia), 41
Eloge de Newton, 170
Emile, L', 139
Encyclopédie, 157
Entretien avec M. de Saci, 107
Entretiens sur la pluralité des mondes, 162, 163–6, 167, 174
Epicurus, 17, 70, 71–2
Essai pour les coniques, 85
Essay concerning Human Understanding, An, 48
Estates General, 3, 143
Examen de conscience sur les devoirs de la royauté, 142
Exercitationes adversus Aristoteleos, 70
Expériences nouvelles touchant le vide, 86, 87
Explication des maximes des Saints sur la vie intérieure, 134, 135–7, 142
Explication du Cantique des Cantiques, 136
Exposition de la doctrine catholique sur les matières de controverse, 120

Fables of Fénelon, 140
Fabri, 76
Fabricius, 179 n. 49
Femmes savantes, Les, 20, 138
Fénelon, 3, 29, 108, 128, 132–46, 147
  and authority, 132, 141, 143, 146
  and Descartes, 134–5
  and economic theory, 134, 142, 143–5
  and Gallicanism, 132
  and Jansenism, 133
  and Protestantism, 121, 133, 140
  and politics, 3, 132, 140–6
  and Quietism, 132, 135–7, 140
  as educationalist, 19, 137–40, 165
  as royal preceptor, 135, 137, 138, 140, 144–6
Fermat, 32, 63, 84, 92
Fontenelle, 11, 12, 15, 116, 147, 161–76
  and authority, 11, 163, 165
  and cosmology, 164–7, 168–9
  and Descartes, 12, 80, 81, 162, 165–8, 170, 172
  and Malebranche, 168, 172
  and Newton, 169–70
  and polemics, 163
  and religion, 161, 164–5, 167, 174–6
  and superstition, 173–4
  and the *Académie Royale des sciences*, 161, 162
  and the concept of progress, 116, 170–4

Gaffarel, 30
Galen, 30
Galileo, 10, 11, 12, 19, 25, 28, 30, 31, 41–2, 70, 71, 80, 92, 151, 164, 167, 170, 179 n. 49
Gallicans, 98, 118–19, 125
Gassendi, 10, 14, 15, 17, 25, 34, 48, 68–72, 78, 164, 194 n. 6
Géométrie, La, 34, 43, 49
Gilson, 33
Grandier, 22
Guyon, Mme, 136–7

Harvey, 12, 30, 58, 78, 183 n. 48
Hauranne, Jean du Vergier de, *see* Saint-Cyran
Haussman, 44
Hazard, Paul, 12, 179 n. 52
Henri II, 1,
Henri III, 2,
Henri IV, 3, 120
Hippocrates, 30
Histoire des Ajaoiens, 174
Histoire des oracles, 162, 174, 175
Histoire des variations des églises protestantes, 120, 126–7
Histoire universelle, 118, 127–31
Hobbes, 34, 78, 123, 156, 182 n. 31
Holy Thorn, miracle of the, *see* Périer, Marguerite
Homme, L', 58, 73
Horace, 171
Huxley, Aldous, 22, 114–15, 182 n. 34
Huyghens, 75, 77

Index, Congregation of the, 19, 76
Inquisition, 25
Introduction à la vie dévote, 7, 136

Jansenism, 19, 33, 76, 94–9, 107, 112, 115–16
Jansen(ius), 96
Jaspers, 33
Jesuits, 9–11, 19, 75–7, 87, 95–8, 193 n. 2
John of the Cross, Saint, 136
Journal des savants, 20, 61, 166, 186 n. 92
Jupiter, moons of, 19, 25
Jurieu, 154

Kant, 160
Kelvin, Lord, 179 n. 49
Keeling, 100
Kepler, 11, 12, 23, 26, 151
Kircher, 30
Koestler, Arthur, 27

Index

La Bruyère, 13, 28, 116, 161
La Flèche, Collège de, 19, 28, 75
La Fontaine, 79
La Mettrie, 187 n. 101
La Mothe le Vayer, 14, 15, 154
La Rochefoucauld, 116
La Rochelle, Fall of, 120
La Voisin, 23
Lacombe, 137
Langer, Suzanne, 81, 190 n. 42
Le Tellier, 121, 124
Leeuwenhoek, 29, 30, 183 n. 48
Leibniz, 21, 31, 33, 77, 93–4, 117, 160
Letter to the Grand Duchess Christina, 80
Lettre a Louis XIV, 133, 142, 145
Lettre|contre les Sorciers, 17
Lettre sur la comète, 151
Lettre sur les aveugles, 134
Lettre sur l'île de Bornéo, 162, 174
Lettres philosophiques, 12, 114
Lettres provinciales, 83, 93, 97–8
Leviathan, 123
libertins, 13, 14–18, 20, 24, 40, 68, 135, 154
Locke, 48, 66–7, 78–9, 123
Loudun, 22–3
Louis XIII, 1, 3, 22
Louis XIV, 1, 4–5, 20, 23, 76, 97, 98, 119, 120, 121, 132, 137, 142, 152, 194 n. 23
Louviers, 85
Luther, 6

Maimbourg, 149
Maintenon, Mme de, 135, 137, 141, 142
Malebranche, 30, 73–5, 77, 133, 135, 172, 196 n. 35
Mallarmé, 53–4
Malpighi, 29, 30, 183 n. 48
Malraux, 110
Manicheans, 158
Maritain, 33, 180 n. 8
Mars, orbit of, 26
Marsak, 170
Martimort, 117

'*matière subtile*', 64
Maximes des Saints, see *Explication* . . .
Maximes et réflexions sur la comédie, 117
Mazarin, 4, 6
Meaux, Bishop of, see Bossuet
Médicis, Marie de, 3, 4
Meditations chrétiennes, 74
Meditations sur la philosophie première, 34, 69, 73
'*Mémorial*', Pascal's, 93
Mercure galant, 161, 165
Mersenne, 20, 21, 61, 69, 84, 85, 172
'*merveilleux, Le*', 21–2, 30
Mésangère, Marquise de la, 165
Mesland, 76
Météores, Les, 34, 43
Michelet, 22
Mill, J. S., 160
Molière, 20, 138, 171
Molina, 95
Molinos, 136, 142
Monde, Le, 16, 34, 40, 42, 43
Montaigne, 14, 107
'Montalte, Louis de', pseud. of B. Pascal
Montespan, Mme de, 23
Montesquieu, 12, 130
Montmort, 20, 61
More, Henry, 78
More, Sir Thomas, 62
Moyen court et très facile de faire oraison, 136
Mundus subterraneus, 30
Mydorge, 38

Nantes, Edict of, 3, 4, 120
Nantes, Revocation of Edict of, 5, 6, 120–2, 125, 133, 154–5
Naudé, 15
New Atlantis, 62
Newton, 12, 31, 33, 78–9, 81, 93, 166, 167, 169, 170
Nicole, 76, 79
Noël, Etienne, 75, 87–9
Nouvelles de la République des Lettres, 154, 164, 165, 174

Observatory of Paris, 20
Ockham, William of, 9, 48
Of the Advancement of Learning, 31
Oratory, Congregation of the, 40, 73, 76, 96

Papin, 184 n. 54, 189 n. 20
Parent, 169
Paris, University of, 10, 19, 34, 76–7
Parlements, 3, 10, 19, 23, 76, 96
'parti des dévots', *see* Church party
Pascal, Blaise, 13, 17, 19, 21, 33, 39, 82–116, 129, 157, 172, 184 n. 55
  and authority, 90–1, 111
  and Descartes, 82, 83, 85, 89, 100–6, 107
  and '*divertissement*', 110
  and experiment, 31, 85–91
  and fideism, 106
  and his 'Illumination', 39, 84, 93, 107
  and Jansenism, 83, 84, 91–2, 94–115, 97, 107–16
  and '*le cœur*', 99–102, 104–5, 156
  and '*l'esprit de finesse*', 102–4
  and miracle, 106, 111–13
  and Port Royal *see* Pascal and Jansenism
  and Saint-Ange, 91
  and philosophy, 82–3
  and the calculating machine, 85
  and the controversy with Noël, 87–9
  and the cycloid, 21, 93–4
  and the Jews, 113
  and the mathematics of probability, 92
  and the *Pensées*, *see Pensées*
  and the '*puissances trompeuses*', 104–5
  and the vacuum, 64, 85–90
  and the 'wager', 113
  as anticipator of Integral Calculus, 93–4
  on man's misery, 29, 108–111
Pascal, Etienne, 84, 91
Pascal, Gilberte, *see* Périer, Mme
Pascal, Jacqueline, 84, 91–2, 112

Pascal's Law, 90
Pascal's Theorem, 85
Pascal's Triangle, 92, 93
Pasquier, 126
Passions de l'âme, Les, 35, 51
Patin, 30
Paul, St Vincent de, 7
Peiresc, 14, 20
Pelagius, 95, 128
Pensées, 29–30, 93, 98–116
Pensées diverses sur la comète, 149, 151–4
Périer, Florin, 89
Périer, Marguerite, 112–13
Périer, Mme Gilberte, 84
Perrault, 198 n. 34
Petit, 86
petites écoles, 19
petits prophètes, 22
Phèdre, 21
philosophes, 12, 141, 153, 156, 160, 163, 195 n. 13
Picard, 21
pineal gland, 57, 64, 66
Plans de gouvernement . . . pour être proposés au duc de Bourgogne, 142
Plato, 8, 46, 145, 157
Politique tirée des propres paroles de l'Ecriture Sainte, 118, 123–6
Pomponazzi, 14
Pontchartrain, 142
Port-Royal, 91–2, 96–9, 112–13
Préface sur le Traité du vide, 86, 90
Principia philosophiae, 35, 42, 167
Protestantism, 1–4, 6, 22, 41, 97
Provinciales, *see Lettres provinciales*
Ptolemy, 8, 165
Puy-de-Dôme, Experiment of the, 67, 89
Pyrrhonism, 14, 80, 107, 149

'Querelle des anciens et des modernes, La', 170–4
Quietism, 135–7

Racine, 19, 21, 96, 116
Recherche de la vérité, La, 73

Index

Recherche de la vérité par la lumière naturelle, 101
Récit de la Grande Expérience de l'équilibre des liqueurs, 89
Réfutation du système de Malebranche sur la nature et la grâce, 133
'Régale, La', 119, 132
Régis, 162, 167
Regius (le Roy), 77
Regulae ad directionem ingenii, 34, 40, 48, 73
Relation de la conférence avec M. Claude, 120
Relation sur le quiétisme, 135
Renati Descartes principia philosophiae, 77
Revius, 77
Rex, Walter, 152
Richelieu, 4, 6, 22–3, 40, 96
Rimbaud, 53
Roannez, duc de, 92
Roberval, 84
Roemer, 27, 64
Rohault, 78, 162, 167
Ronsard, 2
Rosicrucians, 39
Rothkrug, 141, 143, 193 n. 7
Rouillard, 73
Rousseau, J.-J., 124, 139
Royal Society, the, 61, 78, 162, 176
Ryswick, Treaty of, 142

Sablière, Mme de la, 79, 165
Saint-Ange, 91
Saint-Cyran, Jean du Vergier de Hauranne, abbé de, 96
Saint-Evremond, 71, 131
Saint-Simon, 141
Sales, St François de, 7, 136, 146
salons, 20, 79
Scheiner, 75, 179 n. 49, 185 n. 61
Scheuchzer, 31
scholasticism, 7–11, 26, 87–9, 152, 169, 170, 171
Sciences, Académie Royale des, *see* Académie . . .
Scotus, John Duns, 9, 95

Seignelay, marquis de, 141
Sévigné, Mme de, 121
Sextus Empiricus, 71
Simon, Richard, 196 n. 34
Smith, John, 78
Soissons, comtesse de, 23
Sorbonne, the, 10, 96
Sorcière, La, 22
Spinoza, 77, 123, 187 n. 103
stoicism, 50–1, 69, 107
Suárez, 9
Summa theologica, 9
Sun, distance of, 27
Sur l'histoire, 174
Swammerdam, 29, 30
Syntagma philosophicum, 68, 164

Tables de Chaulnes, *see* Plans de gouvernement
Télémaque, 138, 139, 141, 144–6
Teresa, Saint, 136
Theodicy, 160
Théorie des tourbillons cartésiens, 165, 170
Thomism, *see* Aquinas
Torricelli, 64, 85–7, 90
Tourbillons, *see* Vortices
Traité de la connaissance de Dieu et de soi-même, 117
Traité de la nature et de la grâce, 73–4, 168
Traité de la sagesse, 14
Traité de l'existence et des attributs de Dieu, 133–5
Trent, Council of, 7, 9, 95
Triangle, Arithmetical, *see* Pascal's Triangle
Triomphe de la religion, Le, 175
Trublet, 161
Turenne, 120

Ultramontanes, 119, 125
Usher, Archbishop, 28, 127
Utopia, 62

Vanini, 15, 24
Vatier, 75
Vauban, 144
Vesalius, 183 n. 49
Viau, Théophile de, 18
Vietà, 63
Voët (Voetius), 77
Voltaire, 12, 44–5, 79, 80, 82, 83, 97, 113–14
vortices, theory of, 64, 167, 180 n. 14

Vrillac, P. de, 122

White, Thomas, 78
Wilkins, 164

Zwingli, 7